Praise for Peggielene Bartels and Eleanor Herman's

KING PEGGY

"Extremely well-written and amusing. . . . Candid and humble. . . . A captivating glimpse into the mental and spiritual transformation of a middle-aged African American woman as she steps into her royal destiny as an African king." —*The Baltimore Times*

"There's an unlikely new leader in West Africa. . . . Bartels had to quickly and forcefully let tribal elders know that despite being far away and female, she had every intention of taking her position seriously—and being taken seriously in turn." —NPR

"*King Peggy* is wildly entertaining and thoroughly engaging, and Peggy is a true modern hero as she battles her council of elders who try to maintain their old lifestyles of privilege and greed. *King Peggy* reminds readers that the truth is often stranger than fiction; King Peggy herself does not disappoint, neither as a ruler nor a storyteller." —Shelf Awareness

"In the moving story of Peggielene Bartels, all of us can feel a connection to our ancestors, and a reminder of the good that can come from courageously embracing unexpected responsibilities."
—Jeffrey Zaslow, author of *The Girls from Ames*
and coauthor of *The Last Lecture*

"Compelling and heartwarming, [*King Peggy*] is a most enjoyable and absorbing read."
—Deborah Rodriguez, author of *Kabul Beauty School*

"Though it sounds the stuff of fairytale and legend, *King Peggy* is the fascinating true story of her courageous acceptance of this difficult role and her unyielding resolve to help the people of Otuam. . . . Full of pathos, humor and insight into a world where poverty mingles with hope and happiness, *King Peggy* is an inspiration and proof positive that when it comes to challenging roles for women, 'We Can Do It!'"
—*BookPage*

"[A] winning tale of epic proportions, full of intrigue, royal court plotting, cases of mistaken identity and whispered words from beyond the grave. Upon arrival, King Peggy—who left Ghana three decades earlier and has since become an American citizen—found an uphill battle and vowed to tackle the issues plaguing her community: domestic violence, poverty and lack of access to clean water, health care and education. . . . Florid description of the landscape, culture and characters work together to fully evoke the rhythms of African life. Ultimately, readers come away with not only a sense of how King Peggy was able to transform Otuam, but also an understanding of how the town and its inhabitants transformed her."

—*Kirkus Reviews*

"*King Peggy* is the funny, wide-eyed account of [Peggielene Bartels'] struggle to overcome sexism, systemic corruption and poverty without losing her will to lead or the love of her 7,000 subjects. . . . Coauthor Herman says her interest in Africa came from the fiction of Alexander McCall Smith; she thinks she has met in Peggy a real-life Mma Ramotswe, and readers will quickly agree."

—*Maclean's* (Toronto)

Peggielene Bartels and Eleanor Herman

KING PEGGY

Peggielene Bartels was born in Ghana in 1953 and moved to Washington, D.C., in her early twenties to work at Ghana's embassy. She became an American in 1997. In 2008, she was chosen to be king of Otuam, a Ghanaian village of 7,000 people.

Eleanor Herman is the author of three books of women's history, including the *New York Times* bestseller *Sex with Kings*. Her profile of Peggy was a cover story for *The Washington Post Magazine*.

www.kingpeggy.com

Also by Eleanor Herman

Sex with Kings
Sex with the Queen
Mistress of the Vatican

09/07/12

KING PEGGY

Helen

Many Blessings To
You!

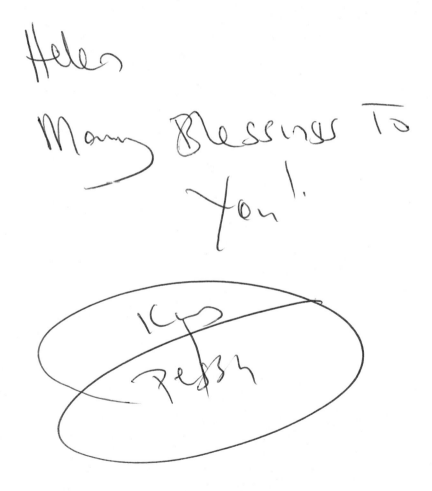

KP
Peggy

KING PEGGY

An American Secretary, Her Royal Destiny,
and the Inspiring Story of How She Changed
an African Village

Peggielene Bartels and
Eleanor Herman

ANCHOR BOOKS
A Division of Random House, Inc.
New York

FIRST ANCHOR BOOKS EDITION, FEBRUARY 2013

Copyright © 2012 by Peggielene Bartels and Eleanor Herman

The Library of Congress has cataloged the Doubleday edition as follows:
Bartels, Peggielene
King Peggy : An American secretary, her royal destiny, and the inspiring story of how she changed an African village / Peggielene Bartels and Eleanor Herman. — 1st ed.
p. cm.
1. Bartels, Peggielene, 1953– Travel—Ghana—Otuam.
2. Ghana—Kings and rulers—Biography.
3. Americans—Ghana—Biography.
4. Ghana— Social life and customs— 21st century.
5. Secretaries—Washington (D.C.)—Biography. I. Herman, Eleanor, 1960– II. Title.

DT512.44.B36A3 2011966.7— dc23 [B] 2011019544

Anchor ISBN: 978-0-307-74281-0

Cartography by Mapping Specialists
Insert photographs copyright © by Sarah Preston

www.anchorbooks.com

Printed in the United States of America
10   9   8   7   6   5   4   3   2

Contents

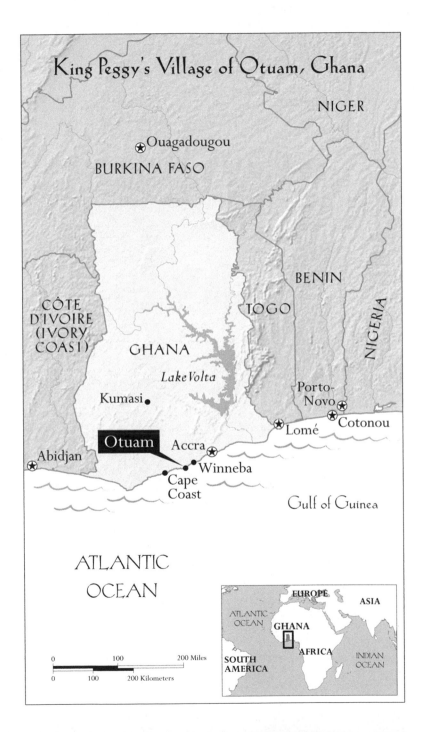

King Peggy's Village of Otuam, Ghana

KING PEGGY

Prologue

In the dream Peggy was back in Kumasi, a child again, walking home from school in her sky blue uniform with the round white collar. Usually the path was dusty in the dry season, pocked with puddles in the rainy season, but now it was smooth as marble; her black sandals glided over it and her feet remained clean.

The sky was a bright turquoise vault above her head, so beautiful it broke the heart, and the warm golden sun on her shoulders felt like a loving embrace. Just as she had every school day when she lived in Kumasi, in the dream she walked behind the king's palace, a rambling brick structure painted blue and white and built around a large courtyard where royal festivities were held. The Ashanti king of Kumasi, known as the *Asantehene,* was a very important leader with millions of subjects, and he was rich beyond measure because he owned some of the biggest gold mines in the world. All day at his palace, important visitors were coming and going—tribal priests, elders, government ministers, ambassadors, chairmen of important companies, and humble people asking him for justice.

She stood outside the rear of the palace and looked at it, wondering what was going on in there. But there was nothing for her, a skinny little girl, in a king's palace. And so she glided down the marble path to her home.

Because Peggy had the dream so many times she knew it must be a message from the spirit world. Like many Africans, Peggy understood that dreams meant something. They were not just random thoughts, fears, or hopes, or something from dinner irritating your intestines. Sometimes a dream was a message from God or Jesus, or from your ancestors, or even from the better part of yourself talking to the stupid part of yourself. Dreams were like encoded letters from the spirit world that must be carefully decoded and interpreted. They guided you in your choices, warned you of deception and accidents, or showed you the future.

"What does the dream mean, Mother?" Peggy asked when she called her mother in Ghana.

Mother thought about it a long while. "It's been thirty years since you walked behind that palace to go to school in Kumasi," Mother said. "Perhaps it's just a memory."

"But why would I have it so often, thirty years later?" Peggy insisted. "Here I am living in the United States all this time; there's nothing to remind me of the king's palace in Kumasi. The dream has to mean *something*."

A moment of silence dangled in the transatlantic air. Peggy could picture Mother's long smooth face and shining dark eyes as she considered the question. Finally, she said, "Pray for God and the ancestors to show you what the dream means, Peggy. Perhaps, in time, they will."

Mother was right. God and the ancestors would show Peggy the meaning of the dream in their own time, but it would be long after Mother had joined them.

Part I

WASHINGTON, D.C.

August–September 2008

1

Is the king dead? Peggielene Bartels wondered as she stood in the small mail room off the lobby, rubbing her thumbs across the front of the envelope, the ugly red stamp—UNDELIVERABLE—splayed across the blue ink of the address carefully penned in her own hand. For the third time a letter to her uncle Joseph had boomeranged back from Ghana. Another resident jostled her apologetically as he took out his little silver key and opened his mailbox, but Peggy just kept staring at the letter.

Uncle Joseph was her mother's brother, and for twenty-five years he had been king of Otuam, a community of seven thousand souls where Peggy's family had originated hundreds of years earlier. Periodically, when she had returned to Ghana to visit her mother, the two of them would drive to Otuam to see Uncle Joseph, known there by his royal title Nana Amuah Afenyi V.

The king of Otuam was a tall man with heavy-lidded eyes, the lower lids revealing a great deal of white below the iris. He had been director of all the prisons in Accra, Ghana's capital. In 1983 at the age of sixty-seven, he had retired and, upon the unexpected death of his sixty-three-year-old cousin, Nana Amuah Afenyi IV, was chosen the new king.

Peggy remembered Uncle Joseph as a gentle, smiling man who never raised his voice. A man always ready to forgive. A man everybody liked. Sometimes Peggy wondered how such a man could be a king when kings were supposed to be tough and strong. If she had been in his position, she wasn't sure she would have been so kind. She wouldn't have cared if some people disliked her as long as she was a good king, punishing evildoers who took advantage of the weak.

The last time she had seen Uncle Joseph was at her mother's funeral in 1997. He had arrived at her mother's home in Takoradi with a group of his elders, a kindness that even in her overwhelming grief Peggy had appreciated. For years she had regularly sent her mother money, and once her mother was in a better place where no money was needed, Peggy decided to send the money to her uncle out of respect. It was only one hundred dollars a month, but it went a long way in a Ghanaian town where many people lived on a dollar a day. And Peggy knew that even though Uncle Joseph was a king, he was not rich. His palace was falling down around his head, with a leaking roof and mildewed walls begging for spackling and fresh paint. And she worried that he might need medicine.

He had been grateful for the money, and the two had kept in touch in the eleven years since her mother's passing. Earlier that year—had it been January?—he had had a stroke and been hospitalized, but he had seemed to be recuperating. She had spoken to him on his cell phone now and then during his months-long stay in the hospital in Accra, and someone had picked up his mail for him at his post office box in Winneba, the city nearest to Otuam with mail service.

But for the past three months, her letters had come bouncing back. Nor had he collected her Western Union wire transfers. She had tried calling Uncle Joseph on his cell phone, but it was disconnected. How old would he be now? Ninety? No, ninety-two.

Truth be told, if he was dead she probably wouldn't hear about it immediately. In Ghana it was considered terribly disrespectful to say *The king is dying* or *The king is dead.* When the king was very ill in the hospital people said, *The king has gone to his village for a cure.*

If it didn't look like the king was going to make it, his elders said, *The king is still in the village taking care of himself.*

When they said, *He'll be in the village a long time. He won't be coming back anytime soon,* that's when you knew he had died.

But a king's elders didn't even say that right after the king died. They waited for weeks, even months after his death, before they said he wouldn't be coming back anytime soon from the village.

The funny thing was that at a king's funeral, the embalmed body sitting stiffly on a royal chair, even then nobody talked about him as dead. People said, *We hope the king is getting a good cure in the village, but we probably won't see him for a good while.*

How had this strange custom started? Peggy wondered. Maybe kingship raised kings above mere mortals, rendering it disrespectful to talk about them as dead or dying like the rest of humanity, just as royalty wasn't supposed to be seen eating and drinking in public or running off to the toilet. Perhaps it was because kings, even after death, were thought to still rule over their kingdoms from the Asamando, the place of good ancestors.

Or maybe it was because the villagers, knowing the king was dead, would start to misbehave. Especially the men, she thought, because it was well known that men misbehaved a lot, drinking and fighting and beating their wives. So it was better if they didn't know for sure where the king was, and whether he would be coming back to punish them for their bad behavior. This tradition kept misbehaving men in line, and in this world of misbehaving men anything that kept them in line was a good thing.

Peggy roused herself from her reverie and walked to the elevator. The doors opened and she stepped inside, still staring at the letter. Well, she figured, if Uncle Joseph was in the village for good somebody would call her. She had dozens of close cousins in Ghana, and though none of them lived in Otuam they had an informal network of gossip and news that eventually reached everybody. Indeed, gossiping cousins seemed to be the liveliest form of communication throughout Africa.

Stepping out on her floor, she walked down the long narrow corridor to her one-bedroom condo and unlocked the door. For years she had saved money for a down payment, for the chance to own property and have her slice of the American dream. She would never forget the enormous pride she felt at the settlement a year earlier when she realized she actually owned her own place. It was in an old building from about 1960 shaped like a giant block with hundreds of units and a laundry room in the basement. It wasn't in Washington, D.C., but in the less expensive suburb of Silver Spring, just north of the Maryland line. Still, the condo was *hers.*

The down payment, closing costs, renovations: Peggy knew before she made the deal that the costs would wipe her out. "Property values are rising rapidly," the real estate agent had told her with a smooth smile. "Once you redo the kitchen and bathroom your unit will be worth more. Then you can refinance and get a load of cash back."

But as soon as she had bought the place and made the improvements real estate values plummeted. Almost immediately, Peggy owed more to the bank than the condo was worth. Then they raised her monthly condo fee by $150. Old buildings like hers, she was told, needed a lot of maintenance.

Because she didn't earn much working as a secretary at the Ghanaian embassy, for the past few years she had supplemented her income by working Saturdays and Sundays as a receptionist at a local nursing home. Working seven days a week also filled up the pockets of time that would otherwise have been empty.

Periodically she asked someone to cover for her at the nursing home so she could sell Ghanaian art and handicrafts at weekend expos and church bazaars, which brought in much more money than her hourly wage. But as the U.S. economy began to tank, her African art customers became more careful in their spending. Sometimes she sat there all day and didn't sell a single thing, and the booth space cost her hundreds of dollars. Soon she stopped going altogether.

Peggy threw herself on her couch, still holding the stack of mail, looking at the empty space where her dining room table should have been. After all the expense of buying and renovating the condo, she had decided to build up a nest egg again before making any large purchases, and so the dining room set would have to wait. *Oh well,* she thought, *I am an African. I'm not spoiled. I can sit on the floor and eat and be grateful for my food.*

But tonight she wasn't hungry. It was too late to eat dinner—past ten. Her boss, Ambassador Kwame Bawuah-Edusei, had kept her late, typing letters and preparing his schedule for the following day. Peggy had worked at the Ghanaian embassy in Washington for twenty-nine years in a variety of administrative positions, but the two years in the ambassador's office had been her favorite. She loved the busy excitement—

meeting African heads of state and U.S. senators and planning glittering receptions.

In Bawuah-Edusei's office the people she dealt with were extremely polite, unlike some of the people she had come in contact with years earlier when she worked in the consular section. There, people had called her up and cussed her out when their visas weren't ready, as if it had been her fault. But Peggy never let anyone disrespect her; she had yelled back at them, and in some cases hung up on them. "If you step on my toes," she liked to say, "I will bite your leg." She was transferred to the embassy's administrative section.

Growing up in Ghana, Peggy never imagined she would leave the country forever. She had been born to Joseph Ankomah Foster and Mary Vormoah in Cape Coast, a bustling city of eighty-three thousand. Her home name, or tribal name, was Amma, indicating that she had been born on a Saturday. For centuries, the southern people of Ghana had named their children after the day of the week on which they were born. *Kwame* was given to a boy born on Saturday; *Kwesi,* born on Sunday; and *Kwadwo,* born on Monday. Kofi Annan, the Ghanaian former secretary-general of the United Nations, was born on a Friday. Women, too, had day names: *Adjoa* for those born on a Monday, *Abenaa* for those born on Tuesday, etc. If more than one child in a family was born on the same day of the week, they were given an additional name referring to their birth order (*Piesie* for firstborn, *Manu* for second born, etc.). Sometimes extra names referred to the parents' feelings for the child: *Nyamekye* meant "gift from God," and *Yempew* meant "we don't want you."

When Peggy was six, her family moved north to Kumasi, where her father had found an excellent position as a railroad engineer, which allowed the growing family to live fairly well by Ghanaian standards. After graduating from high school in 1971, she studied catering at Kumasi Polytechnic and at Southgate Technical College in London. Energized by living in the United Kingdom, Peggy wanted to experience a year or two in the United States, after which she planned to return to Ghana to become a gourmet chef at a fine restaurant or hotel. Her father's old school chum, Alex Quaison-Sackey, was Ghana's ambassador to Washington and arranged for her to work there as a receptionist. And so Peggielene Foster began her job at the embassy in 1979. Somehow the years had slipped by, and she never left.

Peggy looked at the clock: 10:15. She had to be in the office by 7:30 the next morning to prepare for the ambassador's visitors. She needed to make sure the coffee cups and trays were clean, and that there was sufficient cream and sugar. She hadn't gotten around to doing that before she left for the day.

Peggy set the undelivered letter and all the bills down on the little glass tea table next to her old white leather couch. She was too tired to bathe or even wash her face. But she went to the kitchen and filled a glass with water and poured it in front of her door. For many Africans, pouring libations was a way of showing respect to God and honoring the dead, who were always thirsty, and it helped her stay close to her mother in the spirit world.

"Help me, Mother," Peggy said, and tears came to her eyes as they always did when she spoke to her, because she would never get over the emptiness of a world that no longer held her mother. Even though Mother had been eighty-four when she died, Peggy had been so deeply distressed that she decided she would probably never return to live in Ghana, and after eighteen years in the United States she had finally become an American citizen. "Mother, I know that you are with God," Peggy said. "Go to him and speak to him about me. Ask him to look out for me."

She poured water for her mother every night, and every morning she poured a little Gordon's gin. In Ghana the ancestors liked schnapps, and the brand used was from the Netherlands—introduced by Dutch slave traders centuries earlier—packaged in square dark green glass bottles. But the only kind of schnapps Peggy could find in the American liquor stores was peppermint schnapps, and she didn't think her mother would like that.

Her relatives in Ghana told her that the closest thing to Ghanaian schnapps was Gordon's gin, so that's what she should use. You were supposed to pour it on the ground right outside your door. Since Peggy had a condo, she couldn't very well pour it in the hallway—it would make the place smell like a saloon and leave a stain—so she poured it just inside the door on the cream-colored carpet. Though clear, the alcohol soaked through to the wood floor below, and the wood stain seeped up and discolored the carpet.

She went into the bedroom, took off her pantsuit and blouse, slipped on a pink cotton nightgown, and sank into her bed. Then she wrapped her head in her blanket, a cocoon of safety that somehow made her feel warm and cozy and loved.

Though Peggy enjoyed her work in the ambassador's office, the best part of her day was her sleep. When she was asleep she didn't have to worry about unpaid bills, or office politics, or undeliverable letters. Nor did she have to ponder how to lose the weight she had been gaining due to a slowing metabolism forced to sit in a chair twelve hours a day. She didn't have to miss William, her husband who had returned to Ghana, or resent her body, which had failed to bear them children. She didn't have to question whether her life had a purpose.

Peggy had never had problems sleeping in her life, and she usually slept deeply. It was as if she went to another world, a world where everything was beautiful and there were no worries at all, a place where she was never lonely or aching for her mother.

2

Peggy's sleep was disturbed by the phone ringing. She pulled the blanket closer around her head. Maybe if she ignored it the noise would go away. It didn't.

She flung off the blanket and sat up, turned on her light and looked at the clock. It was a few minutes past four a.m. Peggy hated it when people called her that early. Sometimes her brother, Papa Warrior, who lived in Australia, got the time confused and called at that hour, but usually it was relatives in Ghana who got up at four a.m. every day because the chickens woke them. If they wanted to talk to her, they would wait patiently the five hours until it was four a.m. in Washington and then call her, thinking perhaps the chickens would be getting her up, too.

She stood up, walked to the dresser, and stared at the phone. The caller ID said "unavailable." It was an overseas call all right.

Peggy picked it up. "Hello!" she barked.

"Hello, Nana!" said a male voice on the other end. It added in Fante, "This is your uncle, Kwame Lumpopo."

Kwame Lumpopo. She remembered him. He was her mother's sister's son, so technically her cousin. But Africans weren't too technical about family relationships. They called their great-aunts *mother,* and their nieces and nephews *children,* and their distant cousins *brothers* and *sisters.* For some reason, Kwame Lumpopo always referred to himself as Peggy's uncle, even though he was about her age. He was a tall, good-looking man with a wide white grin who lived near her mother's old home in Takoradi. She had seen him at family gatherings at her mother's, and he had been on her uncle's royal council in Otuam.

"What do you mean, *Nana?*" she asked groggily. *Nana* literally meant "ancestor" and was an honorary title reserved for royalty and people of stature. Children might call their grandparents *nana*, but Peggy had no grandchildren. And she certainly wasn't royalty or a person of stature.

"Congratulations!" Kwame Lumpopo boomed. "You are the new king of Otuam!"

She rubbed her eyes. This had to be a joke.

"Kwame Lumpopo, you'd better stop your nonsense because it is four a.m. in the United States, and you have woken me from a sound sleep," she said briskly. "I have to go to work in a couple of hours to arrange the ambassador's coffee cups, and I don't appreciate this foolishness. Why are you bothering me? I'm going to hang up now." She pulled the phone away from her ear.

"No, no, please! Don't hang up!" Peggy could hear Kwame Lumpopo's loud protests hovering in the air. "Nana—I'm serious! This is no joke!"

She put the phone back against her ear.

"What is it that you want really?" she asked. "Tell it to me straight. I don't talk nonsense before the sun is up."

"Your uncle, the king of Otuam, will not be coming back from the village anytime soon," Kwame Lumpopo said quickly, before Peggy could hang up.

Oh.

Now she understood the returned letters and the disconnected phone. Hearing of her uncle's death was like losing a part of her mother all over again. That generation was going, going, gone. All anger drained from her. Tears stung her eyes.

"When did he die?" she asked quietly.

"I don't know," Kwame Lumpopo replied. "He's been in the hospital . . . er, in the *village* curing himself for a long time now. You know, they don't tell you exactly when the king . . . when they know that the king isn't coming back from the village."

That was true. If you weren't in a king's immediate circle, you wouldn't learn the date of his death until the funeral program was printed.

"Where is he now?"

"His children have put him in the fridge at the Accra morgue. We will have to keep him there until his funeral, whenever the new king—you—decides to hold it."

The new king? In Ghana the king wielded executive power over the people. So yes, *theoretically* the person who held the office could be female, just as in the United States the president could be female. But a female king was a new phenomenon and very rare. Peggy had read about two lady kings in Ghana during her morning perusals of the national news website, Modernghana.com, but her royal family, the Ebiradze, had never had one.

Was Kwame Lumpopo trying to scam her? African people scammed each other a lot, she knew, and while men around the world liked to take advantage of women, Peggy believed that Africans were the international experts.

Long ago Peggy had decided that African men were aided and abetted in taking advantage of African women by African women themselves, who were usually too timid to stand up for themselves, put the men soundly in their place, whack them on the head, or whatever the situation required. Most African women wouldn't even look a man in the eye when he spoke. Sometimes Peggy wondered how on earth she could be an African woman. She was much more like an American woman, always had been. When talking to a man she fixed her eyes on him with an unblinking stare, and the moment he disrespected her she let him have it with her big mouth.

Maybe Kwame Lumpopo thought she was a rich American and a stupid woman, and he was trying to scam her by telling her she was the king and had to wire him funds for rituals or something. If so, he obviously didn't know her well. Though right now the real problem was that she didn't know *him* well. The few times she had seen him he had smiled and greeted her warmly and asked about her American life, and that was it. She racked her brain to remember what her mother had told her about him. His wife had left him because of something heinous he had done, though that happened to a lot of African men.

"What do you mean that I'm the new king?" she asked sharply. "No woman has ever been king of Otuam. I haven't even been there since we celebrated my mother's birthday at the palace ages ago. I'm a U.S. citizen, living in Washington, D.C. It doesn't make any sense."

Peggy wondered if perhaps Kwame Lumpopo was confused and the elders had actually chosen her queen mother. In Ghana the queen mother, who was usually not the king's wife, looked after the affairs of women and children. She was supposed to be compassionate and patient, a diplomat smoothing over difficulties, gently persuading the king to follow her advice and calmly accepting it when he overruled her.

Come to think of it, Peggy would make a lousy queen mother. She wouldn't be able to kowtow to any man, even the king. She would be a big nuisance to him, yelling at him to do more for the women and children. Then she would scold the women for going to bed with ridiculous men and having so many babies they couldn't afford. No, with her loud voice and strong sense of justice, she would be better as king. But how could she be *king*?

"Your uncle always wanted you to be the next king," Kwame Lumpopo said. "He was so proud of you. 'My sister's daughter is so sensible and strong,' he would say, 'stronger than I am. She has educated herself and lived in the USA for many years, which is no joke for an African woman. She has qualities that would really help Otuam.'"

"Did my uncle pick me to be his successor then?" she asked.

"No no, Nana. You were picked by the elders and ancestors," he explained. "Once we knew that the king would be in his village for a very long time, the king's elders looked over the lists of his relatives. We chose twenty-five people who were healthy and under sixty years old, who had a good moral character, were not drunkards, and who were educated. Your name appeared on the list, Nana, the only woman among the twenty-five, because the king had always recommended you. Uncle Moses, in particular, wanted you on the list. He was the one who consulted the genealogy and insisted you be on it, even though you are a woman."

Uncle Moses. Yes, the bald-headed one with a broad nose and glasses, with full cheeks and a long mustache that made him look like a walrus.

"What happened next?" she asked.

"We took the list to the *obosomfie,* the sacred ancestral shrine where the spirit, the *obosom,* lives. All the elders went, along with some good citizens who were not relatives—to make sure there was no cheating, you know. The chief priest, Tsiami, said each person's name and poured schnapps into the ground."

Peggy remembered Tsiami, a stiff, wiry little man who had an odd habit of avoiding eye contact.

Kwame Lumpopo continued, "When the schnapps sank into the

ground, it meant the ancestors did not want that person to be king. When the schnapps steamed up, it was a clear sign they wanted that person to rule."

"And when Tsiami said *my* name, the schnapps steamed up?" She had never heard of this custom before.

"Ah-henh!" Kwame Lumpopo assured her, the *henh* coming straight from the deepest nasal passages. This was Ghanaian for "That's it! You got it!"

"You were the twenty-fifth person on the list," he continued, "the last one. We were worried that maybe God and the ancestors didn't like anybody we had put on the list, but then the schnapps steamed up when Tsiami said your name."

"It really steamed up?" She was having a hard time picturing this. What did steamed-up schnapps look like?

"Yes. Not once but three times. Some of the elders were surprised because you were a woman. They wanted to be sure. So they made Tsiami perform the ritual two more times, and each time when he called your name the schnapps steamed up."

A shiver went down her spine. There was a long pause.

"The ancestors picked you, Nana," Kwame Lumpopo said earnestly. "Will you take it?"

Would she take it? Peggy had absolutely no idea. Here it was four o'clock in the morning and she was still groggy and this person was telling her that her uncle was dead and she was an African king because the schnapps had steamed up.

"I'll have to think about it," she said. Peggy always said this when most other people would say *I don't know*. It gave the impression of being in control rather than being indecisive, and at the moment she was feeling extremely indecisive. Panicked, even. "I'll call you later."

"The rituals are done," he replied. "The ancestors want you."

Peggy slowly hung up the phone. Clearly, she wouldn't be able to get back to sleep. She walked out into her living room, sat down on the sofa, and looked at the empty space that should have been her dining room. *How can a secretary be king?* While she supposed there was no reason why a secretary couldn't, it must still be highly unusual.

If she accepted she would have to go over there soon for her enstoolment, the Ghanaian form of coronation. In Ghana, going back into the mists of time, hand-carved wooden stools were not just the symbol of royalty, they were also holy items, the focus of prayer and veneration. Each king was given a new stool, the *ahengua,* into which the *tsiami* put the king's soul along with the souls of the previous kings, the ancestors, and the unborn. Royal stools were so holy that they were never allowed to touch the ground; no one, not even the king, could sit on them. For the enstoolment ceremony, the king's *tsiami* held him above the stool, which was on a platform, and lowered him three times in a symbolic sitting. On official occasions, kings sat on their public stools, which contained no ancestral spirits.

The spirits in the royal stool could see and hear everything everyone did within the borders of the kingdom and often cried when they were upset. Peggy recalled a story her mother had told her about Otuam's sacred stools; long ago, enemies had broken into the stool room and stolen them. Fortunately for Otuam, the stools made such a ruckus— angry voices, the sound of breaking crockery, and the slamming of doors—that the thieves brought them back, eager to get rid of them.

If Peggy became king, her behavior in public would have to be regal, in order to honor the stool spirits. She wouldn't be allowed to dance in a club, though she hadn't done that since before she was married. But kings weren't supposed to eat or drink, joke or argue in public either. Peggy loved to laugh, and sometimes she did get in arguments if some one tried to push her around, or butt in front of her in the checkout line at the grocery store. And if she saw an injustice, a man yelling at a woman, or a big kid picking on a little one, or somebody kicking a dog, she would scold the malefactor without fear, shaking her finger in his face. *Somebody* had to tell people when their behavior was disgraceful.

If she became king, she would have to watch herself, certainly when she was in Ghana, and probably in the United States as well. She would hate to see her picture under a headline in *The Washington Post,* "Ghanaian King Caught Behaving Badly in Silver Spring Supermarket." No, it wouldn't matter if she was here in America, or in Otuam, or in Timbuktu, for that matter. Once she was king, she would have to *become* a king.

As king, Peggy would be the personification of government to her people, more so even than the president of Ghana, who was democratically elected but, like most presidents around the world, lived surrounded by layers of impenetrable security in a palace. Though they were different in many ways, Peggy knew that tribal kings and government officials lived in easy camaraderie. When the British colonized Ghana in the nineteenth century, they had relied on local kings to support them. In return the British government had brought a variety of benefits to the tribes—jobs, roads, churches, schools, and other improvements. The kings themselves had often received income from the British to rule their kingdoms and keep their subjects in line with British law.

When Ghana declared independence from Great Britain on March 6, 1957—the eve of Peggy's fourth birthday—many questioned whether kings were necessary anymore. Were they simply a colorful relic of the past that should be put aside like a curio inside a cabinet? But no, the ancient tradition remained too strong. For one thing, kings were the custodians of Ghana's vibrant cultural heritage. Getting rid of them would obliterate most of Ghana's rich history, leaving only the sterile, Western, white part. Kings and all they stood for were what made Ghana Ghana, rather than just another former British colony like, say, Canada.

And there were real advantages to having a king. Citizens could easily obtain justice by simply marching up to the palace and asking to speak to him. Resolving disputes through the king was far easier than hiring a lawyer and taking an opponent to civil court. For one thing, it was inexpensive, costing the plaintiff perhaps a few bottles of beer or a chicken, and for another, the king or his advisors usually knew the characters of all the people involved in a case, their parents, their childhoods, their habitual misbehaviors or exemplary virtues. Such knowledge helped a king decide a dispute fairly, with no lawyers involved.

Lawyers, it was well known, were people professionally trained to meddle in the affairs of others by concealing the truth. Certainly a defendant knew the facts of a case better than his lawyer, who had not been present when the disputed event occurred. Therefore, in Ghana, a defendant who refused to speak for himself and was prepared to hide behind the dazzling verbal legerdemain of a lawyer was felt to be guilty before the trial even began.

Kings knew who was telling the truth simply by looking into the eyes of the person speaking, an ability that came from the wisdom of the stool, which gave the king special powers. Therefore it was useless, even dangerous, for anyone to lie to a king. Moreover, when a king settled an argument, he usually guided both parties to an amicable consensus, using his charm and diplomacy to settle a contentious matter once and for all.

Similarly, kings put their diplomatic skills to work when dealing with elected officials, whom they accepted with regal grace, regardless of party affiliation, and whom they often asked to help their communities build schools, pave roads, or run water lines. Politicians, on the other hand, respected kings for keeping their people in line, keeping civil court dockets clear, and working with government authorities to help their communities. As king of Otuam, Peggy would straddle the worlds of modern democratic politics and ancient tribal traditions.

She tried to remember what she could of Otuam. There was one paved road, she recalled, Main Street, lined with little shops and rambling concrete block houses. There were few cars—taxis, mainly, which residents took to the nearby market towns of Mankessim or Agona Swedru to shop or sell their wares—so the chickens and goats usually had free run of the road. The chickens, Peggy recalled, were painted different colors so their owners could identify them. During her last visit, she had seen chickens with big yellow stripes on their backs, and others with blue or red.

The little blue and white police station was on Main Street, along with the most impressive building in town, the salmon-colored Methodist church with its tall spire that the British missionaries had built a century ago. Between Main Street and the sea was the fishing village of mud huts with thatched roofs, and on the beach the fishermen kept their long, handmade canoes.

On the other side of Main Street, a bit farther afield, was the royal palace. It was a T-shaped, two-story whitewashed building constructed in the early 1960s by her mother's first cousin, Nana Amuah Afenyi IV, whom she had always known as Uncle Rockson. He had been a wealthy man, educated in London, who had brought the first razor blade factory to Ghana. The palace courtyard was flanked by two long rows of housing for the king's relatives called "the boys' quarters," though families lived there. And beyond that were dozens and dozens of small farms, with tin-roofed concrete block houses.

Otuam's farmers worked all day in the fields, cultivating pineapples, yams, and papayas, planting and weeding, fertilizing and harvesting. But it was the fish that brought the town a measure of prosperity and its immunity from famine whether the rains came or not. Six days a week the fishermen hauled in heavy nets of fish—mackerel, herring, red snapper, tilapia, and salmon—from hundreds of feet out at sea, sometimes pulling for eight hours straight, while their wives cleaned the fish and sold it on Main Street from large silver buckets on their heads.

Whether the wives of fishermen or farmers or owners of their own little Main Street shops, Otuam's women spent some time every day outside. Peggy could picture them sweeping the dirt with palm fronds, feeding chickens, smoking fish in large clay ovens, washing clothes in vats, and pounding cassava root into a white paste called *fufu*, which was something like mashed potatoes.

The town hadn't changed much over the decades Peggy had visited it and seemed to be a world unto itself. Even its dialect of Fante was heavy, archaic, using riddles and proverbs the way people had spoken centuries earlier. The Otuam dialect was linguistic proof of the town's scant interaction with the wider world. It seemed that few people ever left Otuam, and even fewer moved there from elsewhere.

Otuam's slow pace gave it one great advantage over more modernized towns: its original gods and goddesses hadn't been chased away by traffic jams, blaring horns, and the hectic lifestyle the spirits despised. Peggy recalled Tsiami telling her once that Otuam had seventy-seven gods and goddesses who lived on the beaches and in the fields and woods, while their counterparts in the cities had long ago fled the noise and bustle. Otuam's spirits, Tsiami had said, were exceptionally strong and intervened frequently in the lives of the town's inhabitants, rewarding good people and punishing evil ones.

But there wasn't much evil to punish: no murders, rapes, armed robbery, or arson that she had ever heard of. Peggy tried to remember something her mother had told her years ago, something unpleasant about the town. Yes, that was it. Some of Otuam's men got drunk and beat their wives, and that was certainly a mark against the place. If she decided to accept the crown, her first order of business would be to put an end to that. But overall, most people were kind and friendly, often taking the time to chat with a friend or visit a neighbor, or sit quietly under a shade tree and watch the shafts of sunlight slanting down through green branches.

Peggy loved Ghana because its twenty-four million inhabitants were known as the friendliest, most peaceful people in Africa and probably in the whole world. They didn't want to rule over anybody, or steal other nations' resources. They just wanted to work hard, stay healthy, and enjoy their friends and families. This was even true in centuries past. Peggy's Fante tribe had, for the most part, interacted harmoniously with the European traders who built fortresses and towns on the coast. The Portuguese first arrived in the late fifteenth century, and within a few decades the Dutch, British, and Danes joined them to trade in slaves, ivory, and gold, developing the local economy and bringing in what the native people considered to be luxury goods. By 1874 Great Britain had either conquered or purchased the other nations' forts and made Ghana, then called the Gold Coast, into a colony.

English became the official language, though every region had a tribal language, which in most of southern Ghana was Fante. Across the colony, school instruction was in English; businesses and streets had English names. Many Ghanaians in the cities even took English surnames, as Peggy's father's family had, and gave their children English first names, often from the Bible.

The Fantes' acceptance of colonization was fueled by their fear of their aggressive neighbors to the north. The powerful Ashanti tribe was building an empire of its own and fielded half a million soldiers by the mid-nineteenth century. The peace-loving Fantes realized they, too, would be conquered by the Ashantis if the British didn't protect them, though by 1902 even the Ashantis had been forced to submit to British rule.

The Fantes embodied the nonviolence, hospitality, and friendliness of modern Ghana, and Peggy supposed that the people of Otuam were the most peaceful of the peaceful. The symbol of Otuam, the figures carved on top of the chief priest's speaking staff, Peggy remembered, were a gun, a snail, and a turtle. During her last visit there, she had asked Tsiami what those symbols represented. He had told her that they came from an old Ghanaian proverb that said a hunter in the bush wouldn't bother himself with a turtle or snail, peaceful creatures that stayed low and quiet on the ground. The hunter would shoot a lion or rhino, pow-erful, aggressive creatures. The people of Otuam felt no shame in seeing themselves as the snail and the turtle. In fact, they felt it was a clear indication of their intelligence; snails and turtles would never get shot. Yes, it seemed to Peggy that it would be fairly easy to rule over the peaceful people of Otuam.

If there was one thing holding Peggy back from accepting the crown immediately, it was Otuam's poverty. The town had no gold mines or factories like other parts of Ghana. It couldn't boast any of the large Ghanaian cocoa plantations owned by Nestlé or Cadbury where local residents earned good money by harvesting the basic ingredient of chocolate to make world-famous candy bars. Otuam had its fish, mostly, which was enough to keep the people fed and healthy, and that was about it. No one starved, but many lived hand to mouth.

Did the king collect any taxes or fees? She didn't know. All the land in a town or village belonged to its king, she knew, as well as to the dead and the unborn. But the king had the right to decide who would live on it. Did he do so for a price? Even if there was some income in Otuam, it probably wouldn't be sufficient for the king's many expenses. During her last visit to Uncle Joseph in the royal palace, Peggy remembered, a chunk of plaster had fallen from the ceiling and no one had seemed surprised.

The derelict condition of the palace had been the root of family dissension for many years. After the death of Uncle Rockson, who had built it from scratch and lovingly maintained it, his successor never lifted a finger. The rainy season in coastal Ghana did a lot of damage to roofs and walls, and when the heaviest rains ended in late August, most families brought out ladders and cement to patch things up. But not Uncle Joseph. When a big hole opened in the ceiling over the king's bed, he put a bucket in the middle and lay on one side of it, and his wife on the other.

Uncle Rockson's younger brother, Uncle James, was horrified. He bought cement with his own money to patch up the walls and brought the bags to Otuam as a gift to the king, and he even offered to have his own workmen do the repairs. But Uncle Joseph seemed offended by the offer. The bags sat in the courtyard, and during the next rainy season, they got wet and turned to cement blocks.

Peggy suddenly remembered a day long ago when she was on break from catering school in London and visited her mother. "I'll be going to Otuam," Mother said. "There's trouble afoot between Uncle Joseph and

Uncle James about the palace. So the family is meeting to try to resolve the dispute. Do you want to come?"

Peggy had yawned. What did she care about falling-down palaces and the arguments of old men? "I'll stay here," she said.

And now, ironically, if she accepted the kingship, the falling-down palace and the arguments of old men would land squarely in her own lap. For if she became king, she would have to arrange Uncle Joseph's funeral, which she couldn't begin to do until she had entirely refurbished the palace.

A magnificent royal funeral, held in an impressive locale, reflected glory not only on the deceased, but on his successor and his people. Such events typically lasted three days and were enormously expensive. Hundreds of the late king's subjects would show up, along with neighboring kings and their elders and relatives, and they all drank whiskey and ate meat from freshly slaughtered cows. The deceased would be interred in a tomb within the palace.

If, in her haste to put Uncle Joseph to rest, she gave him a poor funeral in the crummy courtyard of a decrepit palace and entombed him behind a tottering, leaky wall, his spirit might haunt her for the rest of her life. Then again, if she left him in the fridge in Accra for a long time, that would make him mad, too. He would be wandering in limbo, that gray world in between life and death, not fully welcomed by the ancestors until after his funeral. Peggy winced at the prospect. Either way, if she became king, it looked like she would be haunted.

Peggy wondered if she could count on the late king's children to help her with these expenses. There were five of them, two boys who had moved to Houston and become U.S. citizens, and three girls who lived in Accra.

She strained to remember what Mother had told her: something about the children's anger at their father for leaving their mother and not supporting them. He had gone from woman to woman, finally settling down with an Otuam fishmonger in the palace, ignoring his children's requests for financial help. So the children went without, just as the palace now did.

Far more serious than the falling-down palace was the water situation in Otuam. During her 1995 visit there had been no running water, and she doubted they had gotten any since then. The British colonial government had put in pipes in 1950, and many houses had a toilet, sink, and shower. But the pipes had gone dry in 1977, and no one knew why. Was it a massive rupture underground? The faulty new pumping station thirty miles away? The Ghanaian government never investigated because it didn't have the money to fix the pipes whatever the cause. Thousands of villages needed water, and the funds simply weren't available.

Since then the town had dug a couple of boreholes on its outskirts, pumps where you would set your bucket under the faucet on one side and jump up and down on the long handle on the other side to make water come out. Most families relegated their children to water duty, and kids as young as five walked every day for miles before school to carry heavy buckets on their heads.

As an American she couldn't let her people live without running water. It was unthinkable. Yet how would she fix whatever was wrong with the pipes? How much would it cost? Who would she ask to look into it?

The truth was, if she became king, seven thousand people in Otuam would be counting on her to improve their lives. It was a huge responsibility. And daunting as the job was, she couldn't devote herself to it full-time, at least not yet. Right now she had a job, a condo, a life in Washington. She would have to rule the kingdom from afar, returning perhaps once a year for as many days as her boss permitted, and move to Otuam once she retired. Would the elders be okay with that?

And then there was the question of whether she could do the job at all. Peggy had never been trained for an executive position. She had never run a company, sat on the city council, or even managed a store or restaurant. For twenty-nine years, she had carried out the instructions of others who gave her documents to type, people to call, and coffee trays to set up. For decades, she had followed the vision of her bosses, not her own.

Could a good secretary be a good king? She turned the dilemma around in her head, examining it from different angles. As a secretary, she had to think on her feet, understand people's needs, and find solutions to a wide variety of problems, whether technical, interpersonal, or financial. She had worked diligently to acquire new administrative skills, which, she believed, could be quite helpful in running a small kingdom. In some cases, she had advised her bosses on improving efficiency, troubleshooting problems they were unaware of. Surely that ability would help her rule in Otuam. And after doing her boss's expense accounts for years, she could organize the town's financial matters.

As king, she would have to deal with a variety of conflicting personalities—her elders, her subjects, government officials, and potential investors. As a secretary, she had dealt with embassy staff from all of Ghana's tribes—the Fantes in the south, fun loving and friendly; the Ashantis in the middle, shrewd businessmen; the Ewes in the east, extremely conservative and trustworthy; and the "northerners" in the arid region, a complex group of Muslim tribes feared for their generations-long blood feuds. She also dealt with pencil-pushing U.S. government bureaucrats, flamboyant African heads of state, and members of the general public, who ranged from the polite to the insane.

Yes, being a good secretary required its own kind of leadership and vision, as well as flexibility and resourcefulness. The one blip in her personnel file—her prickly, autocratic spirit—could be seen as proper in a king. Perhaps those very qualities that made some consider her to be arrogant or aloof might help her to be a truly good ruler.

As king she would have to work closely with her council of elders. Technically, the royal council was advisory in nature, counseling the king on all matters that required his attention, from settling disputes among townsfolk to organizing royal ceremonies. However, it was very bad form for a king not to consider the elders' advice and stubbornly go his own way. Arguments were permitted between a king and his council, but in the end they were expected to reach a consensus.

She pictured herself meeting with Otuam's council of elders, men in their seventies and eighties, set in their ways and used to telling women what to do. And not only was it awkward that she was a woman. There was another consideration: Peggy was significantly younger than her elders. Even if she were a man, they would have a hard time hearing criticism from a younger person. Age seniority was so important in Ghana that someone might say, "Hush, you youngster! I am older than you are! Have respect for your elders!" even if he was older by one day. Twenty to thirty years younger than her elders, Peggy would be considered almost a child in their eyes. How on earth was she going to rule over a council of traditional old men? An amicable consensus on important issues would be impossible if they tried to boss her around, she knew, because a king shouldn't meekly follow orders from anyone, except God.

She sat there and thought and thought about it until the sun came up and it was time to pour libations. For centuries, perhaps millennia, African tribes had poured libations to their ancestors and worshipped the divine in every living thing, even in objects. Souls, they believed, were not limited to human bodies, for God was all-powerful, and everything in the world he made must therefore possess an immortal spark. Spirits could inhabit bodies, clearly, for such was the case with human beings. Or they could inhabit plants, rocks, or even man-made objects. Peggy often spoke to the female spirit of her car, a 1992 Honda, begging her to keep going for just a little while longer.

Like many Ghanaians, Peggy mixed Christianity with her ancestral religion, animism, into something that you might call Christianimism. To the dismay of the missionaries who brought Christianity to Ghana, many of those who had jubilantly converted also continued their ancestral traditions. They saw Jesus, born of a virgin and resurrected from death, as one of God's countless miracles, along with thirsty ancestors and objects that could think.

There were, of course, some Christians in the big cities who scoffed at the pouring of libations as a tragic waste of good liquor and some animists in the bush who ridiculed Christianity as a tool used by white men to colonize black ones. Peggy was raised to see truth and beauty in both traditions and combined them flawlessly. While pouring her morning libations to the ancestors, she also asked Jesus for guidance and wisdom. Afterward, she read the Psalms and the Gospels.

Today she prayed with particular fervor. "Mother," she said, tears sliding down her cheeks. "Wherever you are, I know God and Jesus are there. Please ask God and Jesus to help me because I have a big decision to make, and I honestly don't know what to do." She poured the gin, and it pooled on the carpet.

What would Mother advise Peggy to do now? Her last words on this earth, before Peggy could get to Ghana to see her, had been about her favorite child: "Tell my daughter I have been climbing the hill a long time, and now I am on the top. I am very tired, so I am going. But tell Peggy that she is very special, and she must stand up loud and clear for what she knows is right. She must be strong, but always remain humble." And then she was gone, and the world was empty.

Peggy prayed to Uncle Joseph for the first time ever, now that she knew he was in the village for good. "You wanted me to be king after you," she said. "And I have been chosen. Now I need your help in making this decision." She poured some more gin.

Then she prayed to all her ancestors going back in time. "Please help me," she said. "Show me the way." And she poured the gin a third time. Now there was a big puddle on the carpet, which slowly sank in and darkened the stain. One of these days when she could afford it she would have to get some new carpet. Maybe in a darker color.

And then it was time to get ready for work. In the bathroom she studied her face in the mirror. "Hello, king," she said out loud. "King *Peggy,*" she added, and burst out laughing.

Was this the face of a king? She ran her fingers over the smooth golden brown skin. Other than the folds that ran from her nose to her mouth, there were no lines on her face, though that was likely because of her weight gain. If she lost the weight, would her skin sag like that of so many women her age? Would she look like a bulldog? She didn't know. Women, she thought, were relegated in middle age either to a wide rear end or a crinkled dog face. Perhaps it was better to have the wide rear end, all things considered.

The eyes looking back at her were large, dark, widely set, and expressive. Her nose turned up, like that of a child. Her lips were full, her teeth white and even. She turned her head from side to side, looking at the angles. It was a strong face, a noble face, perhaps the face of a king. She didn't have much in the way of eyebrows, though. Maybe if she became king she should pencil them in to look tougher. No, she liked them the way they were.

She looked at herself straight on. It was still a beautiful face, she realized, a face that in her younger years had made several men chase her around like the maniacs they were. But there was only one man she had ever wanted. Her husband. William.

3

Peggy walked through the long, dark basement corridor, past the laundry room and trash room, and out into the parking lot, the resting place of cars whose owners couldn't afford spaces in the garage under the building. On this warm August morning, as she approached her green 1992 Honda she burst into laughter. *A royal carriage,* she thought. *A chariot fit for a king.* At least it had been paid for long ago, and that was a great advantage.

"Good morning," she said to the spirit of her car. "Thank you for taking me to work and back today. I know you are old and tired. I will get you a tune-up soon."

She drove to work through Rock Creek Parkway, as she always did. It was a lovely route that cut right through the heart of the nation's capital, following a little stream. Huge old trees arched over the winding road, and elegant houses sat high on hills. It was a much nicer drive than the traffic lights and brake lights of Connecticut Avenue. Plus, her car tended to break down a lot, and if it broke down on the main road in rush hour traffic everyone would honk their horns and yell at her and flip her the finger. If she broke down on the parkway, no one would yell at her, and someone would eventually come by to help her. Her car was like an old person whose health you could determine depending on how she coughed and wheezed. On good days, her car made a noise like *cha-cha-cha-choo,* and on bad days it went *pah-pong pah-pong.*

Today was evidently a good day, and her car's spirit was happy. As Peggy rounded the bends, the car cried *cha-cha-cha-choo.* She came to a stop sign and flicked on her left blinker. And then she heard a voice, as if a person were sitting right beside her in the car. *Nana, kofa wara wodzea,* it said in Fante. Nana, go for it; it's yours. The voice was very powerful and yet quiet. It was neither male nor female. Or maybe it was both.

Peggy looked around, alarmed. What voice was this? She knew that many Africans heard voices, saw visions, and had dreams that came true, but she had never been one of them. Except . . . a memory of something struggled to reach the surface of her mind before falling back down. She brushed a hand over her forehead. Maybe she was so tired and shocked from the short sleep and strange phone call that she was imagining things.

She arrived outside the Ghanaian embassy at seven thirty. To one side was the embassy of Bangladesh, which was usually quiet, and to the other, the embassy of Israel, with its cameras and steely eyed security guards who chased away any hapless non-Israeli trying to park in front. Sitting serenely alongside so much security, her building was made of cream-colored stone, and the front fence was decorated with large tribal symbols called *adinkra.*

Peggy recognized some of the twelve *adinkra* symbols on the embassy wall. There was the large X-shaped symbol, *Nyame Nnwu Na Mawu,* which meant "God never dies, therefore I cannot die," and stood for life after death. Another, shaped like an apple with a diamond in the middle, *Nyame Biribi wo soro,* meant "God is in the heavens," a symbol of hope. And a square with knot-like loops in all four corners, *Mpatapo,* stood for reconciliation and pacification after strife.

There were dozens of *adinkra* symbols, which long ago Peggy had had to learn in school. One suddenly sprang to mind: *Nea Ope Se Obedi Hene,* a V inside a circle inside a square, which meant "He who wants to be king in the future must first learn to serve."

Peggy chuckled. "This king served indeed," she said to herself. "I served coffee, and I served tea." Peggy pushed open the tall metal gate and greeted the security guard in his little kiosk.

The block-shaped building was less than twenty years old, on International Drive, a horseshoe-shaped street lined with large, modern embassies. In the late 1980s several nations, including Ghana, fed up with the bad parking and dilapidated century-old mansions on Massachusetts Avenue and Sixteenth Street, had moved their embassies to this new neighborhood farther north. Ghana's old embassy building had been a turreted stone castle, imbued with Old World elegance, which the new one, with its tinted windows and vast reception rooms, lacked. But the new embassy offered far more space; its heating and air-conditioning worked, and when it rained you didn't have to put a bucket on the floor to catch the water dripping in from the leaky old roof.

Ghanaian embassy staff in particular had had a special fondness for their original building, where Peggy had worked for a decade, because it had been purchased by Ghana's independence leader and first president, Dr. Kwame Nkrumah himself. That building had always reminded them of their heroic struggle for freedom.

Citizens of the Gold Coast had been agitating for greater rights from Great Britain for decades, but after World War II calls for outright independence became louder and stronger. Gold Coast men had fought and died bravely beside the British in both world wars, and after fighting for the freedom of others expected some freedom of their own. They were heartened to see India shake off its British shackles in 1947, and some of them rioted against colonial rule in 1948. Dr. Nkrumah, a bright young politician who had studied in Britain and the United States, organized strikes and nonviolent protests. When Britain granted independence in 1957, Dr. Martin Luther King Jr. flew to Accra to attend the celebrations. President Nkrumah set up the new government according to the British parliamentary system, and the colonial name of Gold Coast was changed to Ghana in memory of a great African empire that had existed a thousand years earlier. As the first African colony to achieve independence, Ghana became a beacon of hope to other colonies struggling for self-determination in the 1960s and 1970s.

Like many of the Ghanaians she knew, Peggy had no hard feelings toward the British, who had brought Ghana roads, railroads, schools, hospitals, and courts of law. She was proud that her country had been a colony of the well-organized British and not the French, who had colonized so many West African countries. Many Ghanaians saw the French as chaotic, greedy, and corrupt, qualities that continued unabated in their colonies long after the French themselves had packed up and left.

Once inside the embassy, Peggy walked to the left of the vast sunken reception room with its floating spiral staircase and Ghanaian art and took the elevator up to her office on the third floor, where she went about preparing the coffee service for the ambassador's visitors. She decided she wouldn't tell the ambassador about this offer of kingship unless she decided to take it. She would continue to pray about it.

It would have been an average day if she hadn't received that phone call. The ambassador arrived, and his visitors came and went. Peggy took his messages and typed his letters. But as the day wore on, she thought she would burst if she didn't talk to somebody about the life-changing choice that lay ahead of her.

She didn't have close friends in the embassy. But she was on friendly terms with many, and she decided she could certainly tell a couple of embassy staff about what had happened. Maybe they could advise her on what to do.

Sighing, Peggy pushed back her swivel chair and took the elevator down to the second floor to see her friend Elizabeth, a lovely doe-eyed woman in her thirties with velvety dark skin. As Peggy told her the whole story, Elizabeth's eyes opened wide. "Should I take it?" Peggy asked.

"Yes, you have to take it!" Elizabeth replied, slapping her desk so hard a stack of visa applications fell over. "God alone makes kings. He must have chosen you."

"But I'm worried about all the money it requires, and the responsibility. And I will lose my freedom. I won't be able to do whatever I want in public anymore."

"God will show you the way!" Elizabeth said, nodding vigorously.

That made Peggy feel a lot better. Elizabeth was right. Still, in the interest of a second opinion Peggy took the elevator up to the fourth floor to talk to Gladys. Gladys was a heavyset woman with large glasses who liked to wear African dresses and lots of jewelry.

"You would be a damned fool to take it!" cried Gladys, her huge gold earrings clacking as she shook her head. Then she waved her hands, and her countless gold bangle bracelets tinkled and clattered. "It will be a lot of responsibility and cost you a pile of money. And you would have to behave yourself in public and stop arguing with people. Tell them to forget it and choose someone else."

That made Peggy feel terrible. Gladys was right. What had she been thinking even to consider becoming king? Then Peggy looked into Gladys's eyes and saw something there—was it jealousy? Perhaps Gladys was jealous because no one had asked *her* to be a king. As she trudged down the long corridor to the elevator, Peggy realized that this was a decision she would have to make on her own.

After work she went home and ate dinner sitting on her sofa. She had picked up pea soup and roasted salmon with caper sauce from the Parthenon Restaurant near the embassy, and as she ate, ignoring the news playing on the TV, she pondered how her predictable average life had become quite strange: in the course of mere hours she had been chosen king of a faraway land, and she had heard a disembodied voice in her car.

She finished eating and flipped through the stack of bills that had arrived in the mail that day, asking herself how she could afford to be a king with huge financial responsibilities when she could barely afford to be a secretary with modest expenses. The people of Otuam needed so much, and Peggy alone couldn't provide it.

She decided to call her brother and ask his opinion. Two years younger than Peggy, his Christian name was Peter but somehow everyone had always called him Papa. His middle name, Ankomah, meant "warrior." As a child, Peggy took good care of Papa Warrior because he was smaller than she was and being a boy was sure to get into trouble. When their parents finally divorced—Father had slowly crushed the life out of the marriage with his unceasing adultery—Peggy and Papa Warrior had become even closer. They protected each other during forced visits to their father, when their new stepmother subjected them to violent beatings for the sin of not being her own blood.

Papa Warrior was a slight, wiry man, bursting with ambition and energy. His voice was several times louder than what an observer might expect to bellow forth from his slender frame. At the age of eighteen, he had shaken the dust of Ghana from his shoes and gone into the world seeking adventure. He had worked as a sailor cruising the seven seas, lived in Greece and Sweden, and more recently owned a security consulting business in Sydney, where he had become an Australian citizen.

A few months earlier, Papa Warrior had been finishing up his second university degree when his studies were interrupted by a terrible car accident. He was currently living in the hospital, undergoing numerous surgeries on his leg.

When Peggy told him about Kwame Lumpopo's phone call, Papa Warrior said with characteristic brusqueness, "Sounds like a joke to me."

"I don't think so," Peggy said. "They want me to come over soon for my enstoolment."

Papa Warrior paused. "In that case, you should accept it. Kingship is a destiny."

"It will be hard though, Papa. The town is a mess. The palace is a mess. I think my elders might prove difficult."

Papa Warrior chuckled. "You will keep them on a short leash, as you do me."

Even after they both became adults (and now they were in their fifties), Peggy couldn't seem to stop telling Papa Warrior what to do. She badgered him to quit smoking, which he finally did, and to drink less and eat more, which he did not do. More disturbing to Peggy than his diet was that when Papa Warrior drank in pubs (which seemed to be the national sport of Australia), he wasn't afraid of fighting if a bigger man insulted him.

Peggy often called Papa Warrior several times a day to check up on him, something their mother had never done. "He's an adult now," Mother had said gently. "Maybe we should leave him be."

But Peggy couldn't leave him be. If she wasn't able to reach him, she pictured him in jail for causing a public disturbance, or even in the morgue, killed perhaps by an enormous Australian weight lifter who had crashed a bar stool over poor Papa Warrior's head. She called his friends to see if they knew where he was. Papa Warrior often returned to his apartment to find yellow Post-it notes on his door with the message *Urgent. Call your sister in the U.S.* After all the drama, it was usually discovered that Papa Warrior had turned his phone off because he had been with a woman. Such frequent calls hadn't been necessary lately, what with Papa Warrior in a hospital bed with his leg in the air, a position in which he couldn't get into too much trouble.

"Take it, Peggy," Papa Warrior urged. "You can call your elders four or five times a day to check up on them, and stick your nose into everything they are doing, and tell them all that they are doing wrong, and check up on me less often. It will be a good thing for us all."

That night Peggy barely slept. She tossed and turned, thinking about her bizarre predicament. She saw Elizabeth's lovely dark face rise before her, saying, "God alone makes kings!" and Gladys's wide bespectacled face saying, "You would be a damned fool to take it!" and Papa Warrior's impatient face saying, "Don't call me so much!"

The next morning, on her way to work, it happened again. The voice. As soon as she hit the stop sign in Rock Creek Parkway, it said, *Yafawo, Nana! We chose you, Nana!*

She looked around her car, decided to pretend it hadn't happened, and kept driving. She was extremely tired, after all. Two nights with very little sleep.

At the embassy the day was like any other, except for Elizabeth and Gladys stopping by to find out what she had decided and urging her in two different directions. The president of Ghana, John Kufuor, would be making a state visit to Washington in three weeks to visit President Bush, and Peggy worked with the ambassador on the schedule of events.

Unfortunately, Ghana's political fortunes hadn't remained stable after independence in 1957. President Nkrumah, who would always be beloved for obtaining independence from Great Britain, veered toward dictatorship himself. He was proclaimed president for life in 1964. He dismissed judges whose decisions he disagreed with and appointed others to make decisions he liked. In 1966 a military coup overthrew President Nkrumah when he was visiting China, and he died in exile. Three years after the coup, democracy was ushered in again, only to be overthrown three years after that by another military coup. Sometimes the military coups themselves were overthrown by military coups.

Ghanaians knew a coup was happening when the television stations stopped broadcasting. Since the first two or three weeks of a coup were dangerous—army men might shoot anyone in the street—schools, courts, and businesses were closed until the television came back on. That meant that the coup was successful, the new government had settled in, and the threat of violence was over. Peggy was in London or the United States when the worst coups took place, but she had heard of how the soldiers raped women—from small girls to great-grandmothers—as a matter of routine.

Ironically, while the democratically elected first president of Ghana had dipped toward dictatorship, it was the leader of a military coup who brought democracy back to Ghana. In 1981 Air Force lieutenant Jerry

Rawlings, a pivotal player in the 1979 coup, threw out the president he had helped install and installed himself in his place. He stabilized the government and put in motion constitutional changes to hold a democratic election. In 1992 he won by a landslide in what international observers hailed as a largely free and fair election. Four years later he was elected to another four-year term. John Kufuor won the presidential vote in 2000 and reelection in 2004. It seemed that finally the pandemonium at the pinnacle of Ghanaian power had settled down. Now elections, not coups, would decide who ruled.

President Kufuor was admired for his efforts to improve the national economy and help entrepreneurs. He raised the diplomatic status of Ghana by helping to broker peace among neighboring countries—Liberia, Sierra Leone, Ivory Coast, and Guinea-Bissau. In 2007 he became chairman of the African Union, a kind of African United Nations, with representatives from all fifty-three African countries. The purpose of the African Union was to resolve conflicts and assist in economic and social development, though it was often referred to in the press as "the dictators' club."

Despite their president's accomplishments, many Ghanaians clucked in disapproval when he built a fifty-million-dollar presidential palace in Accra, shaped like an enormous five-story royal stool. One leg of the stool contained the president's residence, the other leg the presidential offices. The long curved roof represented the seat upon which a gigantic ancestral rear end would, perhaps, emerge from the clouds and sit. Some Ghanaians laughed at it. Others angrily asserted that the palace money should have gone to digging boreholes for the many Ghanaians who had no water, or for buying beds for hospitals where patients still had to trudge in dragging their own mattresses.

President Kufuor's supporters pointed out that if the taste of the Golden Jubilee House was questionable, so was the history of the president's current palace—a Danish slave castle in the port. True, the president and his staff worked in a breezy new wing built in the 1960s, but not far from the dungeons in which so many had suffered and died. The presidential palace, they argued, should be impressive, a symbol of national pride to all citizens, a sentiment with which Peggy agreed wholeheartedly.

At the end of another day, Peggy ate dinner with a tray on her lap with the news on, though she wasn't really watching it. She had stopped by the African supermarket and bought spicy fried fish and *kenke,* a favorite Ghanaian dish of hers, made from boiled cornmeal rolled into fist-sized balls. She ate it the African way, elegantly using the fingers of her right hand to pinch off a piece of food and sweep it into her mouth. Although the younger generation seemed to have forgotten it, Ghanaian etiquette considered it rude to use one's left hand to point, wave, touch others, or, heaven forbid, eat, and while dining it was usually left limply on one's lap.

As she ate, she realized that something was bothering her. There was something almost forgotten, stuck uncomfortably in the back of her mind. She wanted to either spit it up into conscious thought or swallow it entirely so it left her alone. But try as she might, she couldn't seem to dislodge it.

Peggy pushed herself up from the sofa, walked over to the kitchen, and filled a glass with water. "Help me, Jesus," she begged as she poured it onto her carpet. "Only God can make kings. Help me learn if God wants me to be a king."

She fell into another fitful sleep. The following morning, with deep bags under her eyes, she stumbled into her car to head for work. She entered Rock Creek Parkway and tensed up as she neared the stop sign. Would she hear anything?

Nana, oye waeyimyam, nye biara na wobonde onye ohene, the voice rang out. Nana, it is your destiny. Not all human beings are born to be kings and queens.

There was definitely an ancestor sitting in her car. Should she *say* something to it? What do you say to a ghost sitting next to you while you're driving? What if you said the wrong thing? Peggy decided to just keep driving.

A few seconds later, as she went over the little bridge, she heard it again. *It is your destiny. Not all human beings are born to be kings and queens,* the voice repeated, louder, as if to make sure she got the message.

Peggy got it. "Okay," she said to the voice. "All right, already. I'll go for it."

She would go for it? She supposed she had to, now that she had told the voice she would. You couldn't lie to an ancestor and get off easy; he would surely come back and punish you. The silence beside her seemed satisfied, but Peggy was trembling and wasn't sure if it was from fear or excitement, or perhaps a mixture of both. Whatever her emotions, she knew the die had been cast. She would become king.

That evening when she got home, she called Kwame Lumpopo and said, "Tell them that I have accepted it."

"Nana! That is wonderful! There will be great rejoicing in Otuam! To have a new king who is a woman and an American! Do not forget it was I who called you with the news. I would like to help you in Otuam when you are not there."

"Yes, all right," Peggy said. Surely she would need someone to help her rule from Washington, and Kwame Lumpopo was her cousin. He had been there when the ancestors had chosen her, he had been the one to call her with the news—that would forever be a special bond between them.

"Do the elders understand that I won't be able to move there right away?" she asked. "I will go over once a year for as many days as I can, but for the next few years I will need to stay in D.C. and keep my job at the embassy. I will, however, call the elders several times a week."

"Yes! Uncle Moses said just that as soon as we saw the schnapps steam up. It's no problem. Uncle Moses will help you, and I will help you, and you will come when you can."

"That is fine," she said.

"Very good. I will call you tomorrow once I have informed the elders and the people of Otuam of your decision."

"But I am worried about the late king who is in the fridge," Peggy lamented. "I won't be able to hold the funeral anytime soon. How long can we leave him there?"

"Oh, a long time," Kwame Lumpopo replied. "He's in a refrigerated room, in bed, tucked in next to all the kings and queens whose families can't afford to bury them right now or are having some dispute. He'll be fine in the fridge, except for when the electricity goes out. Maybe even then he'll keep cool. They have a generator."

Ghana had rolling power outages, sometimes every day when the grid was overloaded. Peggy hoped the generator would work. Otherwise she might feel the hard slap of an icy hand from the fridge on the back of her neck. She shuddered.

Suddenly Peggy remembered the thing that had been nipping at her memory for three days—it was the dream she had had repeatedly about fifteen years earlier. In it, she had been a little girl walking home from school behind the king's palace in Kumasi, wanting to be inside. At the time, neither she nor anyone in her family had been able to interpret it. But now Peggy understood what it meant: the ancestors had been preparing her to be king.

4

The following morning before Peggy left for work she dialed Kwame Lumpopo's cell phone. "Have you told them?" she asked when he picked up.

"I have told them," he said. "First I gathered the elders and let them know they had a new king. Then we sent the town crier to walk around the entire community banging on the old muffler he carries, announcing that since Nana Amuah Afenyi V had gone to the village for a cure and wouldn't be coming back anytime soon, we had chosen a new king, an American, female king. You, Nana."

"How do the people feel about having a lady king?" she asked.

"There is great joy in Otuam today!" he cried. "The people have gathered in front of the royal palace applauding, yelling, beating drums, and dancing for joy. They want to see their new king soon. Uncle Moses is leading the town's celebrations."

How unexpected, Peggy thought, *that the elders should be happy to have a lady king.* She felt her spirits rise.

"What will my royal name be?" she asked. The elders, she knew, chose the new king's official name.

"Nana Amuah Afenyi VI," Kwame Lumpopo replied.

The past four kings had been called Nana Amuah Afenyi after the town's seventeenth-century founder, Nana Amuah Afenyi I. She was pleased to continue the tradition and take a male name: she would need all the male energy she could get.

Kwame Lumpopo continued, "They want to have you enstooled right away."

Enstooled. *There goes my freedom,* she said to herself, *the one thing I had.* But then she quickly reminded herself, *God alone makes kings.*

"I will talk to the ambassador about my schedule and let you know when I can come. What is the least amount of time I must stay for the rituals?"

Kwame Lumpopo paused. "Well, I'd say at least ten days."

"Ten days. I think I can get that much. They owe me two months' vacation so ten days shouldn't be a problem."

"Nana," he said, more seriously now. "There is something you must do before the enstoolment can take place. Your late uncle who is in the fridge had an argument with some townsfolk and threw them in jail for a long time, which he should not have done."

"Oh?" she said.

"And to resolve the argument among the families, the late king agreed to pay them twelve million cedis." Technically, Kwame Lumpopo should have said twelve thousand cedis, per the new Ghanaian currency system. After the rampant inflation of the 1970s and '80s, the government had revalued the currency in 2007 by taking away two zeros. But he, like many Ghanaians, used the old currency out of decades of habit. Whatever the case, Peggy quickly did the math and realized he was talking about at least eight hundred dollars.

"Yes?"

"But he never did. He didn't have it, and he got sick and went to the village for a cure. In order for you to be enstooled without any problems or disputes, you should wire the twelve million cedis to disburse to the families."

Peggy's heart sank. Eight hundred dollars? Plus the airfare over there, which would be about $1,500, she figured. Together that $2,300 would have been enough money for her to take a trip to the Holy Land, to see Jerusalem and Bethlehem and Nazareth, which had always been her dream. But now, it seemed, she would use it to return to Ghana.

"I will send it," she promised.

"All right," he replied. "And remember, I was the one who told you the good news!"

"I will!" she agreed.

"Oh, and there's one other thing," he added. "The council of elders and I will drive to Accra to call on your husband with the good news that his wife is a king."

"My *husband?*" Peggy asked sharply. She had never spoken to Kwame Lumpopo about William's return to his family business in Accra, hadn't even been back to Ghana in the six years since then, but obviously her entire extended family knew all about it. And now they would tell William the wife he had left behind was a king?

"Yes, we must do it according to our tradition," he replied. "We will bring him bottles of beer and whiskey."

Peggy sighed. They would tell her husband.

Until she was well into her thirties, Peggy hadn't been sure she ever wanted to marry, given the sadness of her parents' marriage. She had spent her first decade in Washington intentionally avoiding men and concentrating on improving her secretarial skills, obtaining a diploma in computer information systems from Strayer University. For a time, she even considered becoming a nun, though she wasn't Catholic. She had always had a spiritual calling and felt that nuns, in their habits and veils, seemed to be shielded against all the violence and injustice of the world.

She started visiting the Dominican convent on Sixteenth Street, where the kindly Sister Catherine offered to work with her to determine if she had a true vocation. There she learned that nuns fasted often and didn't eat much at other times as they believed food took away from their closeness to God. That was when Peggy decided she wasn't suited to being a nun.

Shortly after that, a Ghanaian friend of hers in New York called her and said he had found the perfect man for her. She had laughed and told him he was being ridiculous. But on her next visit to New York she had met William Bartels and liked him. He wasn't like most African men, and this was what impressed her. Instead of wielding swashbuckling bluster aimed at seducing women, William possessed an almost painful shyness, which was probably why he was still unmarried in his late thirties. Two years older than Peggy, he was of average height and had an athletic build. He had intelligent eyes and a full, pleasant face. He courted her slowly, politely. *Here is a man of character and moral values,* she thought. *Here is a man who will never hurt me.*

For eight months they talked on the phone daily, visiting each other now and then, and in 1990 they married. They had a very small ceremony because William was uneasy in crowds, shy with people he didn't know well. He moved to Washington and got a good job in the communications department of C&P Telephone.

They would have been happy, so very happy, if she could have given him a child. Though she was thirty-seven when she married, Peggy knew that many African women had children later in life. Peggy had been born when her mother was forty, the seventh of ten children Mary Vormoah had delivered, most of them in her thirties and forties, including two sets of twins, though one set had died at birth. Peggy felt no need for concern because of her age.

But the months, and then the years had come and gone with no sign of pregnancy. Peggy and William spent all their savings on fertility doctors. Three times after the treatments she became pregnant. Their hearts soared with hope, and their dream of the future became rich. Three times she started to bleed a few weeks afterward, shaking her head in denial, pushing on her abdomen to hold the child in. *No, no, no,* she had keened, curled up in a ball on the bathroom floor. *Not this, not after all the money, and all the humiliating treatments, and the sudden burst of joy and hope. Not this.*

I failed, she often thought. *I failed so miserably at doing the one thing expected of every woman. Even aided by the most sophisticated American science money could buy, I failed.*

After the third miscarriage she didn't want William to touch her anymore and avoided intimacy as much as possible. During their rare lovemaking, she lay there thinking, *What is the point of all this?* Within a few days or weeks her period would come, proof in bright red blood of yet more failure.

And all the time William's family back home—especially his mother—was telling him that if Peggy couldn't do something as basic as give him a child, he should leave her. It wasn't that they were being cruel, Peggy knew. African families expected their sons' wives to produce children, and many of them. Those women who failed to do so were usually discarded for the good of the family. After all, a woman's main role in life was continuing the family line.

Peggy knew that she was lucky she lived not in Ghana but in Washington, a place where many women chose not to have children, a decision incomprehensible to Africans. She knew that she was also lucky that William loved her and stayed. The strain on their relationship was heightened when he was laid off during a downsizing. He stayed home, with no child and no job and a wife who didn't want him to touch her, despondently perusing the *Washington Post* classified section for a position, while Peggy worked to support the two of them. Such a situation would have been humiliating to any man, much more so to an African man whose self-esteem is measured in how well he can support his family. Sometimes she cajoled him into getting out of their apartment and attending an embassy reception, but he just sat with his back against the wall, shy because of all the people he didn't know. Those were his good nights; on his bad ones he sat in the car, and she brought him a plate of food and a drink.

In 2002 William's brother in Accra received a large government contract to provide Ghana's hospitals with beds. He invited William to come back for a while, join the family business, and make some good money. Peggy could join him later, or he could return to Washington. With Peggy's blessing, William left, with a spring in his step and a twinkle in his eye. He would have a good job. Earn money. Be proud of himself again.

But no sooner was William back in Ghana than his family set to work on him. He should stay there, they advised, and have children with a younger, fertile woman. When, in that terrible phone call consigning her to loneliness, he had sadly told her he would not be coming back, she had cried, "Have the child and bring it back to me! I will be its mother. You and I will raise the child together."

Such a solution was acceptable when a wife was infertile, and Peggy was willing to raise another woman's child as long as it was also William's child. At first he seemed to agree, but the years passed and eventually he had two children with two different women and never returned to Peggy. His hospital bed business was booming, and the mothers of his children seemed reluctant to part with them.

Peggy wasn't angry with her husband. The happy years they had lived together as man and wife were no match for the strong traditions of the African family. William Bartels had found himself in an impossible situation—choosing between disappointing his wife or his large family.

She understood why he had chosen to jettison her rather than his mother, brother, sisters, aunts, uncles, and cousins. She understood. She grieved every day for the companionship so rudely taken from her, and for the children she hadn't been able to carry, those tiny clots of lost hope that she still cherished because they had had heartbeats for a few days, warm and nourished inside her, and no one could ever take that memory away from her. But despite her grief at loss upon loss, she loved her husband still, and always would.

Peggy realized the great irony of her marriage. She had waited to marry until she had found a man who was moral and good and wouldn't break her heart. She had been correct that William Bartels was moral and good. He was moral and good enough to make his family happy by following African tradition. And in so doing he had broken her heart.

After he left, Peggy let her friendships slowly unravel. After all, if gentle William, who loved her, had hurt her this much, what would other people do to her? She needed to fill up her time so that she didn't get to thinking about it. She could barely stand to have a day off from work and didn't mind her long hours as the ambassador's secretary. The best thing was to arrive home too exhausted to think.

Yes, she thought, as she hung up after her conversation with Kwame Lumpopo, *William has to be told.* How would he feel about it? She supposed he would be happy for her. He was a kind person who still cared for her and felt guilty about leaving.

Then another thought occurred to her: *Maybe this is why I had no children despite all the fertility treatments, all the money, pain, and heartbreak. Now I will have seven thousand of them, and that's enough for anybody.*

On her drive to work she tensed up as she approached the stop sign. But today there was no voice. Evidently the ancestors didn't need to say a word now that she had accepted. She exhaled. She had been afraid that perhaps every day they would talk to her in her car on the way to work.

Peggy knew it was time to tell the ambassador she was a king. What would he say? Well, it was usually best to be direct with unexpected news, and come to think of it, Peggy didn't know how to be any other way. As soon as she arrived at her office she buzzed the ambassador. "Boss, I want to talk to you."

"What have you done now?" snapped the crisp voice over the intercom, cutting the air like a knife. "Have you argued with somebody in the embassy again?" The ambassador had heard about Peggy's time in the consular section, and he knew that even among her embassy colleagues, if people stepped on her toes, she bit their legs.

Fortunately for Peggy, Ambassador Bawuah-Edusei had many diplomatic talents. It was fortunate for Ghana, too. A medical doctor, he had convinced the World Bank, the U.S. Congress, and the State Department to provide medical assistance to poor areas in Ghana, areas where he himself had provided care at his own expense for nearly a decade. Appointed ambassador in 2006, he lobbied tirelessly to convince American corporations to open branches in Ghana, convincing the agricultural giants Cargill and Archer Daniels Midland to open cocoa processing plants, and Coca-Cola to expand its operations there.

"Boss, I'm coming to see you now," Peggy said, and hung up the phone.

Bawuah-Edusei's face was somber when she entered, and instead of remaining seated at his desk to talk to her as usual, he offered her a seat on the burgundy-colored leather sofa set against the wood-paneled wall. He sat down in the chair next to her.

The ambassador was a distinguished man with a high round forehead that made him look like a brown egg. He had small, piercing dark eyes that glowed like embers behind his gold-rimmed glasses, and a pencil thin black mustache. He was always beautifully dressed, and his manners were impeccable. Peggy thoroughly enjoyed working for him and had always felt she could tell him anything. But now the words stuck in her throat. She opened her mouth, and a little croaking sound came out, and then she closed her mouth.

"Well, Peggy?" he asked.

She took a deep breath, ran her hand over her short curly hair, and said, "Boss, do you know that your secretary is going to be a king?"

The ambassador cocked his head to one side and looked at her strangely. "Are you feeling okay?" he asked.

"I'm tired," she admitted, thinking that one good night's sleep hadn't entirely made up for three sleepless ones. "But I'm fine."

"Then what are you talking about?"

"Boss, I have been chosen king of Otuam because my uncle passed away. They did all the rituals, and the ancestors want me because they made the schnapps steam up, and I have accepted it."

The ambassador frowned. "King, Peggy? Are you sure they don't want you to be the queen mother?" he asked. "Perhaps you got it wrong."

Peggy had a feeling that she would be getting this question a lot. "It's true that there aren't many lady kings in Africa," she agreed. "But now you are looking at one, the same one who types your letters and makes your appointments, and I have to leave you in the near future to go to Ghana for my enstoolment."

"How many days will you be gone?" He frowned again as if struggling to absorb this turn of events.

"Don't worry, I'll stay until President Kufuor leaves D.C.," Peggy offered. "Then I'll be gone for about ten days. They say that's the minimum that I will need for all the rituals."

The ambassador nodded. "Very well," he said. "Congratulations." He stood up, and Peggy stood up, and she went back to her desk.

A few minutes later the ambassador buzzed Peggy and called her into his office. This time he remained sitting at his desk.

"Is it true, what you told me just now?" he asked. "Or was it a joke? Or are you perhaps not feeling well?" He rubbed his forehead as if it were he who wasn't feeling well.

"Boss, why are you so shocked?" she asked.

"Because in Ghana we don't *have* female kings. It doesn't make sense." He shook his head back and forth and put his palms up toward the ceiling in the ancient gesture of shocked agitation. If she wasn't mistaken, she seemed to be witnessing the crisp, cool, polished ambassador coming undone.

"We have two female kings in Ghana," she countered. "I read about them on the Ghana news website. Now I'm the third."

The ambassador sighed. He shifted in his chair and frowned thoughtfully. Beneath his trim mustache, his mouth formed into a little O that swung first to the left side, and then to the right. Looking into space, he finally said softly, as if speaking to himself, "You will be a good one. You are very strong, very focused, and you don't take nonsense from anybody. You stand up for what is right. You run this office beautifully, so I can see you running your kingdom efficiently as well." He nodded curtly, and Peggy got up and went back to her desk. The buzzer rang again.

"How did you get to be the king?" he asked over the intercom. "What is this about schnapps steaming up?"

She told him about the genealogical list and ancestral libations. "They have chosen a good one," he said again. "I guess I'm the only ambassador in the whole world whose secretary is a king!"

Word spread quickly throughout the embassy, and most people congratulated her heartily, calling her *Nana* and bowing playfully in front of her. Elizabeth, in particular, was happy. "Only God creates kings!" she said, smiling broadly. "God has a purpose for you!"

Some others looked a bit sour and told her she was crazy to accept such a responsibility. But when Peggy looked into their eyes she knew that these were the jealous ones. A lot of them were career diplomats with a much higher rank and salary than she possessed, full of themselves because, for a time at least, they had been sent to the best diplomatic posting in the world, Washington, D.C. And yet she was the king, not them. When the government recalled them from Washington and sent them to, say, Somalia, she would still be king, and they would be in Somalia.

William called to congratulate her—they usually talked about once a month—and told her about the Otuam elders' visit to give him the news. When Kwame Lumpopo arrived at William's house in Accra with a gaggle of traditionally robed elders bowing and bearing bottles of beer and whiskey, William had been startled. Then, when he heard of Peggy's accession to the throne, he had thought about it a moment before saying, "My wife will make a most excellent king. But I hope you people know what you are in for. Because if anybody in Otuam is doing anything wrong, Peggy will bust their ass." William told her that Kwame Lumpopo and her elders had laughed at this remark, but he had been dead serious and hadn't even cracked a smile.

During the call, Peggy and William caught up on the news of their respective families. There was no bitterness between them, just goodwill tinged gray with sadness now, and unspoken regret for what might have been. Toward the end of their conversation, William surprised her by saying, "I will visit you in Otuam. I will try to make it for your enstoolment, but if I can't, I will visit you another day."

Peggy's heart leaped. William would visit her. Only now she wouldn't be a barren, discarded wife. She would be an enstooled king, mother of seven thousand people. Maybe, when they saw each other again after six years, things would be different. Maybe William, now a father and a successful businessman, would be stronger, more independent in making his personal choices. It was a small, secret hope that she hardly dared to admit, but it was there, nonetheless.

After all the turmoil of making the decision, Peggy was happy that she had accepted. She had no idea what awaited her over there in her new kingdom, but she trusted that God, Jesus, and the ancestors would take care of her. And so she cheerfully kept up with President Kufuor's ever-changing schedule for his visit to Washington.

The evening that President Kufuor was guest of honor at a state dinner at the White House, Peggy saw clips of it on the news as she packed her bag. Ghana's president looked splendid in a tux, but his wife wore a striking gown of Ghana's traditional fabric, kente cloth, narrow strips of hand-woven cotton or silk with designs that dated back to the seventeenth century. In the past, kente had been worn exclusively by kings and dignitaries, but nowadays anybody could buy it. The price deterred many, however: about nine hundred dollars for a single eight-by-twelve-foot cloth.

Kente could be made in any color, though most people preferred bright colors with orange or gold predominant, woven in geometric shapes and bold designs. Each color represented a virtue of some sort: Black for the intense spiritual energy of the ancestors. Red for death and mourning. Yellow for fertility. Maroon for Mother Earth. Purple for tenderness. And blue for the sky, the home of the Great Creator Spirit. Each pattern also had a meaning, such as *The extended family is a force, One person does not rule a nation, To err is human, It's not my fault,* and *If you have something to say about me, let me first give you a stool to sit upon.*

An African wearing kente, or even regular cloth decorated with *adinkra* symbols, walked out into the world proclaiming what he or she stood for: strength, family, or forgiveness, powerful concepts that helped you get through your day. Peggy opened her closet and looked at the row of black and brown pantsuits she usually wore to the office. How sad, she thought, that we Americans dress like this. We walk outside every morning with no power, no symbolism, no added bit of spiritual heft to help us meet our challenges.

Most of the clothes Peggy would be wearing were already in Otuam. Kwame Lumpopo had said that every day during her visit she would have to wear the royal kente cloths of the late king who was in the fridge, thrown over her left shoulder the way men wore them. This was because until she was enstooled, the old king, who had merely gone to his village for a cure, was still technically alive and in power. Peggy would be standing in for him, wearing his cloths and carrying his regalia. Only after her enstoolment could she buy her own cloths.

Peggy considered what to do about jewelry. Ghanaian kings wore lots of colorful beads, bracelets, rings, and anklets. But as men they didn't wear earrings, which queen mothers weren't allowed to wear either. Peggy decided that since she was now a king she would give up earrings entirely, but she would go heavy on the traditional beaded necklaces and bracelets.

She opened her jewelry box and took out her beads, examining them carefully. Ghanaian beads were made of recycled glass, smashed to a fine powder and shaped in a heated mold. Half-inch-long tubes were the most popular shape, often interspersed with spherical beads. They were all hand painted. The background color, blue, for instance, would be overlaid by white, yellow, or red designs: a combination of circles, dots, stripes, zigzags, and squiggles.

Underneath her beads she found the delicate gold bracelet her mother had given her, and a quick stab of pain seared through her. She hadn't worn it since her mother's death, had intentionally buried it beneath her beads, because it hurt her so to look at it. In Ghana, mothers gave their daughters a collection of gold jewelry upon their first menstruation, a gift welcoming them to womanhood. Women wore the gold on their wedding day and on important occasions throughout their lives before passing it on to their own daughters. The gift included four bangle bracelets (two for each wrist), a few long necklaces, and four long belts with antique beads. If a woman had more than one daughter, she worked and saved for years, if necessary, to make sure each one received a substantial gift of jewelry.

When Peggy menstruated, her mother told her she would give the gold to her later when she left the house to get married or continue her education. The day before Peggy left for catering school in London, she told her mother the time had come for her to receive her birthright, the beautiful gold that had been passed down in her mother's family and cherished for generations. But Mother sagged and started to weep.

"What's wrong, Mother?" Peggy asked.

Mother went miserably to her bedroom and came back with the dainty gold bracelet. "This is all I have for you," she said. "When your father left me, I had to sell the rest of your gold to support the family. I sold it for our future, Peggy, for your tuition in London. You can put gold on the table, but you cannot eat it."

In Ghana there were no laws to force men to support wives and children. Many of them, like her father, like her Uncle Joseph, simply walked away and never paid a dime. They left their old families in the lurch while they ran off and started new ones. Some men had several wives, each with numerous children, and the men only provided for the families they were currently living with.

To support her children, Peggy's mother had opened a store in the market, selling brightly colored bolts of cotton cloth and lace trim. She had worked hard, with Peggy often helping in her free time, and the family had never gone hungry. It had never occurred to Peggy to wonder where she got the money to open the shop, but now she knew.

Now Mother sat on the couch and rocked back and forth, crying for her failure as a mother to do the most traditional thing a woman was supposed to do for a beloved daughter. Peggy held the little bracelet and began to weep, too. Not for the loss of the gold; she didn't care about that. But now she finally understood the sacrifices her mother had made for her, the pain she must have endured while making them, and the dread she must have had of this very moment.

And it was all her father's fault. She wondered if he had any idea that he had caused such wretched sadness. If he *had* known, he probably wouldn't have cared. Where was he now? Eating and drinking with his awful new wife? Enjoying the children he had had with her when he had still been married to her mother? Peggy wanted to spit on him. She went to the couch and threw her arms around her mother and cried with her, their tears and sobs blending together until they were too exhausted to cry much more.

"I failed," Mother said through her hands, "I failed you as a mother. I can't give you the gold. My great-grandmother's beautiful gold."

"It's all right, Mother," she said, "I don't care about the gold. You are giving me an education. Your little shop put food on the table. That is so much more important than some stupid jewelry. I don't need the jewelry. But I will treasure this little bracelet all my life."

She pulled her mother's hands away from her face and cupped her wet cheeks. "This bracelet means more to me than all the gold in the world," she said. And she meant it.

Now Peggy examined it closely. There were two thin bands of gold held together in the center by beautifully carved family symbols so old that their meaning had been forgotten. Her tears fell on it, shining for a moment like liquid diamonds before disappearing. She would wear this bracelet in Ghana, to have her mother with her there when she became king.

Failure, she thought, can follow you anywhere, like a lion tracking its prey in the bush. It can find you as a wife, or as a mother. It seemed to impact women more often than men, who usually didn't pay it much mind. There were many men who, when faced with failure, would go to a bar to get drunk and watch a football match, perhaps go home with a strange woman, and forget about it. Such men bounced around doing exactly what they wanted, not thinking of how their behavior hurt others, until they knew they were dying and then they started to think about it. Her father had been one of those men. In 1987 he had called her from a hospital in Kumasi. He was dying, he explained, and begged her to come see him before he left the earth. He had something he needed to say to her.

This was the traditional time when African men, maybe men all over the world for all she knew, asked their women for forgiveness. And the women always showed up ready to give it. Maybe we are partly at fault, she thought, because we make it so easy for them. Men know that no matter how badly they treat us, they can always make a deathbed confession and leave this earth unburdened by guilt. Maybe we should say, *Hell no! After what you did to us, I will never forgive you. In fact, I will pour libations right now begging the ancestors to drag you down to hell.* Maybe that was what she should say to her father right now.

"Well, Peggy, are you coming?" he asked, his voice trembling. Now, she thought, was the time to let him have it with both barrels.

"Yes, Father," she said. "I will take the next available flight."

She hadn't seen him in years, and now he looked shriveled. Old age and illness had reduced this once hale and hearty man to a dried-up shell, a corn husk that could speak. She approached his bed.

"I'm sorry," he said, and his voice was ragged and raspy. "I have been lying here thinking how badly I treated your mother and you kids. I hope you can forgive me so that when I go to meet the ancestors in a few days, or hours, I can tell them you have forgiven my bad behavior."

At first Peggy was exasperated. Why did men so foolishly wait until the last minute? They were like bulls in a china shop, running riot, doing damage, and never thinking twice about it until someone presented them with the bill. Only then did they say, *Gee, did I do that? Sorry.* And they only did it then because, being selfish creatures, they didn't want the ancestors to drag them down to hell.

She wanted to make him a sharp retort, the kind that stabbed the soul like an ice pick. But then she looked at the shrunken old man in the hospital bed, with the tubes going into his skinny veined arms. She looked at the human soul behind eyes glazed with approaching death. She had hated him for so many years, but she couldn't hate him now. Also, even if it had only been done in a moment of selfish pleasure, this man had given her life, and she must always be grateful to him for that, and honor him, no matter how bad his behavior.

"I forgive you," she said, and for a moment the dull eyes shone with light. "Go to the ancestors knowing you are forgiven. We all forgive you. Mother, too." She knew her mother would have wanted her to say that.

She left him then, and he died the next day. He had, evidently, been waiting to die until he was forgiven, and that was probably the smartest thing her father had ever done. It would be terrible to leave your body bowed down with the crushing weight of unforgiven sins. The ancestors waiting to take you to the other side would yell at you, possibly beat you, before they dragged you down.

Peggy wondered if Uncle Joseph's children had obeyed his summons at the end. Had his sons in Houston flown to Accra? Had the daughters living in Accra gone to his side when he was in the hospital, dying? Had they told him that he was forgiven to speed his soul to God? She hoped so.

Part II

GHANA

September 2008

5

Kwame Lumpopo was standing in the visitors' waiting section and flashed her a white grin as she emerged from the terminal. There he was, just as she remembered him—tall, well built, and good-looking. A charmer.

Though Accra was only sixty miles away from Otuam, you never knew how long the trip would take. This afternoon it took them two hours just to get out of Accra. The road was jammed all the way to the city limits and for a mile or two beyond. They crept alongside beat-up cars with black smoke roaring out of the tailpipes and lopsided public minibuses called *tro-tros*, stuffed with passengers and crowned with a tottering heap of luggage roped to the roof. There were large dust-covered trucks carrying merchandise between Accra and the hinterland, and the occasional shiny SUV so popular with top government officials and successful businessmen, always in black or steel gray. Peggy smiled to see the air-conditioned SUVs and stifling *tro-tros* all equally stuck in the same unmoving line.

Local residents made good use of the tie-up to sell idled travelers a startling variety of goods: blankets, bath and dish towels, boxes of Kleenex, rolls of toilet paper, children's toys and rubber balls, meat pies, phone cards, dog leashes, superglue, pens, apples, fried plantains, and sunglasses on a large square board. They hawked machetes, which were used to open coconuts or cut grass (most people didn't have lawn mowers), and water, large and small bottles, as well as little plastic baggies of water for those who couldn't afford the luxury of a whole bottle; people bit the corner off and squeezed the water into their mouths. And they sold tiger nuts, which looked like small, dimpled peanuts and for centuries had been eaten by aging men as a sexual stimulant, a kind of African Viagra.

Sometimes there was a veritable stream of vendors, one right after the other, marching between stopped cars, deftly dodging the motorbikes that drove between the lanes. As bad as traffic was, the vendors made it worse. Often, when a ten-minute light finally turned green, drivers were waiting for change from a vendor who kept it in a basket on her head. When, due to violently honking horns, the driver started rolling forward, with the vendor running alongside the window, by then the light might have turned red, and everyone would be forced to idle with windows open, since very few people had air-conditioning, and breathe in the retch-inducing exhaust fumes belching out of a thousand cars. Bored to tears, they might decide to buy something, and then the delay would happen all over again.

Peggy knew that the street hustlers were the kids who never went to high school. Only grades one through nine were free in Ghana and most families couldn't afford the fees required to send their kids to four years of secondary school, or S.S., as they called it. Those kids who turned to farming or fishing in their village could usually support themselves adequately, but those attracted to the glitter of the big city usually ended up peddling stuff on the street twelve or fifteen hours a day for a few pennies profit.

Otuam, she knew, had no high school. How many Otuam kids—*her* kids, now—left for Accra or Cape Coast to hawk stuff at traffic lights? As king, what could she do to protect them from such a hard life? She would have to bring a high school to town, she realized, though that was another thing she had no idea how to do.

Zigzagging in and out of the crowds of hawkers were handicapped young men on skateboards, their tiny shriveled legs tied up around their waists as they propelled themselves with their hands encased in flip-flops. Many of these young men, Peggy knew, were highly intelligent. In the United States, they would have university degrees in computer engineering, say, and whisk themselves to work in a handicapped-modified car, slide into a motorized wheelchair, and roll unimpeded into their offices using handicapped-accessible ramps and elevators. As far as Peggy knew, in Ghana only a few modern hotels and major hospitals had elevators, and she had never seen a handicapped ramp.

Here, as in all of Africa, there was no place for the handicapped, because there was already no place for so many of the able-bodied. It was almost impossible to get a good job in the private sector unless the owner was a relative. And even a relative wouldn't hire a handicapped person, an object of pity and ridicule. Peggy sighed, watching the bright-eyed young men rolling themselves quickly up to cars with their hands outstretched. The best place in the entire world to be handicapped, she knew, was in the USA.

Once outside the city, they had about thirty good miles on the Accra–Cape Coast Highway, and as the car sailed along west Kwame Lumpopo chattered charmingly about all the ceremonies and family gatherings over the next nine days, the work he had done to help organize them, and how he would help Peggy rule Otuam. They sped down the highway past pale green fields dotted with termite hills up to seven feet high, cones of golden-red earth sticking up like minivolcanoes. Every so often, rising like an elegant umbrella above the celery-colored meadows and dark green bushes stood the *onyina*, or silk cotton tree, with silver-white bark and black-green leaves.

Many houses along the road dazzled with colors that jolted the eyes, having received free paint jobs from the cell phone companies: an explosive yellow with a blue MTN logo, a screaming red with a white Vodafone logo, and a clamorous blue with a white Tigo logo, occasionally all three of them in a row.

At six p.m. the sun set rapidly and local farmers closed up the little stands from which they sold home-grown coconuts, tomatoes, papayas, yams, and pineapples. Twice they passed groups of thirty or forty people sitting outside on plastic chairs, watching a soccer match on a television perched high on a cabinet.

Suddenly Kwame Lumpopo veered off the coastal highway onto a rutted side road between the wooden stands of two street vendors. At first there was just the occasional pothole, which really wasn't any worse than the roads in Washington, and Kwame Lumpopo swerved neatly around them in a series of undulating semicircles that reminded Peggy of figure skating.

But then they got to rougher patches where there were so many potholes that they had no choice but to drive over them. The car pitched and rolled from front to back and side to side, bouncing up and down like a small vessel tossed by a hurricane. Kwame Lumpopo had stopped talking now; he gripped the steering wheel tightly and concentrated on avoiding the deepest potholes, which could flatten your tire or tear off your muffler. The car didn't seem to have any shock absorbers, and with no seat belts in the car their heads kept hitting the roof. Peggy felt that every bone in her body and all her teeth were rattling.

African roads are no joke, she thought. *Oh boy. I had forgotten. As king I will also have to fix this pitiful road at some point. No one is going to want to invest in my town if they crack their heads going over these potholes. When was the last time they paved this road? Forty years ago?*

They drove a long way through the bush and through some small villages of mud and concrete block houses lining tiny twisting roads. After about thirty minutes on the unpaved roads, they finally reached Otuam. Built on a slight hill, sloping gently downward to the beach, it was topped by its most recognizable feature, the salmon-colored Methodist church with its tall steeple. As they drove down Main Street, Peggy saw people—her people—sitting at tables selling food and phone cards on either side of the road with kerosene lamps burning. Technically, they weren't lamps so much as thick wicks jammed into large tin cans of kerosene and set ablaze. There were no streetlights, but Kwame Lumpopo's headlights lit up short-legged goats scurrying out of their way.

The people milling about Main Street were slower to get out of their way than the goats as they walked from one table to the other, laughing, chatting, examining merchandise. Peggy studied them, but they ignored her. Little did they know the lady in the passing car was their new king.

Kwame Lumpopo turned onto a road that was more like a sandy patch of ground than a road and swerved around tree trunks until they passed behind the royal palace, totally dark now what with the king in the village for good. Peggy wouldn't be staying there. When she had asked Kwame Lumpopo about the condition of the palace, he confirmed her fears that it was completely uninhabitable. He had arranged for her to stay in the home of a distant cousin of theirs just a few hundred feet away.

They swung around the back of the palace and bounced under some trees, past a few low houses. Then they stopped in front of a one-story concrete block house with a long front porch, painted blue with yellow trim, lit outside by a single lightbulb next to the front door. For the next nine days this would be the king's residence.

Kwame Lumpopo honked the horn and within seconds a gaggle of women ran out the door, arms outstretched, clucking and cackling in gleeful welcome.

"Welcome, Nana!" they cried, waving their arms above their heads. As Peggy emerged from the car, she recognized Auntie Esi, who at eighty-five held the status of the eldest female in Peggy's family. She was a petite, spry woman with a narrow face and lively sparkling eyes. Auntie Esi was everybody's mother and grandmother. They embraced affectionately.

Standing next to Auntie Esi was Cousin Comfort. At seventy-six, she was beautifully dressed in an elegant printed blue robe, edged with lace and embroidered with gold, and a matching head wrap. She wore a thick black wig, flawless makeup, and real gold jewelry. Cousin Comfort lived in Tema, a suburb of Accra, and had been driven to Otuam earlier that day by her son.

"Nana, we are so proud!" Cousin Comfort cried, hugging Peggy. "Your mother would be so happy to know her daughter is a king." Peggy felt a little stab of pain but managed a smile.

Cousin Aggie had come in from Accra to cook and clean for the royal entourage and would be staying in the little bedroom next to the kitchen. Her brother lived in Otuam, so there would be plenty of time for her to visit with him. Aggie was probably fifty, though she looked ageless. She had long limbs, broad hips, and a thousand braids, which she wore in an oblong bun covered by a kerchief, making her head look something like a hornet. Aggie, too, gave Peggy a hug.

And there were three other elderly aunties who made up Peggy's entourage, Auntie Esi explained, introducing them. Together they would teach her about Otuam and instruct her in royal etiquette. They would help her dress and undress, provide her with company, and fan her with towels when it got too hot, an honor accorded to kings. Peggy remembered elderly women fanning Uncle Joseph in shifts at royal events.

Cousin Charles, with his thick glasses, big muscles, and booming baritone voice, was also there to welcome her. At forty-five, Cousin Charles lived in Cape Coast and worked for an optician. He was married, with three grown sons who worked in the building trade. Cousin Charles was known for his sturdy reliability: always there when you needed him, always ready to help.

"Nana, we are so happy for you!" he said, giving Peggy a big bear hug.

As Kwame Lumpopo moved his bags into Cousin Charles's room in the front of the house, Auntie Esi took Peggy on a quick tour. All the rooms except one had old linoleum floors and a few sticks of furniture. The dining room had a table, six chairs, and an ancient fridge that shuddered and rumbled. There was a big fan above the table, with three lightbulbs, two of which were burned out. The kitchen had a kerosene stove and two large rusty tanks in the corners where the kids dumped the buckets of water in the morning, for which Aggie carefully counted out the coins. The five bedrooms each had a bed, and that was it, except Peggy's corner room, which also had a couple of plastic chairs. She would have to live out of her suitcase, since the closet had no shelves and no clothes rod. Luckily, there was a fan on the ceiling, which she would keep on twenty-four hours a day, as long as the electricity held out.

Though the rest of the house was spartan, the parlor was lush, plush, and Victorian in décor, with overstuffed chairs and sofas on a beautiful new linoleum floor. It had lacy drapes, and several fans and chandeliers crowded the intricately carved ceiling. One wall had bookcases filled with china and dainty knickknacks. Oddly, the walls were covered with plastic vines and flowers. The owner of the house, Comfort Mensah, also known as the Other Cousin Comfort, was the widow of Peggy's cousin and used the Otuam house as a weekend getaway. She had bought these luxury items at one of the new Western-style furniture stores in Accra, where she resided most of the time.

Peggy sat down with her relatives on the comfortable furniture while Aggie served beer and water. They asked her about her journey and her life in the United States and told her how excited they were that the ancestors had seen fit to choose a woman king. "We couldn't believe it when we heard it!" Auntie Esi said. "This is a new day for Otuam."

Looking around at her relatives chattering happily, Peggy realized that she had suddenly been enveloped in the warm embrace of African family, something she hadn't felt since her mother's funeral. Here there were so many layers of people around her, aunties, cousins, nieces, nephews, and neighbors, an interconnectedness of human spirits that she had never developed in the United States.

At that moment she wondered how she could have stood to live without it for so long, the shining eyes, the kind words, the laughter and stories and humanness that bound them all together. In the United States, she did her job and came home to her condo. Sometimes she feared that if she died in her condo or had a stroke, no one would find her for weeks. That would be impossible in Ghana. There would always be relatives calling to see how you were, banging on your door, bringing you plates of fish and rice, inviting you to church and family events. Even if you told them to go away and leave you alone, they wouldn't. They would bounce back with gentle chastisement of your bad behavior and more invitations and perhaps a few bottles of beer.

Then Auntie Esi turned to Peggy and said, "We will be sleeping with you. Just as a pride of lions sleeps surrounding its leader, as a king you must have attendants in your room at all times."

Peggy frowned. Suddenly the warm embrace of family did not seem so desirable. Enjoying the company of others in the waking hours was one thing, but Peggy did not relish a slumber party at her age. That was one great advantage after her husband left. No one snoring, coughing, getting up to pee, trying to talk to her, or tossing around in the bed like a Sea World dolphin so she bounced up and down.

"But I am an American," she replied. "I need to sleep alone, not with a bunch of people."

The aunties roared with laughter and shook their heads.

"You are a king now, and you need our spirits to protect you!" cried Auntie Esi. She explained that as Peggy's closest female relative, Cousin Comfort—her mother's sister's daughter—would share the bed with her. The other four relatives would sleep on mats on the floor.

There was no arguing with them. As king, it seemed, Peggy would have to give up certain things.

She asked the aunties to show her where she could bathe. They opened a narrow wooden door off the hall, and she saw a small tiled shower room with a shower head, faucets, and drain. Then she saw the bucket on the floor. It was as she had thought—no running water in Otuam. Peggy nodded. All Africans knew how to get very clean with a bucket of water. Even if they were born and raised in a big city, they always had relatives who lived in a town or village in the bush. And you didn't need to heat the water because room temperature water in Ghana was already quite warm.

Right next to the shower room was the toilet room, which had a toilet and sink that didn't work. Instead of flushing the toilet you had to throw a bucket of water into the bowl to push everything down the pipe. Peggy laughed. Truly, a toilet fit for a king.

After she bathed, she chatted with her aunties for a while and as soon as she got in bed fell into a delicious sleep.

Peggy was awakened at four a.m. by roosters right under her window shrieking cocka-doodle-doo in a variety of discordant tones. The birds must have awakened the goats, which immediately started a raucous baaing. She rolled over and put the pillow over her head.

At four thirty she was again shocked awake by the pounding of drums somewhere nearby, which reverberated through her pillow. Drums had always been an important part of Ghanaian culture. There were the royal drums, the *fontomfrom,* which were played only for the king by royal drummers. Chest high, these drums were made of wood carved with ancient symbols. Six-inch-high elephant tusks projected around the front of the drum, and a piece of cowhide was stretched tightly over the top. Each drumstick was made of a piece of wood naturally angled like the number seven, the dark bark stripped off revealing the naked whiteness of the wood beneath.

The regular drums, the *djembe* and *kpanlogo,* were smaller, knee-high, and anybody could play them with bare hands. The drums sang out an ancient rhythm, the heartbeat of the earth, which the loud chatter of modern civilization had long ago drowned out in most parts of the world. They started slowly at first, then gradually increased until the beat became the very tongue of the ancestors calling in a voice far more powerful than any human voice.

Peggy pulled the pillow off her head and listened to the drums. From the uneven staccato beat she knew that these were the talking drums, an ancient form of tribal communication, like Morse code. Ghanaian languages had a tonal component in which each syllable had a different pitch. Using a set of drums of different pitches, therefore, the drummer could communicate as if he were speaking. Such messages easily traveled five miles in days when the world was silent, before cars and planes and general noise pollution. Then the village five miles away would drum the message so other villages would hear it and repeat it. Within minutes, an important message could be drummed dozens of miles away, much sooner than even the swiftest runner could deliver it.

Peggy wondered if this particular beat was to inform the people of Otuam that their king had arrived. Her hunch was confirmed shortly afterward when she heard several bangs of the porch gate, followed by the repeated slams of the screen door. A moment later Aggie knocked on her door and poked her turban inside. "Nana," she said, "the elders are here to greet you."

The aunties, she knew, had also been awakened by the drums. She had heard them yawning loudly and stretching. Now Auntie Esi leaped up from her sleeping mat and said, "We will dress you, Nana."

The aunties wrapped Peggy in an over-the-shoulder cloth, red for mourning the late king, and threw on several layers of bead necklaces and bracelets. She stood as the aunties walked around her, examining her and, after a few more tucks at her cloth, told her she passed inspection.

As they dressed themselves in colorful two-piece print dresses and head wraps, Peggy sat on the bed holding a little hand mirror and made up her face. She had given great thought to her makeup. Kings wore eyeliner to keep evil spirits at bay, and Peggy would wear plenty of that as she always had. Not only did she like the look, but as king she would probably attract more jealous spirits than ever before, so she would really lay it on thick. Her one concession to being a lady king would be lipstick. Bright red lipstick. Peggy could never give that up. She applied a thick coat.

Auntie Esi stood next to the door, ready to open it so Peggy could lead the way. Just before she stepped outside her bedroom, it occurred to Peggy that this was her first moment of kingship, meeting her royal council, and she inhaled sharply, feeling a wave of dizziness wash over her. This was real. It was no longer merely an amazing story, an exultant twist of fate that made her feel special. The reality, the responsibility was here.

She stood up straight and squared her shoulders. She was a king. She had lived alone in America for decades, no easy thing for an African woman. She had the strength to do this. She touched her mother's little gold bracelet, and suddenly her spirits soared.

Taking a deep breath, she glided down the corridor, ready to meet her elders, and found them already seated in the parlor on the comfortable chairs and sofas, leaving a chair for her between Tsiami and Kwame Lumpopo.

"*Akwaaba,*" she said, smiling cordially and nodding at each one as she took her seat. Welcome. The elders greeted her and smiled back. Were they, too, just a little bit nervous to meet their new king? The thought calmed her rapidly beating heart as the aunties trudged in carrying in the handmade wooden bench from the dining room and set it against the wall. Jostling one another, they sat down.

Peggy recognized some of the royal council from her mother's funeral and her previous visits to Otuam. A few years earlier, there had been fifteen in all, Kwame Lumpopo had told her, but several had died, moved away, or become too old and ill to attend council meetings. Today there were six of them, all members of the royal Ebiradze family.

Peggy's priest, Tsiami, was sitting at her right hand, the proper place for her chief elder. Now he stood and bellowed in a reedy voice, "Nana! *Akwaaba* to Otuam. In the name of the ancestors who chose you and of your royal council, I welcome you."

Peggy had inherited her late uncle's *tsiami,* seventy-six-year-old Kweku Mensah, who had held the post for about forty years. Tsiami, as everybody called him, was a lithe man, all bones and sinews. His face was intense, his dark skin stretched taut over angular bones. He had a large square forehead, a snub nose, and perfect white teeth despite a lifelong absence from a dental chair. While most men his age were bald, Tsiami still had a full head of black hair, graying at the temples.

Like so many elderly men in the villages, Tsiami had never learned to read or write because he had started fishing full-time as a child. He had fished for more than sixty years, but at the age of seventy decided the sea was too dangerous for an old man. The riptides in Otuam's Atlantic waters were so strong that even young fishermen who fell overboard in rough seas were swept away and never found. Usually Otuam lost several fishermen a year, good swimmers all.

Tsiami had bought a large plantation not far from the palace with several acres of pineapples, papayas, and cassava, which he tilled with his strapping sons. They were building a new house near his fields for the expanding family, which now included numerous grandchildren. The decades of fishing and farming had left Tsiami with the slender muscular arms and shoulders of an athlete in his twenties.

Also known as a "linguist," a *tsiami* was the king's official spokesman. On grand official occasions, such as royal funerals, the king whispered into the *tsiami*'s ear and it was the *tsiami* who spoke, holding the royal speaking staff, while the king sat silently and serenely, too majestic to utter a word out loud.

Tsiamis were chosen from the royal family for their eloquence and were often called upon to polish and edit the king's words. They handled money in public for the king, to pay the royal drummers, for instance, as kings weren't allowed to be seen in public with demeaning wads of cash in their hands.

Most importantly, *tsiamis* were the bridge between the living and the dead and conducted all of the rituals to keep God and the ancestors happy. Peggy's *tsiami* could actually talk to the royal stools and understand when they talked back. Many *tsiamis* performed the rituals for decades but never developed this enviable ability. Sometimes these less talented *tsiamis* received messages in dreams, which was almost as good. As a person who could hold conversations with ancestors and gods, Tsiami didn't believe in Christianity at all. He felt that white European religions detracted from the ancestral beliefs, pulling Africans away from their own culture and wasting their time in bad singing and useless clapping.

Watching him take his seat, Peggy felt there was something stiff and prickly about her *tsiami*. She remembered from her earlier trips to Otuam that he rarely smiled and usually stared straight ahead or at his lap, even when he was speaking or listening to someone. He could sit for hours as still as a statue, as still as one of the pineapples he grew.

"It is indeed very good to have you back with us, my daughter," Uncle Moses Acquah said enthusiastically, waving his hands about. Uncle Moses was the walrus who had consulted the genealogical records to compile the list of candidates for king, and he now proudly took credit for having put Peggy on the stool. "I can't tell you how happy we are that the ancestors chose a Ghanaian-American lady king! It is so very exciting. You are like a bird that has flown far away and has now returned to its nest." His emotional manner and wild gestures contrasted sharply with Tsiami's stony coolness.

Uncle Moses was considered the most educated of her elders because he had finished ninth grade and could read and write in both Fante and English. He had been a military policeman for twenty-two years, but after his retirement returned to his roots in Otuam and joined the royal council. Because of Uncle Moses's literacy, the late king had put him in charge of the fishermen to settle disputes that arose from the tangled nets of competing canoes and such matters.

The aunties had mentioned that Uncle Moses worked as a part-time security guard at one of the cell phone towers located a few hundred yards from the royal palace. There were two of them right next to each other, white with red lights at the top, which was why Otuam, which didn't have a drop of running water, had some of the best cell phone coverage in Africa. The town had been thrilled when Tigo and MTN had built the towers there as part of their new networks along Ghana's Atlantic coast.

Cell phones had first come to Ghana in 1992, and they took off like wildfire because few people had land lines. Until then, whenever someone needed to contact a relative in another village they would take a message to the local radio station, which would transmit it to the radio station in the broadcast area of the intended recipient. There, during the message hour, the announcer might say, "Would Auntie Dorothy Mensah of Mankessim please contact her cousin Martha Boateng in Kumasi, as she has important news for you." Even if Auntie Dorothy wasn't listening to the radio at that moment, one of her friends or relatives would surely hear it and give her the message.

Given the clumsiness of this form of communication, it wasn't surprising that nineteen thousand Ghanaians bought cell phones the first year they were introduced. By 2008, more than six million people had cell phones, a quarter of the population. Cell phones themselves were cheap, and even in the most remote village cell phone users could buy a prepaid phone card for a set amount, scratch off the waxy coating over the long code on the back of it, and type it into the phone. Prepaid cards were efficient, as many Ghanaians didn't have addresses or postal service for bills to arrive, nor did they have bank accounts from which to pay the bills.

Otuam's Tigo cell phone tower needed security guards because the little concrete block station at its base contained a lot of wire, and several years earlier some enterprising thieves had broken in, stolen all of it, and twisted it into beautiful necklaces and earrings, which they sold on Main Street. After that the cell phone company hired elderly men to lounge on a bench under a shade tree outside the station in shifts, twenty-four hours a day. No one had broken in since. Several days a week Uncle Moses put on his brown security guard uniform and lay down on the bench under the popo tree to guard the wire.

Next to Uncle Moses sat his good friend, Isaiah the Treasurer. At sixty-eight, he was the youngest of the Otuam elders and eschewed traditional robes for high-waisted pants, held up well above his trim waist by a large belt. He was considered highly educated as he, too, could read and write quite well, and he was very active in the Methodist church on Main Street. He had flashing, intense, deep-set eyes, full cheeks, and a pointed chin, which made him look something like a turnip. Peggy remembered him well for his polished flattery.

"Nana," he said now, smiling widely, "we are so happy you are our new king, indeed, truly delighted. Speaking on behalf of your entire council, may I say that we will do our best to help you, and when you are in Washington, we will take care of everything for you. Uncle Moses and I are, you know, very well educated." Peggy thanked him for his kind words.

Across from Peggy, Uncle Eshun reclined on the overstuffed sofa. She had heard about Uncle Eshun's stroke a few years back; one side of his body was lame, but he could shuffle around well enough on his cane and still had a kindly, gentle air. He had Bambi eyes, large and dark and widely spaced, fringed with curly eyelashes. Beneath his wide cheekbones, his cheeks had sunken in since there were so few teeth to hold them out. "Nana, I, too, can read and write. I am in charge of recording all funerals in Otuam," he said proudly in a voice shredding with age, "and issuing death certificates."

Sharing the sofa with Uncle Eshun, Baba Kobena was heavier than the others, with an energetic face and a square jaw sporting an underbite. When he smiled he flashed a full row of lower teeth. He wore a lozenge-shaped black hat, which he kept taking off, playing with, and putting back on his head. He, too, had been a fisherman for more than half a century, and like Tsiami was completely illiterate. Peggy was taking notes in a little notebook on her lap (a habit she had picked up as recording secretary at countless embassy meetings), and when she asked him how he spelled his name, he merely shook his head. Uncle Moses and Isaiah the Treasurer tried to spell it for her, arguing over which vowels to use in *Kobena*.

As they exchanged small talk about her journey, Peggy decided she would give it to them straight. She was never one for beating about the bush, and her elders needed to know what they were getting themselves into with her as their new king.

She took a deep breath and said, "You may be the men and I the woman, but you really have to be ready for me. I am not going to take nonsense from anybody. You are also much older than I am, but you have given me the power to rule. And I will do the best I can for you, but don't think that you are putting me there for *you* to rule *me*. *I* will be ruling *you*. I am your king, and the king rules. God put these people in my charge, and I am going to do great things for the sake of the coming generations."

They nodded, smiling. Peggy couldn't tell whether they were taking her seriously. Well, if they didn't now, she was pretty sure they would later.

Aggie served the elders "minerals," the Ghanaian term for soft drinks, as at five a.m. it was still a bit early for beer—and Peggy looked carefully to see that all of them drank something. In Ghana, if someone comes to your house and doesn't touch his drink, not even a sip, it means he doesn't like you. Had all these elderly men approved of her, a woman, becoming their new king? One by one, they all sipped their Cokes and Fantas. Yes, they had approved.

Peggy noticed that Aggie, having served the elders drinks, was standing at the door, one hand on her hip, the other holding a spatula. Evidently she wanted to watch the council meeting, perhaps so she could take drink orders or perhaps because she was nosy. And her spatula, which she could just as easily have left in the kitchen, seemed to be a weapon that she held at the ready to defend Peggy, if need be. *Well,* Peggy thought, *it wouldn't be a bad idea to have another woman from a big city keeping an eye on these men.*

Periodically, Peggy heard a strange sound coming from the other room, like a deep groan. She realized it was the fridge, an ancient machine whose spirit was exhausted and in pain. Perhaps no one here talked to it, encouraged it, and complimented it, the way she did the tired spirit of her 1992 Honda.

"So what is there that I need to know about ruling Otuam?" she asked. Silence. A few elders shrugged their shoulders. "Surely there is *something?*" she prodded. "What does the king do?"

Silence again. Then Uncle Moses began to speak. "You meet with us to resolve various disputes in families and between neighbors. You are present for rituals at shrines and the pouring of libations at the stool room in the palace. You attend the funerals of kings in the region."

That didn't sound like very much. That's all the king did?

"What about my queen mother?" Peggy asked. She remembered from her visit to Otuam in 1995 that the position of queen mother had been vacant for years, and the late king who was in the fridge hadn't bothered to fill it. But at the start of a new reign the elders would have selected a new queen mother as well as a king, probably using the same methods. "Who is she?"

"Your cousin Elizabeth's oldest daughter, Paulina Nyamekyeh," Tsiami replied. "She has taken the royal name of Nana Kodzia III."

Peggy made a face. "Isn't she a little girl?"

"She is fifteen."

It was unfortunate that the queen mother was so young. Usually a more mature woman was chosen, one who could provide the king with advice to help the women and children, based on decades of experience as a woman and mother herself. Paulina was a child, still in school. And it suddenly struck Peggy as very odd, the selection of the new king and queen mother of Otuam: a lady king living thousands of miles away, and a little girl who didn't know anything. How was anybody going to rule Otuam?

"And the ancestors also selected Paulina's ten-year-old cousin, Faustina, to be your Soul," Tsiami told Peggy.

"My soul?" she asked. She could have sworn she already had one.

"Jealous evil spirits like to zoom in on kings like vengeful wasps," he explained, staring into space, "but they can be deflected by the innocence of a little girl sitting directly in front of the king, a kind of human shield. For all your official events, you must have the Soul in front of you or the evil spirits might make trouble for you."

Peggy hadn't heard about this tradition, but she knew it was best to avoid evil spirits at all cost. "What happens when the innocent little girl grows up?" she asked. "They do grow up, you know." Lots of them got pregnant, and then she wouldn't be any good at all diverting evil spirits.

"When your Soul is sixteen, we go to the shrine and pour libations to choose another one and wait for the schnapps to steam up. But Faustina will always have the honor of having been the king's Soul."

The next topic was the stool Peggy would choose for her enstoolment, which would sit on a shelf in the stool room near all of the male kings' stools going back for generations. Royal stools were carved from the wood of one of three trees—tweneboa, nyameduah, or sese—which were known to have very vindictive spirits that stayed in the stools even after the souls of the kings and ancestors had been put inside. These trees had the power to walk through the forests, and their roots could turn into venomous serpents. Some of them became so angry at being cut down, that no matter how strategically the carver placed the cuts, the tree would fall over right on top of him, crushing him, unless he sacrificed eggs, chickens, and sheep to the tree before cutting it down.

Peggy had thought long and hard about the important question of her stool. She wanted something different, something to stand out from the rest, the kind of stool that would proclaim to the big masculine stools, *I contain the spirit of a lady king.*

"I want a small stool," she said, "a white one."

Once Peggy's royal stool had been purchased, Tsiami would conduct the rituals to put her soul into it, along with the souls of the kings who had gone to the village for good, the souls of all the ancestors of Otuam, and of those yet to be born. Then he would ask her stool what libations it would like to drink; though almost all stools liked schnapps, once in a blue moon a new stool said that it wanted something else. She would not be present for these rituals but would first see her stool on her enstoolment day.

The conversation drifted to her enstoolment celebrations. Tsiami said, "You will need to buy many crates of beer and Coke, Fanta, and other minerals for the party we are going to have here after your enstoolment, some whiskey, too, for the most honored guests, as well as fish, chicken, and rice to feed all the guests."

Peggy had to pay for her own food and drinks? She hadn't expected this. "Are there no funds that can be used to pay for it?" she asked.

She turned to Isaiah the Treasurer. If he was the treasurer, that must mean that *money* went through his hands, right?

"Isaiah, is there no money at all?"

Isaiah the Treasurer shook his head. "Not a penny, I'm afraid," he said, smiling apologetically. "Nana, having lived in the United States for so many years, you are probably not aware that in African villages the king usually spends his own funds for celebrations, as well as providing any assistance to the people."

Peggy had stuffed a few hundred-dollar bills from her last paycheck into her bra, which she figured was a very safe place because nobody had any reason to go messing around in there. She had assumed there weren't enough royal funds to repair the palace, or the road, or the water pipes. But she had also assumed there would be at least enough cedis in the treasury to pay for her food, the enstoolment reception, and any other small costs that might arise, and the money in her bra, which she had brought for an emergency, would accompany her back to Washington. But now she was beginning to fear it wouldn't even last her the nine days in Otuam if unexpected expenses kept popping up.

Seeing her concern, Uncle Moses said, "During your enstoolment, we will set up a table under a tent next to the royal palace. The distinguished guests you invited, the chiefs and others, will go there to make donations to help you pay for the costs. Some of them will give chickens or goats, and some will give cash."

Peggy was hoping for cash. She looked around the room at her elderly elders and sighed. Being king looked like it was going to be a very expensive proposition.

Outside the parlor, the spirit of the ancient fridge must have sensed her thoughts, because it uttered a loud, shuddering groan.

6

When the council meeting ended at six, the sun was just rising and the world outside was silver. The elders returned to their fields to do some work before the day became too hot. Peggy went to her room to rest a bit and saw a line of children with heavy metal buckets of water on their heads trudging down the path from the borehole behind the house. Some of them were headed for her kitchen.

Auntie Esi stood next to Peggy as she gazed out the window. "How far do they walk?" Peggy asked.

"There are only two boreholes, so the kids that live farthest away have to walk about a half hour in each direction."

"An hour for a single bucket," Peggy said quietly.

"And some kids make two or three trips before and after school. Some walk for six hours a day."

"Is the water clean at least?"

Auntie Esi shrugged. "It's not clean if you haul it from the pond. That water is a yellowish brown, and that's what the entire town had to use when the pipes first broke in 1977. But the local government representatives built two boreholes shortly after that which provide very clean water, though it costs money. A few pennies a bucket."

Peggy scowled. "You mean they charge for clean water?"

Auntie Esi nodded. "The pumps break down a lot, so they use the money to pay for repairs."

"And the people who can't afford the borehole water drink the yellowish-brown water?"

Auntie Esi nodded again. "They don't get sick from it, though. For hundreds of years before the British brought piped water, people in Otuam got all their water from the pond. Many believe the goddess of the pond purifies the water and keeps them healthy."

Peggy sighed, a deep sigh that came from the soul and rumbled through her entire body. Evidently the pond contained one of the seventy-seven gods and goddesses known to protect Otuam. But even so, no American king could allow her people to drink that disgusting water. And besides, it was well known that sometimes nature gods and goddesses left their ancient spots without a word of warning. If the goddess left, those drinking the water would sicken and even die. She would have to get those kids more boreholes, free boreholes, and eventually fix the pipes. How on earth was she going to afford it?

Auntie Esi put her weathered hand on Peggy's shoulder. "You will fix the water later," she said. "Remember the sparrow, who builds her nest one twig at a time. We are going to eat breakfast now, and after that we are going to give you your first royal etiquette lesson. You don't want to disgrace the stool by doing something inappropriate for a Ghanaian king." No, Peggy did not want that.

Sitting at the dining room table, they breakfasted on weak coffee and porridge. After breakfast, the aunties taught Peggy how to walk *majestically*. A king, they said, was never to show any hurry. The whole world waited for a king. Flapping around here and there like a chicken was undignified.

Auntie Esi strolled at a glacial pace down the hall, head up, shoulders back. "Like this, Nana. You bounce around too much and go too fast."

"In the U.S., if I walked that slowly I would be hit by a car," Peggy pointed out. "No one there would wait for me to cross the street. They would run me down, and as I bounced on the asphalt they would keep on going so they wouldn't be late for a meeting."

Auntie Esi smiled. "But there are very few cars in Otuam, and here they wouldn't run over their king. Try it again, slowly."

Peggy sighed. Give just a hint of a smile, they said, showing regal serenity. Shoulders relaxed. Head held high. Chin up. Slow, straight, determined steps. Self-consciously, she walked back and forth in front of them, like an awkward aspiring model training for the runway.

"Too fast!" cried one.

"Hold your chin higher!" said another.

"Don't swing your arms like that!" said a third. "You look like an orangutan."

"You're frowning!" said Auntie Esi. "Don't frown in public."

"Don't frown?" Peggy asked. "What if I see something I don't like?"

"Don't frown!" Auntie Esi repeated. "You can make a mental note of the problem and deal with it later."

"Oh."

"And you can't eat or drink in public. It's unseemly for a king to be shoving things into her face. Plus, if there is a witch in the crowd watching you she can make you choke to death on whatever you're consuming."

Peggy had heard about the no-eating-in-public rule, though she was unaware it had to do with witches. It made sense, though, that witches, known as vengeful, jealous creatures, would want to harm a king, especially one who stood for the good. Witches created havoc for the sheer malicious pleasure of it, and you never knew who in your village was a witch. Sudden illnesses, childhood deaths, accidents: they might all be traced back to the kindly old grandmother next door or the jovial uncle down the street. Only a traditional priest, using tried and true rituals, could determine if bad luck was caused by the ancestors punishing selfish behavior or by a witch making trouble for good people, and then prescribe the proper rituals to take care of it.

Peggy sighed again. As king, she had to worry whether Uncle Joseph would haunt her for not burying him in a timely manner. She had to remain vigilant against evil spirits who might zoom into her. And now she had to defend herself against spiteful jealous witches who could be anywhere. Not eating or drinking in public was simple compared to these more troubling issues.

"In Otuam I will abide by this rule," she said. "But in the U.S., we all work so much that we have to grab a bite in public sometimes because when we get home it is too late to cook. And no one there knows I am a king."

"They know at the embassy. One of *them* might be a witch. And even if they aren't, it would be undignified to stuff your face even there."

Witches. At the *embassy*. Looking back on her twenty-nine years there, Peggy realized this could explain a lot of things.

"And Nana," Auntie Esi said, "the king can't argue in public."

"Argue in public?" she said, all wide-eyed innocence. Surely they hadn't heard anything of her arguments at the embassy. "Me?"

Cousin Comfort chimed in, "Nana, we all know that ever since you were a small child, when someone misbehaves, you can't let it go."

That was true. The most infamous story had occurred in Kumasi when Peggy was about ten. One of her father's girlfriends—who was also a friend of her mother's—would come by the house when her mother wasn't there and hang around to flirt with her father. Peggy soon figured out what the woman was up to. She didn't know if her mother knew her friend had betrayed her, and she certainly wasn't going to be the one to tell her. So she decided to take matters into her own hands and set things right.

One day the woman came in when Peggy was alone in the house. Peggy grabbed a broom and started beating the woman on the backside as hard as her skinny arms could, yelling that she would *never*—whap!—*ever*—whap!—allow anyone to hurt her mother. Peggy followed the woman out the door and into the street, swatting her on the shoulders, back, and rear end, as the woman cried out and begged her to stop. Peggy told her if she ever came back to make trouble in the family, she would beat her again. The woman never returned. At dinner that night, Peggy's father looked at her oddly, and her mother seemed happier than usual, but no one ever said a word to her about it.

"When you see an injustice," Cousin Comfort continued, "you are like a village dog with his jaws locked on a bone. You just don't give it up. But as king you will have to deal with these things in the council chamber and not yell at people on the street or beat them with brooms." The aunties all laughed at that one.

Auntie Esi said, "And if you are wearing the crown and want to say a crude thing, you have to take it off before you speak so as not to dishonor it."

Peggy nodded. That would be easy. She always knew well in advance when she was planning to say a crude thing. When a person was talking nonsense, she could feel the crude thing bubbling up from the place where crude things sprouted. She could feel it taking shape in her chest and rising in her throat. There would certainly be plenty of time to remove the royal crown before the crude thing was launched full force from her mouth in the direction of her opponent.

"And there's one more thing," Auntie Esi added. "It is not regal for a king to always be running off to the bathroom. When you have official events, we will give you a special dish that takes away the urge to urinate for the entire day. Still, it is best not to drink much before or during. Just a little water so you don't faint in the heat."

The heat. Though it was still early, the delicious coolness of the night had vanished, replaced by a stultifying miasma of sticky air. During the etiquette lesson, Peggy and her aunties had glowed at first, then perspired, and now the sweat was running down their faces in rivulets.

Whenever Peggy was back in Africa she realized how spoiled she was by air-conditioning, how she took it for granted and forgot to thank God for it. In Africa only the very rich or powerful had air-conditioning. When you visited someone in an office, you could tell where they ranked because only the bosses had a unit, though sometimes their secretaries benefited from one in the waiting room.

Most houses, including the one Peggy was staying in, had fans that made the temperature just about bearable. But when the government rationed electricity, cutting it off in certain districts for a few hours, the houses became unbearable. Electricity was usually cut off during the hottest part of the day, rarely in the evenings, when it was cooler but dark outside. It seemed to many that the government preferred people to die in the heat rather than get lost in the dark.

Peggy knew that the best drink to stave off the heat was beer, which Ghanaians drank in the morning as the heat rose. But beer was also the very drink to make you most want to run to the toilet. Peggy remembered an American comedian who once said, "It's good to be da king." Except in Otuam the king would have to be thirsty, and hot, with a bursting bladder and witches putting hexes on her. Maybe it wasn't always good to be the king of Otuam.

"And another thing," Auntie Esi said. "As an American, you probably brought deodorant. But here people cut a lemon in half and rub the two halves all over their bodies. They let the lemon juice sink in, and a while later they bathe with soap and water. This works better than deodorant. If you are going to be out in the heat all day for a royal ceremony, you should remember to use lemon." Peggy promised she would.

For lunch they had the staple food of Otuam—fresh fish deep-fried, on white rice, and covered with a spicy onion and tomato sauce. They would be eating it for lunch and dinner for Peggy's entire stay. In the

United States she often didn't think twice about the wide range of food she had and would have complained if she had to eat the same thing all day long. Africans could enjoy the same meal again and again and be grateful for it.

"By God's grace, the people here are never hungry," Auntie Esi explained as they dove into their meal. "They are very poor, and don't possess much, and they have to haul water. But there is plenty of food. Nana, you should see the dozens of fishing canoes that come in every morning, their nets heavy with fish. And the farms produce beautiful pineapples, papayas, coconuts, plantains, and cassavas."

That was indeed a blessing. While the other problems were vexing, hunger among Peggy's people would have devastated her. The people of Otuam would never be hungry, and living in Ghana they would certainly never be cold.

7

For several hours that afternoon, Peggy again sat in the parlor with her elders and her aunties discussing the needs of Otuam. Aggie took up her position leaning against the door frame, spatula in hand.

The heat was rapidly becoming intolerable. After the group placed their orders for beer, Aggie returned from the kitchen with a tray of them, the spatula tucked under her arm. Using the beer opener, she popped off the caps and politely set them back on top of the bottles. This was because in Africa you always had to keep your bottle covered between swigs. Otherwise flies, hovering around in the hope of just such an opportunity, would make a kamikaze dive down the neck of the bottle and do several somersaults in the beer before drowning in ecstasy.

Beer was the most popular drink in Ghana because of its ability to cut the heat, along with its alcoholic propensities, and the national brand was called Star beer. Whiskey was popular, too, but far more expensive. It didn't cut the heat, but it quickly made you not care about the heat, so the effect was the same. Before the Europeans came with their whiskey and beer, Ghanaians drank palm wine, *nsafufuo,* which was easily obtained and shockingly alcoholic. It was made by slicing a small cut in the bark of a palm tree from which the sap dripped out overnight into a tin cup tied just below the cut. The next morning, the cup would be full of clear liquid, which wasn't alcoholic immediately but fermented rapidly over the next twenty-four hours.

Some people still drank palm wine because it was quite cheap. It was sold along the roads from little stands, in reused plastic bottles, with tiny black specks floating in it, which were either bits of palm bark or minuscule bugs, Peggy could never quite tell. There was a good reason, she thought, that as soon as European ships appeared off the coast most Ghanaians quickly ditched the palm wine: the taste, a bizarre mixture of coconut juice, bacon fat, cigarette ashes, and fingernail polish remover. Sipping their beers, the elders started bringing Peggy up to speed on life in Otuam. Every few minutes, the cell phone of one of the elders would ring, and the elder would have a loud conversation while Peggy and the others were trying to talk. Most of the ringtones were songs, such as "When the Saints Go Marching In" or Michael Jackson's "Thriller." When a particularly amusing song came on, everyone stopped talking and burst out laughing.

When one of her elders needed to use the bathroom, he would quietly walk outside. It was considered polite to use the bushes rather than making a mess in the host's toilet, considering there was no running water.

Toying with his black hat, Baba Kobena explained the law enforcement situation in Otuam. The police station on Main Street had one window-less concrete jail cell and five officers, including the chief inspector, who lived on the premises and were on call twenty-four hours a day. There was no phone; people who wanted to report a drunken brawl ran there and brought the police back with them, a necessity since the houses in Otuam had no addresses. Nor did the police have a car; those families wanting the officers to haul away a drunk who couldn't stand up had to pay for a taxi. The person who reported a criminal was responsible for bringing him two meals a day in jail, and many felt they should pay the chief inspector of police a tip for his trouble. These costs persuaded most people to deal with their drunken relatives themselves and not bother the police.

"There's very little theft," Baba Kobena said. "That wire stolen from the cell phone station years ago was a big exception as people here always tell on each other, or jump the thief in the act, or report him when the stolen object is seen in his home. Otuam is pretty much self-policing, which is a problem for the chief inspector, who is bored and doesn't get to pocket many tips."

Though she had never met him, Peggy pictured Otuam's chief inspector as the Maytag repairman in that old American commercial, sitting around all day, waiting for the phone to ring. Except the chief inspector didn't even have a phone.

"The only serious crime," Baba Kobena continued, "is wife beating, which likely stems from boredom. Only a few people here have television or radio, so many of them drink to pass the time, and some of the men, once toasted, start pummeling the women. As a Muslim, I never touch alcohol, Nana, and I can see all too plainly the terrible effect it has on some people."

"A terrible effect on some people," Isaiah the Treasurer repeated. "As a devout Methodist, I generally abstain, myself, from the evils of alcohol. It turns some men into demons, beating their wives black and blue."

Peggy frowned when she heard them confirm what her mother had told her. If two people of equal strength wanted to beat each other up, that was their business. But a stronger person beating a weaker one would not be tolerated under her reign. She would make that very clear. No matter what a woman had done, she didn't deserve to be beaten by a man.

Baba Kobena opened his mouth to continue but Peggy interrupted him. "There is one thing I must let the people of Otuam know," she said, "and I want you all to spread the word. As a lady king, as an American, I will not tolerate any form of brutality against women. Let me make this clear: if any man beats his wife, I will make sure he goes to jail for a long time. Then I will throw him out of Otuam and see that he never sets foot here again."

She studied the faces in the room. The aunties were nodding and smiling and nudging one another. But her elders looked shocked. There was a long uncomfortable silence that Peggy allowed to continue so that the full effect of her words would sink in. Then she said, "I want to know about the health care situation."

Isaiah the Treasurer stood and hoisted his trousers up toward his chest. "Well, Nana, Otuam is very fortunate to have a medical clinic, which serves thirteen communities, including some of the little mud-brick villages you drove through to get here. We are lucky because our sick people don't have to walk far to the clinic. But if I were to take you there right now—it's the single-story tan building not far from the palace—you would see many people waiting on the porch who have walked miles and miles to get there. Can you imagine being so sick and walking for miles?"

Peggy couldn't. The few times she was sick she had planted herself firmly in bed and not budged.

"How many doctors?" she asked.

"No doctors. But there are fourteen nurses who work there and live in the nurses' quarters next door, so there is always someone available to help the sick."

Isaiah the Treasurer explained that malaria was the most common complaint but could be easily cured at the clinic if diagnosed early. The clinic saw infections of the upper respiratory tract and urinary tract, as well as the occasional case of typhoid fever. Cipro and other antibiotics cured these. The nurses dispensed immunizations for diphtheria, yellow fever, measles, influenza, and hepatitis.

Nurses also treated diarrhea, stitched up small cuts, and set simple fractures. Saltpond Government Hospital, a forty-five-minute drive, had X-rays and sonograms, which the Otuam clinic did not, and treated compound fractures, cancer, and heart disease.

"Pregnant women are encouraged to come by for prenatal care," Isaiah continued, "for checkups and vitamin packs. And women have babies at the rate of one or two a day here."

"But there's no doctor to deliver the babies?" Peggy asked.

"No, there's a very good midwife, though. Sometimes she delivers the babies on the floor because there are only a few forty-year-old beds, rusty and corroded from the salt air, which have a tendency to collapse when the patient is thrashing around."

Peggy tried to picture this, but then her thoughts went to a more frightening place. "But some births are so complicated that a midwife, without being able to perform surgery, could very well lose both the mother and child. In the U.S., many women have the babies cut out of them or else they might die."

Isaiah the Treasurer nodded. "If a woman is having a difficult delivery, she is put in a taxi to go to Saltpond. But sometimes she can't even be put in the taxi right away; her family members run through Otuam trying to raise the cab fare from friends and neighbors. Some women and their babies die while waiting for the cab fare, or die in the backseat of the cab bouncing down the rutted road to Saltpond. It's the same thing for those suffering from heart attack or stroke, Nana; they often die in the taxi."

"But it doesn't happen very often that someone gets that sick," Tsiami interjected, studying his fingernails. "If Otuam people survive childhood, they live into their eighties and nineties. I had forty-one children with my two wives; twenty-five of them died before the age of five. But my great-aunt, who never saw a doctor in her life, lived to be one hundred and two."

"Five of my ten children died young," Uncle Moses chimed in, "but most of my aunts and uncles lived to be in their eighties and nineties."

Yes, Peggy thought. *The lifestyle keeps them healthy, with fresh fruit and fish, and hours of exercise every day. Thank God for that, at least.* She knew that the 50 percent childhood mortality rate of Uncle Moses's generation had dipped to somewhere between 12 and 17 percent due to the national effort to vaccinate infants. But even the death of one child with whooping cough, of one woman in labor, of one heart attack victim who could be revived was too many for her town. An ambulance would save lives. With the necessary equipment, a nurse could stabilize patients and keep them comfortable on the rough ride to the hospital. Peggy knew she could never afford a new ambulance, which must cost tens of thousands of dollars or more. But how much did a used one cost, and where would you get it?

Peggy noticed that Uncle Eshun's teeth, those few that remained, looked like the sarsen stones of Stonehenge, long and dark and widely spaced, leaning toward or away from one another at crazy angles. And one of Baba Kobena's front teeth had snapped off near the top, with a dark gray cavity spreading over what remained. Uncle Moses, too, was missing a few, and those that remained were stained and decayed.

"Does the town have a dentist?" she asked. She had been blessed with strong, white, even teeth, which she flossed and brushed with great care.

"I think there's one in Cape Coast Hospital," Eshun replied. "But most people can't afford the fees."

Peggy would need to bring doctors to Otuam, and a dentist, and an ambulance and some sturdy hospital beds. It suddenly occurred to her that perhaps her husband could help with the beds, and maybe he even knew a hospital that was looking to get rid of an old ambulance. But it would be much harder to find qualified medical personnel. Most Ghanaian doctors and dentists left the country soon after medical school. Working in the UK or America they could earn many times a Ghanaian salary and help support their extended families by sending home substantial portions of their paychecks.

Now Kwame Lumpopo spoke. "I suppose you know from corresponding with your uncle, the late king who is in the fridge, that in Otuam
there is no mail delivery," he explained, "since there are no addresses.
People expecting mail rent a post office box in Winneba, which is where
they also have bank accounts, since there is no bank in Otuam. And
there is no trash pickup, not that Otuam really needs it. Being from a
big city myself," he said, smiling at her, "I know how we throw things
away. But almost everything in Otuam is used and reused until it falls
apart. What little waste remains is burned outside."

There was a cave on the beach, Kwame Lumpopo continued, connected to a passage that led to the dungeons beneath the ruins of the old
slave castle, Tantumquerry, built by the British in the early eighteenth
century. Years earlier the people of Otuam had crammed the cave full of
trash bags since it seemed a good, tucked-out-of-the-way place to hide
garbage.

Peggy could picture the cave as it once was, with slaves stumbling
out from the dungeons in chains and coming onto the beach, where
they got into canoes and rode out to slave ships bobbing a mile or two
offshore. She reflected that the cave was a sacred space, a point of no
return for those thousands who left Africa forever. *Maybe I should have
that trash cleaned out,* Peggy thought, *hire a truck and cart it off to the dump
in Cape Coast and make the cave a shrine to the memory of those enslaved.* She
sighed. Of course that wouldn't do any good at all because people would
be delighted to find there was room once more to put trash.

Uncle Moses was next. He reported that Otuam had three schools
that went from kindergarten to ninth grade. Two of them were public,
state-run schools, and one of these had no toilet facilities; teachers and
children alike either had to wait to get home or use the bushes behind the
school. But in 1998, one of Peggy's cousins, Kobina Mensa-Yorke, with
his own hands built a simple open-air school, the International School,
to improve the educational opportunities for local children. Though it
was a private school, the fees were very modest, and the education was
far better than that offered in the public schools. Born in Otuam, Mr.
Yorke, as everyone called him, was highly educated, having won a high
school scholarship and obtained his diploma in accounting at Kumasi
Polytechnic.

Peggy remembered Mr. Yorke. He was one of the children of the
Other Cousin Comfort. He was a dark-skinned, birdlike man with tiny

bones. Mr. Yorke spoke English with a perfectly crisp British accent and was extremely precise in everything he said and did. His words were like the slices of a surgeon's scalpel, cutting through all nonsense and getting directly to the point. Despite his delicate build, Mr. Yorke's ramrod straight posture and precision demanded instant respect. He had a way of fixing his dark eyes on you as if he were silently determining what grade to put on your report card. Yes, Peggy could see him as an excellent principal.

"Mr. Yorke's school fees are very low," Uncle Moses said, "considering how much the kids learn there, and soon after his school opened, those families that could afford it enrolled their children. And, Nana, he's brought educational innovations to Otuam. Three computers from the 1990s are used to teach word processing, and he started night classes to educate kids who had to fish or farm all day with their parents. His night classes are always well attended because otherwise those kids would never learn how to read or write."

Mr. Yorke wanted to bring a high school to Otuam, Uncle Moses went on. Most parents couldn't afford to board their kids in other cities, or if there was some money available, they would send only the oldest boy. Some of the girls fortunate enough to go to high school returned home a few months into the school year shamefaced and big bellied as the nearby cities were full of men who preyed on fresh-faced country girls. These men waited outside the school gates for the girls to come out. They flirted with them, took them to dinner, and gave them cheap presents. The next thing you knew the girls were pregnant and went crying to the men who, they found out, were already married. Though abortion was illegal in Ghana, a girl could have a dangerous back-alley operation. Most Otuam families, however, no matter how poor, preferred to welcome another child rather than get rid of it. So the girls came back to Otuam and had babies, and that was the end of their bright future.

"It's a shame," Uncle Moses continued, "that Otuam has no library. There is nothing for kids to read for fun in English to improve their language skills. In the two public schools, they even share their tattered, ancient textbooks with other students, though Mr. Yorke's school provides every student with his or her own books. And because their English is so poor, and school is taught in English, they don't learn much in the way of math, science, or social studies, either, at least in the public schools. Mr. Yorke's students' command of English is somewhat better."

As they discussed Otuam's ever-lengthening list of needs, they heard the crunch of tires against sand as a cab rolled up out front. A car door slammed shut, and a few minutes later Peggy's nephew Ekow stood at the door of the parlor holding a suitcase in each hand. Ekow was the son of Peggy's late sister Charlotte and lived in Accra.

Ekow had never been completely right in the head. A gentle, self-deprecating soul nonetheless, he had always tried to be helpful. But these days he seemed to be living on the fringes of life, borrowing money, doing odd jobs, living in someone's spare room. It wasn't that he was stupid. His English was excellent, a remarkable accomplishment for someone who had only completed elementary school and had never left Ghana.

For a while Ekow had worked as a car mechanic, and he had been a good one. But when in September 2004 he had lost his mother, father, sister, and eleven-month-old son, he had also lost his mind, descending into an alcohol and marijuana fueled mania. He had always reacted very badly to alcohol of any kind—much the way normal people might react to PCP—but his reaction became even more severe after the death of so much family. And it was heightened by the fact that the causes of three of the four deaths were never fully explained. His father had been elderly, but his mother had evidently died of nothing more than an aching leg, his sister of a bad stomach, and his son of a boil on his neck. At least, that's what the doctors had said. Had the deaths been caused by witchcraft? Medical incompetence? Bad luck? Ekow couldn't stop obsessing over it, and it had derailed him completely.

His family had tried several times to take him to a hospital for a psychiatric evaluation, but he refused to go, howling that doctors would do terrible things to him. Peggy wondered if he had developed a touch of schizophrenia. Possibly he had been bewitched, which was probably the true cause of schizophrenia, but he likewise refused to see a traditional doctor, claiming to be a devout Christian. Whatever was wrong with him, nowadays he seemed to be living in his own world, muttering strange things.

Some three years earlier, when Peggy's relatives had called her about Ekow's steep decline, she thought maybe a year in school would help him. She agreed to send money to a trade school so he could get a higher-level mechanic's certificate. But then a cousin called her to say that she was wasting her money. Ekow had convinced the school that he was transferring elsewhere, and they gave him his money back, which he promptly spent on booze and pot. He hadn't worked a day since his mother's death, Peggy heard. The relatives were afraid to ask how he got his money. Sometimes he showed up at family events with a black eye or cut lip.

Peggy hadn't seen Ekow since well before his parents' death, and now she was surprised at how thin he was. At forty-one, he had the slender arms and undeveloped torso of an adolescent boy. His face appeared older, however, like a narrow squeezed prune, and his ears stuck out at right angles from his head.

"Mama, Mama, you are my mama and I am here for you," Ekow said as he entered the parlor, pushing Aggie aside. She cried, "Hey!" and raised her spatula threateningly.

Ekow dropped his suitcases, threw himself on his knees, and slid across the floor toward Peggy. *Oh boy,* she said to herself. *Being a mother to Ekow might prove more challenging than being a king.*

Who had told Ekow that she was in Otuam for her enstoolment? The last thing she needed was for him to make trouble at the solemn ceremonies. Peggy decided a strict approach would be best. "Ekow," she said, the *k* sound coming from the back of her throat as if it were a cough, "if you are going to stay here, you must behave. I will not put up with any nonsense. No alcohol, no smoking any dope or whatever you smoke."

"Yes, Nana Mama. No alcohol. No dope. I promise. Now, which one is your bedroom?" he asked, looking toward the hall. "I will sleep in there." The aunties were all shaking their heads and waving their hands in protest.

"Not a good idea," Kwame Lumpopo whispered in Peggy's ear. "The men will need to keep him in line at night."

Peggy nodded emphatically. "Ekow, you will sleep with the male cousins in the front room, with Kwame Lumpopo and Cousin Charles." Then she added as majestically as she could, "And if you don't behave, I will throw you on the first *tro-tro* to Accra."

Everyone chuckled, even Ekow. "I will be nice," he said, "and very, very fine." It's what Ekow always said when told to behave. But from what Peggy had heard, he usually wasn't nice or fine.

After the meeting, Peggy retired to her room. If she had felt giddy about becoming royalty, riding high on her new status as King Peggy, the meeting had sobered her up and brought her down to earth. Wife beating, poor medical care, few educational opportunities, no trash pickup, no running water, and no money. She had been aware of all this before she accepted the kingship, but now, face-to-face with the harsh realities of life in Otuam, she found herself coasting downward, her initial optimism punctured. In accepting the kingship, she believed the ancestors would help her to be a good leader of her people. Had this been a mistake? What had she gotten herself into? How on earth was she going to help these people?

Years earlier, the most important thing in the world to Peggy was to become a mother. She had done everything humanly possible to achieve that goal and had still proved a barren and useless wife. Now that kingship had been dropped into her lap, she had the incredible opportunity to give life not to a single individual, but to an entire town. If she couldn't help Otuam, if she were to prove a barren and useless king, her heart would surely break.

Again.

8

If you want the ancestors to bring you blessings, Peggy knew, it is important to thank them for blessings they have already bestowed and not take for granted anything they have done for you. Peggy and the elders needed to thank them for choosing her as the new king, and for her safe arrival in Otuam after a long and potentially dangerous journey. This offering of thanks would be combined with Peggy's first town meeting, where any resident of Otuam could meet her, ask questions, or make their complaints known.

The following morning, as Peggy, the elders, and aunties prepared to walk from the house to the palace, a taxi rolled up. Out jumped a tall, well-built man, who greeted Peggy and introduced himself as her cousin, Kwesi Acheampong, known as Nana Kwesi out of respect for his position as head of the family branch in Winneba. Peggy had never met Nana Kwesi but had heard about him from various cousins over the years. She was impressed that his taxi driver hauled out of the trunk cases of beer and Coke for her enstoolment and a nice robe for her. No one else had given her anything.

Nana Kwesi was fairly well off by African standards. He had been divorced from his wife for four years and lived with his four school-age children in a modern, comfortable house with running water, a wide-screen television, and beautiful furniture.

At fifty-two, he had smooth skin the color of milk chocolate. He was completely bald, and his head had a pleasing shape. His ears were small and tucked neatly against his skull, while his lower lip stuck out farther than his nose. As they chitchatted, it was Nana Kwesi's smile that caught Peggy's attention. It was most unusual, like the smile of a sweet child, a smile of genuine, innocent happiness. It was a contagious, angelic smile that lit up his whole face and radiated out until everyone else could feel it, and you just had to smile back for the sheer joy of it.

As the group walked over to the royal palace, Peggy noticed that Uncle Moses and Isaiah the Treasurer had their heads together, like children telling secrets, while Uncle Eshun trailed behind in the dust, leaning heavily on his cane. Approaching the courtyard, Peggy squinted at the patches of palace she could see behind a large, many-trunked tree, its enormous roots buckling the earth around it. The building had once been white, she recalled, but large chunks of plaster had fallen off, revealing the sandy-colored concrete blocks beneath, and wide vertical streaks of black mildew ran from the old tin roof—which had several large holes in it—down to the ground. As they approached, she could see that the ancient louvered windows were corroded and broken.

Suddenly, Peggy stopped walking and simply gasped at the hulking mess now in full view. The palace looked much worse than it had in 1995. "It will be all right," Cousin Comfort said, taking her by the elbow. "You know the ancestors wouldn't have put you here if they weren't going to provide you with the means to do the work."

Peggy nodded miserably and willed herself forward. They approached a long concrete patio in front of the main entrance, where her elders sat down on benches and plastic chairs. A stool had been provided for Peggy, with a tiger carving supporting the seat, which was covered by a brown and white goatskin. The stool's white paint was faded in some patches, peeling off like dry skin in others, and the tiger looked as if it might collapse in exhaustion. She frowned as she looked at it, realizing that her public stool was as old and as rotten as her palace, and cautiously sat down.

Uncle Moses had the royal cow horn wrapped in a piece of fine red flannel. Now he unwrapped it, puffed up his large walrus cheeks, and blew short shrill toots. This was the call for everyone who heard it to come to a town meeting.

Soon a few people from the surrounding houses came ambling up to the palace, carting plastic chairs from their homes. This was their first opportunity to see their new lady king.

"Is this all there is?" Peggy whispered to Kwame Lumpopo. "Does the town know I have arrived and am holding a meeting this morning?"

He nodded. "We had the town crier put the word out yesterday. But not many came to your uncle's meetings, either. Your people are very busy."

Peggy frowned. Her people were too busy to meet the new king? They had nothing to say to her, to ask her?

Tsiami stood and cried, *"Nana, wonfreye!"* a plea to the ancestors which meant "Let us call all good things to come to us."

Those gathered responded with, *"Yemrah!"* Let the good things come!

When this ritual opening prayer had been completed three times, Tsiami announced that he would pour libations in the stool room as an offering of thanks for their new king's safe journey from so far away.

Tsiami cried, *"Kokoko!"* as he unlocked and opened the palace door, approached the stool room door, and knocked loudly. In Ghana, as in much of Africa, visitors cry out *"Kokoko!"* as they near a house because it is only polite to let people know when you are visiting so you don't frighten them or catch them doing something private. The ancestors in the stools, too, needed to be made aware they had visitors. Perhaps they were sleeping inside the stools, or had traveled elsewhere on some business. The cry would tell them to rouse themselves, or return, to hear what the elders had to say to them.

The stool room was a closet-sized windowless chamber next to the staircase. Tsiami opened the door a couple of inches. That way, the ancestors could see those gathered outside if they wanted to, but the worshippers couldn't see the stools, as they were too holy for most people to observe.

"We are here!" cried Tsiami. "We are with the new king whom you have chosen when you made the schnapps steam up. Nana Amuah Afenyi VI is here. She thanks you for your blessings and for her safe journey home. We, the people of Otuam, thank you for choosing her."

The elders cried, *"Kwa! Kwa!"* and *"Ampah!"* which meant something like "Amen" or "That's right!" Tsiami cautiously opened the stool room door and slipped inside, leaving it slightly ajar. He then removed the goatskins covering the stools and poured an entire bottle of schnapps over them in long splashes while he cried and chanted. When the libation ceremony was over, Tsiami replaced the goatskins and closed and locked the stool room door.

Emerging onto the patio, he stood beside Peggy and asked the five townspeople—four men and a woman—if they had anything they wished to say to the king. They shook their heads. "This meeting is now over!" Tsiami said. The attendees picked up their chairs and took them back inside their tiny houses. Peggy had to admit the turnout was unsatisfying, and those few who had attended seemed to have done so out of curiosity or boredom. She had hoped for a larger turnout, had imagined people talking about their problems and asking for her advice and help.

Peggy had let her elders know that after the libation rituals and town meeting she wanted to inspect the palace to see what renovations were required. As she walked around the outside of the entire palace, a smiling Nana Kwesi beside her and her elders following, she saw more broken windows, missing chunks of plaster, and long streaks of mildew. When they entered the building, Peggy groaned out loud. The leaky roof and shattered windows had damaged the interior walls as well, and water had poured into the stool room, desecrating it. Peggy silently promised the stools that she would fix the leaks as soon as she possibly could and prayed for them to have patience.

Paint and plaster had fallen onto the floors, exposing pipes and wiring. Birds nested in several of the rooms, their feathers and excrement coating the floors. The kitchen appliances were rusted and disgusting. The doors didn't open or close properly. It was clear the whole place would have to be gutted. New wiring; new plumbing for a new rain tank on the roof; new windows and doors; a new kitchen and bathrooms; new walls, ceilings, and floors.

The condition of the palace wasn't anything surprising to her elders, especially Uncle Moses, who lived in the two best rooms on the first floor, rooms he kept tidy but filled with buckets to catch the leaks when it rained. Nor was it shocking to Auntie Esi, who lived in Otuam, or Kwame Lumpopo, who visited frequently. These people now adroitly stepped over bird feces as if it was the most normal thing in the world to do in a royal palace, and chatted with one another as if they were seeing nothing unusual. But coming from Tema, Cousin Comfort hadn't been inside for at least a decade, and now her initial optimism seemed deflated. She kicked an old bird's nest out of the way and clucked in disapproval, her manicured hands on her hips.

Isaiah the Treasurer, seeing Peggy's shock and disgust, sauntered up to her and said, "Well, Nana, I suppose it does need a new coat of paint."

New coat of paint?

Silently, Peggy asked the late king who was in the fridge, *How could you have lived like this? How could you have left such a mess for me? I can't live here. I have to have the whole thing completely renovated before I spend an hour here. And how much will that cost? Tens of thousands of dollars, I suppose. As it is, I can hardly keep up with my mortgage and condo fees. How am I going to restore the royal palace for your funeral?* She was suddenly afraid she would burst into tears in front of her council members.

Ebotum aye! said the voice. You can do it!

Peggy looked around. Where had that come from? She hadn't heard the voice since the day she accepted the kingship when she was driving through Rock Creek Park. But here it was again.

Just then Nana Kwesi approached her. "I know you want to renovate the royal palace, Nana," he said. "I have been a building contractor for many years. I have designed and built many of the new mansions in Winneba. I can help you with the work, especially since, with the economy getting so bad, there has been less work for me lately. As a family member, I won't charge much profit on the work and can do it much more cheaply than any other contractor."

That was wonderful news. Perhaps the ancestors had sent Peggy this kind, generous building contractor to help her renovate the royal palace. "Really?" she said, beaming. Then, nervously, she asked, "How much do you think it might cost?"

Nana Kwesi beckoned her to follow him upstairs, and Cousin Comfort joined them as they walked silently from room to room. In the king's bathroom, Peggy saw a blackened, filth-encrusted toilet, sink, and bathtub so nasty that she ran out of the room in horror.

Chuckling, Nana Kwesi joined her in the hallway and turned to her with his angelic smile. "Obviously, the bathroom needs a lot of work," he said. "But the first thing to do is to put on a new tin roof. That will prevent further water damage."

Peggy nodded. At all costs, the stool room must be kept dry. "And then we can take repairs one step at a time, as you get money," Nana Kwesi continued. "Don't worry, Nana. This will be a beautiful place."

Peggy looked around at the exposed wires and rusty pipes where the walls should have been, the fallen ceilings, and the bird feces on the floor. A bird, or was it a bat, was zooming down the corridor looking for a broken window to exit. *A beautiful place,* she repeated. *One step at a time.* Ekow had silently followed them upstairs, and now he was flapping spastically through the rooms as if he, too, were a bird trapped inside. Echoing her thoughts, he squawked, "Beautiful place! One step at a time!" like a parrot. Then he stood stock still, started to sob, and walked morosely from the room.

Peggy sighed. What on earth was she going to do with Ekow if he acted up, as the aunties warned her he would? As king, she was expected to be strong with misbehaving relatives. But she was also supposed to be compassionate toward the ill and weak-minded. She was further confused by her contradictory feelings toward Ekow. She pitied him, wanted to throw her arms around him and protect him for her dead sister's sake, but most of all, she just wanted him to go away.

Her eyes fell on Nana Kwesi, whose gaze had followed Ekow into the next room. Maybe he was right that the palace could be beautiful. Looking beyond the damaged surface, Peggy could see that the rooms were large and airy. Upstairs, the four bedrooms faced the ocean, a sparkling sapphire blue beyond the green trees, and a cool, fresh breeze danced in through the wide broken windows. She walked to a window and gazed at the view of utter serenity, Cousin Comfort close beside her.

"I will send money for you to start the roof as soon as I go home and get my next paycheck," Peggy promised, wondering what she would use for her condo fee and credit cards. She had put off these bills, paying instead for her ticket to Ghana, which had indeed cost her almost fifteen hundred dollars, and wiring Kwame Lumpopo the eight hundred dollars to settle the debt of the late king who was in the fridge. She had planned to pay her regular bills when she arrived home, but now she would have to start saving money for the palace repairs.

Nana Kwesi seemed to be considering something and looked as if he wanted to speak but wasn't sure if he should. He opened his mouth and closed it; he rubbed his forehead and sighed. Finally, he said, very quietly, "I know this isn't my town, Nana, but don't you think there should be some public funds available to help you pay for the palace repairs and the town's other needs? I know a bit about Otuam because I've come here from time to time for family events, and there is much to do—the water, the schools, the clinic, the road. I feel so sorry for the children here. Yet how can you do everything by yourself?"

Peggy had been asking herself that same question ever since that four a.m. phone call. Now she looked around for her elders and was glad to see they weren't nearby. "Isaiah the Treasurer tells me there's no money at all, that the town is too poor. I have to pay for my own enstoolment party out of money I brought with me from Washington."

Nana Kwesi frowned. "Then why do they call him the treasurer?"

Peggy nodded. "I wondered the same thing."

Nana Kwesi rubbed his cheek and said, "There must be taxes of some kind, don't you think? An annual real estate tax, perhaps? I think that every landowner in Ghana has to pay a small tax on his land. And what about land sales? All the land belongs to the stool, I know—that's true in towns and villages across the country. So when someone wants to buy undeveloped land, to clear a farm or build a house in the bush, they have to pay the king. Who's been selling the land and pocketing the money since your uncle had the stroke in January?"

Peggy was startled to hear him spell it out this way. "I have no idea. I'll ask my elders."

Nana Kwesi shook his head. "Before you bring up the subject of finances again to your elders, we should do a bit of research. As king, you can't very well stroll down Main Street talking to merchants, or amble down to the fishing beach and interview the fishermen. People in small towns are usually very friendly and talkative, eager to speak to strangers. Let me poke around and see what I can come up with."

Peggy felt a surge of gratitude. She suddenly had an idea of her own. It was her duty as king to appoint new elders, and a younger man like Nana Kwesi, educated, with his own business in a major city, would surely prove a welcome addition to the elderly illiterate farmers and fishermen who had sat on the council for decades.

"Nana Kwesi," she said, "I would like very much for you to join my council. I think it needs some fresh blood, younger people who are not set in their ways. I know you live in Winneba, and it's an hour's drive to Otuam, but Kwame Lumpopo lives all the way in Takoradi, four hours from here. He attends meetings on weekends or gives his advice by phone."

Cousin Comfort nodded encouragingly. "A wonderful idea," she said.

"Oh, that's not necessary," he demurred, suddenly looking away, and Peggy realized how shy he was, almost as shy as William had been. Nana Kwesi's natural shyness had been coated by an attractive veneer of maturity, courtesy, and years of business dealings, but it was still there, all the same.

"Of course, I'll help the family however I can," he said bashfully. "For instance, with the palace . . ."

His modest refusal convinced Peggy that she had made the right choice. Here was no swaggering blowhard, seeking to puff up his own importance and his bank account, by joining a royal council. "You can help the family best by joining my council of elders, Nana Kwesi," she said firmly. "I need you."

She hadn't said *that* to a man in a very long time, and as soon as she did so, she regretted it. It dangled strangely between them. Would he say no?

Nana Kwesi's shining eyes latched on to Peggy's and they both smiled. On the surface, she knew, she and Nana Kwesi weren't alike. He was bashful; she was forceful. But there was a certain air of sadness that clung to him that reminded her of her own disappointments. She had heard that there were problems with his ex-wife, which made difficulties for the children. He had also mentioned that his business was down. Now she noticed that buried in the depths of his sweet smile was a touch of heartbreak.

Nana Kwesi had mentioned the gut-wrenching needs of Otuam, a subject very dear to her heart. Perhaps working together they could—

The moment, so full of possibilities, was shattered by a loud, unearthly howl from the next room. Ekow.

One day slipped into the next, what with relatives dropping by, discussions about her enstoolment, and Peggy's royal etiquette lessons. Kwame Lumpopo asked her for money every day to go to Main Street to buy tomatoes, eggs, bread, and drinks; townsfolk usually dropped off gifts of fish every afternoon, so at least Peggy didn't have to buy much of that. Every time Peggy heard the porch gate banging, she hoped that William would walk into the house, smiling and congratulating her. But as many times as the clanging gate heralded visitors, none of them was William. Perhaps he was waiting to come for her enstoolment.

But one day there were female cries of *Kokoko!* outside the screen door and three women tumbled in, one behind the other like boulders. Peggy had been sitting at the dining room table, sipping Coke with Auntie Esi, who, taking one look at the women, rolled her eyes and said, "The late king's daughters, the ones who live in Accra. I met them once before, years ago."

Perpetual, Mary Magdalene, and Dorcas were obviously sisters and might well have been mistaken for triplets: large women of indeterminate age, with chubby faces and round features, though Perpetual wore big round glasses. They all wore African dresses and matching head wraps, bangle earrings and large clattering necklaces and bracelets.

Peggy had never met these cousins before as they hadn't attended any of the family events in Otuam where she had been present, and her mother had told her that they hadn't visited their father in many years. She was surprised that they had come all the way to Otuam to pay their respects.

As they sipped Fantas and chatted, Peggy noticed that Perpetual, the oldest daughter, was the most talkative of the bunch, Dorcas agreed with everything Perpetual said, and Mary Magdalene sat silent as a stone.

"We are so happy, Nana, that you are the new king," Perpetual remarked. "To think, a woman! It is really wonderful."

"Really wonderful," Dorcas said. Mary Magdalene said nothing.

"She will be a very *strong* king," Auntie Esi snapped. "I think Nana will surprise anyone who tries to take advantage of her."

Perpetual ignored this and addressed herself to Peggy. "We don't want to wait long for our father's funeral," she said. "When do you think you will have it?"

"Because we can't wait long," Dorcas said. Mary Magdalene said nothing.

Peggy coughed. "I will have it as soon as I can," she said. "I understand your concern that your father is there in the morgue, and it must be cold for him. I, too, want him to be at peace as soon as possible. But it takes a lot of time and money to organize a royal funeral, so I am asking you for patience."

"We don't need a huge royal funeral," Perpetual said. "We just want him to find his rest soon."

"Very soon," Dorcas said. Peggy began to wonder if Mary Magdalene was mute.

"A king's funeral can't be rushed," Auntie Esi said, staring hard at Perpetual. "It must be done with *dignity.*" She said the last word slowly, loudly. Through her large glasses, Perpetual glared at her.

"You are both right," Peggy said, trying to smooth over the uncomfortable moment. "Believe me, my uncle's rest is something that weighs heavily on my mind, but I must also ensure that he has a truly dignified funeral."

After they said their good-byes, Peggy asked Auntie Esi, "What was that between you just now?"

Auntie Esi sniffed. "They haven't been here to see their father in a long time, Nana, not even when he was very sick. Not even when he was in the hospital slowly dying all those months, begging them to come to him, and they lived right up the road. Now that he's gone, suddenly they've made the trip all the way out here, saying they're concerned about his burial, and it doesn't ring true, somehow."

Sighing deeply she continued, "Part of me feels sorry for the children that they were. Joseph couldn't keep away from women and ran from one to the next like a honeybee to flowers, leaving his own kids to fend for themselves.

"This behavior nourished their hatred and resentment of him," Auntie Esi went on, "fed it, fattened it. But they have been adults for a very long time and should let it go. Joseph was a good man who loved them despite his weakness for women. Their retaliation was successful because they broke his heart. Can you see him, waiting in the hospital for months, calling, hoping? And not one of them ever called, ever came to see him. Don't trust any of the children of the late king. There is a terrible hatred there, one that, I fear, has followed Joseph into death."

Followed him into death? That seemed a bit melodramatic. Perhaps the daughters felt guilty that they hadn't gone to the hospital to forgive him and hoped to make amends by seeing him at peace in his grave sooner rather than later. Auntie Esi was clearly wrong about undying resentment. Peggy was greatly relieved that they had called on her after all those stories she had heard about them, and perhaps at their next meeting she could raise the idea of their sharing the funeral expenses.

The days were so exhausting that she slept like a log every night in the room with her five aunties, even though they always kept the light on so they could make it to the bathroom without stepping on another auntie stretched out on a sleeping mat.

One night Peggy woke up and saw a man sitting in the plastic chair next to her bed. She was surprised because usually visitors didn't come between ten p.m. and four a.m., and whenever they did come, they cried *"Kokoko!"* to alert people to their approach.

His entrance hadn't awakened any of Peggy's relatives in the room either, which was strange because the bedroom door behind him was closed, and to do so you had to make a lot of ruckus, slamming it hard and jiggling the handle.

Her visitor was an elderly man with gray hair and a handsome face of strong, noble lines. Though he had the muscular arms of a fisherman, Peggy assumed that he was about eighty. He wore a multicolored cloth over his left shoulder. She wasn't sure if she recognized him or not—she had met dozens of aunties and uncles and cousins in the past few days and couldn't keep them straight. But she assumed he was one of her many relatives who had come to pay a late call.

He didn't introduce himself, and Peggy was afraid to ask his name because perhaps she had already met him and didn't remember, which he might find insulting. So she just pushed herself up to a sitting position and greeted him pleasantly as if she knew him.

He smiled at her. "Nana," he said, "you must be strong if you want to live the full life of a king. There is nothing for you to be afraid of."

It was an unusual comment for a visitor to start off with, but a wise one.

"I have many responsibilities," Peggy replied. "Many worries, and not enough money by a long shot. I don't know how I am going to do all this, take care of all these people."

He chuckled. "You may not be aware of it yet, but there are so many people taking care of *you* spiritually, mentally, and physically."

He must have meant the ancestors. "I know," Peggy said. "But still it's hard."

He smiled at her and his dark eyes twinkled. "You will find the strength," he said. "You are not alone in this. There is a reason the ancestors chose you as king. This was your destiny before you were born, you know. You will find the way to do great things for the people of Otuam."

Peggy sighed and glanced over at Cousin Comfort, sound asleep beside her. It was strange that their conversation hadn't awakened any of the other five women in the room. She looked back to respond, but the man was gone. The chair was empty, and the door, which made so much noise when closed, was still closed. It had been a dream, Peggy thought. The whole thing had been a dream. She eased back onto her pillow, staring at the chair where the man had been and thinking about what he had said, and finally fell asleep.

A few hours later, Peggy was aware of crowing roosters. She sat bolt upright and looked at the chair. It was still empty. Yes, that had been a dream, surely. Cousin Comfort stirred and turned around to face her.

"Good morning, Nana," she said groggily.

"Comfort," Peggy whispered, "last night I had a dream that an elderly man came in here and sat on that chair and told me things about my kingship. And all of a sudden he disappeared. That's how I knew it was a dream."

Cousin Comfort sat up and smiled. "Oh, no, Nana!" she said. "That wasn't a dream. One of your ancestors visited you last night to advise you."

"But if it wasn't a dream, why didn't anyone wake up when she heard him talking?" Peggy mused.

"That's how it is with the ancestors," Cousin Comfort explained. "When they visit you, they make sure everyone else is asleep and nobody wakes up. If some of the aunties recognized him as a long-dead relative, they would have started yelling and screaming, and then he couldn't have delivered his message to you."

Perhaps he had really been there, Peggy thought, staring at the empty chair, and she had spoken with an ancestor face-to-face. Funny how he had looked like a living person. He hadn't been white or see-through or glowing, as you often hear in ghost stories, nor had there been anything at all frightening about him. Peggy had felt very calm when speaking to him and listening to his wise and encouraging remarks.

Peggy was far more afraid later in the day when she had another supernatural visitor. She was in the bedroom with the five other women when she heard a commotion in the hallway. Suddenly two wild-eyed men came in carrying what looked like a long wooden plank between them, resting on their left shoulders. A square object of some sort was on the center of the plank, but Peggy couldn't tell exactly what it was because it was tightly wrapped in a white sheet.

The men's attire was ordinary enough. They wore T-shirts, shorts, and flip-flops, but they looked very strange. They were sweating, dancing, and chanting, parading all around the bedroom with the plank and shrouded object. Cousin Comfort and Aunt Esi, who had been sitting on the bed with Peggy, stood up to welcome them, but the other three aunties threw themselves on the floor and cowered, their arms flung over their heads.

"What on earth . . . ," Peggy began, her mouth gaping.

"They are the fetish priests of the god Inkumsah," Auntie Esi said knowingly. "These priests go into trances and the god makes them dance and speak in his voice. They tend his shrine in a secret cave on the beach."

Then Peggy understood that the square object was a brass pan that contained a statue, called a fetish, inhabited by a spirit. Spirits, she knew, could glide invisibly across the earth like the wind, until they settled down and attached themselves to a body of water, a patch of forest, a hill, or a beach. Sometimes priests lived on the sacred site, pouring libations to the spirit and even letting it speak through their mouths when they went into trances. Such spirits were often called gods, though everyone knew there was only one Creator God, who had made everything in the universe, seen and unseen. Long ago some of these little gods had been coaxed out of their trees, caves, or lagoons to enter clay fetish images, which the priests kept in brass pans. In times of attack, the priests could run to safety carrying the fetish with them, whereas they couldn't very well carry off a lagoon or a tree.

Inkumsah was, apparently, one of those spirits created at the dawn of time, older than the oldest ancestors, ancient beyond measure, and who knew how powerful. Perhaps he had been born in that cave on the beach, shaped by God along with the molten rock. Or maybe for millions of years he had wandered the earth disembodied, drifted to the cave, and there found repose as one of Otuam's seventy-seven gods. Now this spirit was standing in front of her. Peggy shuddered.

"Welcome, Nana," said the fetish priest carrying the front of the plank. His eyes darted right and left, and sweat poured down his face.

Auntie Esi nudged Peggy. "He's speaking in the voice of the god Inkumsah," she said. Peggy nodded, her eyes wide, her mouth open.

"Why, when you came here, did you not visit me?" the god cried, as the priest who was speaking jumped up and down. "I have known you for many years. Yet you come here for your enstoolment and neglect me."

The god had known Peggy for many years? Really? She had never heard about this god before. How could she have visited him? But the words stuck in her throat. What were you supposed to say to a god dancing in your bedroom?

Peggy was relieved when Cousin Comfort cleared her throat and answered for her. "Nana is from the USA and doesn't know the customs of Otuam," she said. "If an error has been committed, it is not hers but ours for not advising her properly."

"You must pay us something," the god said, as the men jumped up and down with the plank between them.

"Pay?" Peggy asked, astonished. It seemed that everybody in Otuam wanted her money, even the cave god.

Cousin Comfort nudged her again. "Just one cedi. A symbolic act of devotion and respect."

The men were dancing in circles again and shaking their heads, the sweat flying off them. Quickly Peggy grabbed her purse and took out a coin. "Here," she said.

"We are going now," said Inkumsa, as his priest pocketed the coin in his shorts. "You must know that you have been chosen, and we will protect you."

They danced out of the bedroom and out of the house, through the bush and down toward the beach. The aunties who had been cowering slowly raised their heads and looked around. Creakily, they stood up. Peggy just sat on the bed with her mouth hanging open, her pocketbook on her lap.

Most men think they are gods in the bedroom and their women pretend to agree. But that day Peggy had a real god in her bedroom, which is something most women could never say, and it scared the hell out of her.

9

The evening before Peggy's enstoolment, she and her elders and aunties went to a wide concrete house with a large courtyard on Main Street for special ceremonies. The house belonged to a fifty-five-year-old retired engineer, Casely Kweku Mensah, known in Otuam by his royal title of Nana Tufuhiene or just plain Nana Tufu. He was tall and dignified, his gray hair cropped close. He had an intelligent, handsome face, wire-framed glasses, and from the neck up looked like a university professor. He wore a printed tan cloth, a dozen strands of beads around his neck, and several bead bracelets on each wrist.

Nana Tufu had a special role in the area as a mediator, which conferred on him the status of king. It traced back to one of his ancestors who had been known for great diplomatic skill. The ancestor had been drafted to mediate between the king of Otuam and the troublesome Magic Mirror clan, in a quarrel that had been going on for more than three centuries, back to the earliest years of Otuam's existence.

Otuam had been founded by an ambitious young hunter, Peggy's ancestor, Amuah Afenyi of the Ebiradze clan. Amuah Afenyi was the nephew of the king of a farming community, Ampraefu, which means "If you don't weed, it grows."

Amuah Afenyi tracked game wide and far. One day he came across an uninhabited place on the sea, where enormous schools of fish migrated, with rich soil good enough to grow yams. He obtained permission from his uncle, the king, to bring a portion of the clan's burgeoning population to the area and start his own town, which he called Tantum, after a local god.

Once he and his people were well settled, and he had been enstooled as Nana Amuah Afenyi I, he received a visit from a man named Ewusi Kwansa and his wives, children, followers, and slaves. Ewusi Kwansa's great wealth had come from a business opportunity he had seized in his youth: he had obtained a mirror from a Portuguese trader on the coast. In the interior of what is now Ghana, mirrors had never before been seen. Ewusi Kwansa had wrapped his mirror in a cloth and traveled from village to village, promising to show people what their souls looked like—for a fee.

Arriving in Tantum with his entourage, Ewusi Kwansa asked Amuah Afenyi for permission to stay a few days, a request that was granted by the hospitable host. But the Magic Mirror people refused to leave and dug their feet deeply into the ground, like stubborn tree roots that could never be pulled out. Soon they no longer regarded themselves as guests of the stool, but as rightful owners of the land.

After the deaths of Amuah Afenyi and Ewusi Kwansa, their heirs disputed ownership of Tantum, and the Ebiradze family cast out the people of Ewusi Kwansa. But they returned late one night, killing townsfolk as they slept and burning their houses. The Ebiradze rebuilt the town, vowing never to forget the ambush, though they couldn't prevent the Magic Mirror people from eventually returning, claiming land and other rights, and always agitating for more.

More often than not, the peace-loving descendants of Amuah Afenyi I gave in to their claims rather than risking further violence, even ceding to them an acre of land they could legally call their own. But this act of generosity was a grievous mistake. Immediately the Magic Mirror people elected their own king with his own stool to rule over the acre and proclaimed themselves kings on par with the kings of Otuam. They even chose a royal family name that imitated that of the Ebiradze: they called themselves the Aboradze.

Peggy's family looked at them as eternal, unwelcome houseguests who had to be suffered in silence. But in the 1950s some of them committed a heinous crime—Peggy could never determine exactly what they had done—and Nana Amuah Afenyi III changed the name of the town from Tantum to Otuam, which meant "He attacks me unawares." It was a nonviolent slap in the face, aimed to ensure that no one would ever forget the sneakiness and greediness of the Magic Mirror people, who still lived among them.

The fractious relations between the two royal families became so bad that Nana Tufu's family became the official mediators, raised to royal status to give their decrees greater force. Fortunately for Peggy, a few years earlier when the one-acre Magic Mirror king had died, his relatives got into a terrible fight over who should be the next king, with two branches of the family coming to blows. Neither one of the two contenders lived in Otuam or they might have stirred up trouble for her. With the family unable to choose a king, the one acre of the Aboradze remained kingless, which made the Ebiradze happy.

For several years now, Nana Tufu hadn't been called upon to resolve any disputes between the two royal families. But he participated in local festivals, royal elections, enstoolments, and the funerals of kings in the region.

Nana Tufu himself hadn't actually been enstooled because his family alternated kingship between its two main branches (a common practice in much of Africa), and he was sitting in for his cousin who wasn't ready yet to leave his job and move to Otuam. Nana Tufu had taken the position four years earlier, and as each year went by with no sign of his cousin, he sank more deeply into the role and believed he would have it for life, as well he should, he often said, after so much effort.

Otuam's royal mediator was almost always accompanied by his own *tsiami,* fifty-two-year-old Papa Adama. Short and wiry, he had a dark, skull-like face with widely spaced eyes, high cheekbones, a short triangular nose, and a long space between his nose and mouth. He was missing several teeth, yet instead of being unattractive it gave him a cute, friendly look, like a child who had lost his baby teeth and was waiting for adult ones to come in. Tonight he was wearing flip-flops and a pale green knee-length robe.

Like many in Otuam, Papa Adama was an illiterate fisherman. But if he couldn't read or write, he could certainly speak with great authority. And now he cried out the official greetings to Peggy in a loud, ringing voice, perhaps the loudest, most passionate voice in all Ghana. He was like an ancient epic poet declaiming Homer, capturing the absolute attention of everyone within hearing distance. Papa Adama's dramatic inflection put all the other *tsiamis* to shame.

African communication had always primarily been verbal rather than written. Little children were trained by their parents to speak clearly to their elders in family gatherings, prompted to find the right words, put them in a meaningful order, and above all, tell the truth and speak straight from the heart. Therefore most Africans were unfazed by speaking to huge crowds, even if they couldn't read or write, while many Americans, according to a survey Peggy had read, were more afraid of public speaking than of death.

Peggy and her elders, along with Nana Tufu and his elders, gathered in his uneven concrete courtyard where the butcher slaughtered a goat as a sacrifice to the ancestors for Peggy's enstoolment. The skin would be used to make a pouch or sandals, and the meat would be eaten. Then they went inside to Nana Tufu's throne room, a wide chamber with a raised platform at the far end with the royal stool on it, where Peggy would be examined for her suitability as king. To be enstooled as a Ghanaian king, the candidate had to be in good health and show no signs of witchcraft, which were usually manifested in some kind of physical deformity. These included a twisted leg or limp, a bad eye, leprosy or any skin disease. He—or she—would also be disqualified if he were left-handed, or worst of all, had a sixth finger on either hand.

Nana Tufu and his council of elders carefully examined Peggy's skin, looked closely at her eyes, inspected her hands, and made her walk up and down. She was glad for her aunties' royal training because now she walked slowly, with great dignity. After consulting with one another in a corner, they agreed that Peggy was a fit specimen for kingship.

On their way out of Nana Tufu's palace, Tsiami took Peggy aside and remarked, "When I was consecrating your sacred stool, it told me it didn't like schnapps and only wanted to drink Coke."

Ghanaian women usually didn't drink hard liquor, and Peggy found it fascinating that her stool shared this female abhorrence of strong drink. It was clearly imbued with a female spirit.

The next morning, Peggy and the aunties were up at four a.m. They bathed in their buckets, dressed, and breakfasted. Peggy was given a special anti-urination breakfast of yams, boiled and mashed, with palm oil and hard-boiled eggs mixed in. Her aunties assured her that this dish would take away all urge to pee for about eighteen hours. It would be terribly undignified if the new king had to instruct her bearers to put down the palanquin in which she would be carried so she could run off to the nearest toilet.

Peggy wore her late uncle's red, green, black, and gold kente cloth slung over one shoulder. The red stood for sacrificial rites and death, the green for spiritual renewal, the gold for royalty and glory, and the black for the intense spiritual energy of the dead. But she wore something under her kente that most kings didn't bother with—a long-line strapless bra.

Peggy also wore Uncle Joseph's royal sandals, leather flip-flops with wide round toes and heels. The V-shaped strap was made of woven strips of brightly colored leather and decorated at the top with a multicolored pom-pom.

She had rented a van, which now drove her and the aunties through town to a school where the women would adorn her as a king. It was at the far end of Main Street, beyond the little blue and white police station and the salmon-colored church.

The queen mother, Paulina, was already there, along with her cousin, Peggy's Soul, ten-year-old Faustina. Paulina was a strikingly beautiful girl with the startling bone structure of Nefertiti and a lovely figure. Faustina was quiet and patient, qualities required of a Soul, who had to sit still in front of the king for hours at a time, deflecting evil spirits.

As her official dresser, Peggy had chosen Grace Bentil, a plump seamstress in her forties who also worked as a makeup artist, helping women prepare for weddings and funerals and making dead bodies look better for the viewing. Kneeling, Grace clasped golden anklets around Peggy's ankles, then adorned her with heavy beaded necklaces, thick gold bracelets, and large gold rings. She placed a heavy crown on her head, solid gold, which had been in the family for generations and was only used for enstoolments. As the final touches, she lined Peggy's eyes with black kohl, and put bright red lipstick on her lips.

Holding a hand mirror, Peggy studied herself, moving her face right and left. *I look tough,* Peggy thought, *like a man,* and she nodded in approval. Grace then ground a rock onto a smooth stone palette and added a bit of water to make a paste.

"What is that?" Peggy asked.

"Myrrh," Grace explained as she took the top of a perfume bottle with a perfectly round edge, dipped it in the paste, and applied it to Peggy's arms, chest, and shoulders, leaving pale circular shapes. "We put it on kings and queens to keep the evil spirits away." Peggy nodded. What with her Soul sitting in front of her, and all the eyeliner, and now the myrrh, she couldn't imagine she would have any evil spirits attack her today.

Once Peggy was ready, they all stepped outside so that Tsiami could pour a libation to the ancestors. Before he opened the bottle of schnapps, she thought she got a whiff of alcohol as she neared him and wondered if he had already started pouring some of the ancestral libations down his own throat. It would be the perfect job for an alcoholic, she thought. People gave you bottles and bottles of liquor to pour, and they couldn't always be sure exactly where you poured it. She made a mental note of this and filed it away for further use.

The enstoolment was a holiday for the entire town and the streets were jammed with people, which delighted Peggy after the meager turnout for the town meeting. A group of young men had brought the late king's palanquin, a large wooden cradle covered with black and white kente cloth and attached to long poles. In Africa, palanquins were used to lift a king high so all the people could see him and he could get a good view of his people. Before Peggy and the Soul climbed in, Tsiami poured schnapps again outside the school entrance, praying the ancestors to give strength to the men who would carry the palanquin. If they dropped the king, it would mean the ancestors were angry, and bad luck would come to all of Otuam, a drought perhaps, or a flood or epidemic, and several cows would have to be slaughtered to appease the angry spirits.

Peggy sat down in the back of the palanquin, and her Soul sat in front of her. Several strong young men picked them up. Peggy clung to both sides as they lurched forward, and then she settled back as the men started carrying her through town so the people could see their new king. Cousin Charles carried the massive red umbrella, the symbol of royalty, to shield her from the sun. The queen mother was hoisted aloft alone in her own palanquin behind Peggy. Uncle Moses was blowing the cow horn, other men were banging drums, and Peggy's subjects were bowing before her and dancing wildly in the street.

Peggy had mixed emotions as she was carried forward. On the one hand, she was giddy with excitement. *This can't be happening,* she said to herself. *This must be a dream. Here I am, a king, with hundreds of people bowing down before me. I have power over all these people!*

Then she thought, *What am I going to do with it? Can I really help such a backward place? With power comes responsibility. Maybe I should think about that instead of getting puffed up with my own importance.* She continued to smile broadly at her people and wave regally, but she heaved a sigh. *Lord help me,* she said to herself.

She scanned the crowd, wondering where William was, and then told herself she was being foolish. William would never be standing in the middle of such a crowd. Perhaps he was waiting for her back at the house.

The circles of myrrh on her arms and chest had melted, Peggy noticed, and a delightful fragrance rose up. That, and the lemons she had rubbed on her skin that morning, kept her smelling sweet in the unbearable heat.

Peggy was carried up and down Main Street for about two hours, though her palanquin bearers were switched out every five or ten minutes, new ones sliding beneath to shoulder the weight as the old ones slipped out of the way. The bearers were all exhilarated at the honor of carrying the new king. As one was relieved of his burden, he wiped his brow with a handkerchief, looked up at Peggy, and said, "You are the heaviest Nana we ever carried."

Yes, she thought, *I really must go on a diet.*

But her crown also was heavy; the dense gold seemed to dig through her scalp and into her brain, setting her head throbbing. Finally, the royal bearers carefully put the palanquin down, and Peggy, preceded by her Soul, walked under the red umbrella down Main Street and over to the royal palace. Peggy and her elders made their way through the courtyard thronged with people and through the main door of the palace. This was the crucial moment of her enstoolment.

There, in the little hallway at the foot of the stairs, Tsiami unlocked the stool room. Those stools that had belonged to the kings who were in the village for good were laid reverently on shelves. There, too, was Peggy's new stool. She gazed at it in wonder. *My stool,* she said silently, *you are my stool.* It was as if she were seeing her own child for the first time: she had known for some time it was on the way but was overwhelmed with emotion now that it was right in front of her. *I never thought I would have a stool, but there you are.*

Now Tsiami, begging the ancestors in all the stools to hear his words, took the oldest one, the centuries-old stool of Nana Amuah Afenyi I, off its shelf and carefully placed it on a low, wide table as it would have been a desecration for it to touch the ground. "We have a king!" he cried in ringing tones. "You have chosen her for us, and we have accepted her as ruler of Otuam. We beseech you to give her the wisdom and justice to lead her people, to bring them health and prosperity!"

He turned to Peggy, "Nana," he said, "do you promise the ancestors to be available to your people whenever they need you, to meet with them, guide them, advise them, and judge them, except in the case of your serious illness?"

"I do," Peggy said solemnly. This was the most sacred vow anyone could ever make in their lives. If she forsook it, the ancestors would probably kill her horribly.

Tsiami put his scrawny arms around Peggy and grasped her elbows, lowering her to within a few inches of the seat of the stool. It was important that no part of the new king's nether regions touched the stool because it had such intense spiritual energy that it burned away sexual potency in an instant. It was well known that men whose penises had dangled onto it were rendered immediately and eternally impotent, which was why they generally held these parts up and out of the way during this ceremony. Similarly, a female king whose reproductive parts touched the stool would be hopelessly barren and frigid as an iceberg forever.

Peggy wasn't afraid of being barren or frigid, but she made sure to cling tightly on to Tsiami as she was terrified of touching the stool with her rear end. She suspected that the initial searing pain might be followed by lifelong hemorrhoids or constipation. She hadn't asked Tsiami about it for fear she might not have the nerve to go through with the ritual. It was particularly unfortunate that Tsiami was so skinny, and Peggy was not skinny, and at first it seemed as if he would drop her. But Tsiami was surprisingly strong for his size, each thin arm a braid of long muscles toughened by nearly seventy years of fishing and farming.

"Give her the wisdom that your ancestors acquired here on earth!"

Tsiami cried, lifting her back up. "Help her to be strong and compassionate! Give her the power to reconcile enemies!" With great ease he lowered her and hoisted her up a second time, all the while calling loudly on the ancestors.

After the third symbolic sitting, Peggy stood up, grateful that no part of her had touched the stool, while Tsiami carefully put the stool back on its shelf and took down another one. Finally, when the ceremony had been done for all the ancestral stools, Tsiami brought forward her small, plain stool. He had taken her at her word, Peggy realized. It was quite tiny, something a small child might sit on, with no special symbols on its central section, just two smooth pieces of wood holding up the curved seat.

"This stool is your sister," Tsiami said to her. "Its spirit will travel with you when the big stools cannot. It will be with you always." He turned to the stool. "Oh, stool of Nana Amuah Afenyi VI, you have received her spirit inside you. Give her wisdom. Protect her on all her voyages. Help her to rule with justice for all her people."

Peggy would not be lifted over her own stool, but she was expected to speak to it. And suddenly the gravity of the moment almost crushed her. Her soul had been placed inside that stool, along with the souls of all the kings of Otuam who had gone to the village for good, and all her ancestors going back thousands of years, and all the unborn of Otuam. She suddenly found herself trembling before it. What was she supposed to say at a time like this?

"Help me," she said softly, her timid whisper a stark contrast to Tsiami's loud cries. "I want . . ." She tried to collect her thoughts. *What do I want?* she asked herself. "I want to be a good king. I want to use all my advantages as an American citizen to help these people."

She paused as Tsiami waited respectfully. "But there are so many problems here, and so many obstacles to solving them, that I don't know yet what I can do." She took a deep breath. "You had a purpose in choosing me king," she said, her voice louder now. "Give me strength and show me the way! Never leave me alone to face all these problems! Stay with me every minute, guide and comfort me!" Now she was practically shouting. "I will honor Otuam and the late king by fixing the royal palace and holding the most magnificent funeral this place has ever seen! I will bring water! Education! Medical care! I want to be a good king!

I want to help these people! I will always put them first, before myself. I swear it, but I need your help!"

She bent over at the waist, suddenly exhausted. Tsiami took her by the arm in case she was going to faint. But she didn't. She stood up and smiled. She was truly king now.

When Peggy returned to the house, the party was well under way. Aggie was serving beer and whiskey, and many of the guests, who had been drinking since sunrise, were in serious states of inebriation. As king, the aunties had told her, Peggy had to watch carefully how much she drank because the ancestors would be angry if she became inebriated and shamed the stool. Luckily, Peggy never drank more than a glass of wine at a meal or a beer to cut the heat.

The house was overflowing with relatives—aunts, uncles, cousins— as well as the leading townspeople and neighbors. Everyone greeted Peggy warmly as if they were old friends. She smiled and said hello, though she didn't think she had ever met most of them before. She looked around, scrutinizing every face, but couldn't find William.

At one point, when she was sitting at the head of the dining room table, Nana Kwesi sat down beside her. "Well, Nana," he said, "as I promised you, I have been walking around town and talking to people about how things are run here."

Peggy smiled. Nana Kwesi was taking his responsibilities as her newest elder very seriously.

He leaned forward in a confidential pose. "I spoke with one person who had bought land this year, and another one whose cousin bought land, and they gave the money to your elders. Which elders they couldn't say as they don't remember their names, and although the elders gave them signed contracts, the buyers can't read. Also, every year all those who own land are supposed to pay a small real estate tax to the stool. It's not much for each parcel, but it adds up with seven thousand people, and it was collected last month."

"Don't tell me—by my elders."

Nana Kwesi nodded. "I also hear that there's a land records book, where all land sales are registered, that you should ask for."

Peggy shook her head. "If Uncle Joseph was in the hospital or dead, then that money should have been given to Isaiah the Treasurer to hold for town needs, such as my enstoolment party. Yet he told me there was nothing in the treasury. And when I asked about town income, my elders told me there wasn't any."

"Ah-henh," Nana Kwesi said, leaning in even closer. "And that's not all. The fishermen are supposed to pay the king a daily tax on their catch for the right to live on your land, fish in your waters, and store their canoes on your beaches."

Peggy's eyes opened wide. Uncle Joseph had probably died in May, when his cell phone stopped working and her first letter had come bouncing back undeliverable. And she knew for a fact that he had gone into the hospital back in January. "Who has been collecting the fees since January when he had the stroke?" she asked.

Nana Kwesi said solemnly, "Your elders have always collected them, even when the king was in good health. That's the tradition, as the king can't be seen handling money. The elders are supposed to collect it and turn it over to him. But your elders collected it right up until last week. The fishermen I talked to couldn't name the elders but said they would recognize them."

The hope flitted across Peggy's mind that perhaps the elders had collected the fishing tax, the real estate tax, and the land sales and spent it on legitimate purposes: buying coffins for the destitute, medicine for the aged, school fees for bright but impoverished kids. In the severe illness or absence of a king, that is what his council of elders should do with town funds. But in that case, they would have informed her of the money and given her a written accounting of where it had gone. Instead, they had just told her there was nothing.

Peggy had a feeling that even before he got sick, Uncle Joseph hadn't seen much of the town's income. Gentle and forgiving, he probably wouldn't have insisted too strenuously that the elders turn it over. That must have been why he let his palace run down; he didn't even have enough money for a patch on the roof or a bucket of paint, and he hadn't felt like fighting his elders to get it. And his pride had prevented him from accepting help from Uncle James.

Then another thought hit Peggy right between the eyes: had the elders selected her not *despite* but *because* she was a woman? Did they assume she would be weak? At the very least, she lived five thousand miles away, so she couldn't keep her eyes on them most of the time, couldn't insist on a daily turnover of fishing fees. They would be free to keep on stealing the town's funds with impunity. It had been Uncle Moses who insisted her name be on the list. Why? Did he have anything to do with town finances? It had been Uncle Moses who jumped for joy when the schnapps steamed up. It had been Uncle Moses who said it was fine that she wouldn't spend much time in Otuam.

A shiver ran through her. There she was, a king, with a crown on her head, sitting at her own coronation party, and maybe they had chosen her just to cheat the town. Could that be possible? And they had chosen a girl as queen mother, practically a child, who wouldn't even dare to look them in the eye, much less question men sixty years her senior about finances.

No, Peggy said to herself. *It wasn't the elders who chose me. It was God and the ancestors. Nobody but God and the ancestors could make the schnapps steam up. And even if the elders lied about that, manipulated the steaming schnapps somehow, I had the dream fifteen years ago, again and again, about walking up to the royal palace. And I heard the ancestral voice three times in Washington and one time here. And I saw the ancestor sitting by my bed.*

Peggy had been staring into nothingness. When she looked up she saw Nana Kwesi thoughtfully sipping his Coke.

"You don't want any beer or whiskey?" she asked.

He shook his head. "I don't drink alcohol."

Peggy looked around and noticed that most of her elders were very drunk. Tsiami was tipped sideways on the couch, though his eyes were still open and blinking, and Uncle Moses had collapsed in a chair in the corner with his glasses askew, next to Uncle Eshun, who seemed to be asleep and whose cane had fallen to the floor unnoticed. Baba Kobena, devout Muslim, was drinking Fanta and talking sensibly to Cousin Comfort, Peggy saw. But Isaiah the Treasurer, devout and abstemious Methodist though he proclaimed himself to be, was swaying like a tree in a violent wind and arguing with a relative.

And here was Nana Kwesi sipping Coke. Of all of her elders, only Nana Kwesi had looked into the financial issues of her realm and provided her with necessary information. Peggy had noticed that he was a quiet person and opened his mouth only when he had something important to say. He impressed her much more than Kwame Lumpopo, she realized, as she watched her cousin gulping down whiskey and flirting outrageously with a young townswoman. Nana Kwesi had brought her crates of beer and minerals for the party. Kwame Lumpopo hadn't brought her anything.

As if in answer to her thoughts, a distant cousin, Kwadwo Boateng from Takoradi, came up to the table with interesting news about Kwame Lumpopo. Kwadwo was a short, plump man in his forties who owned a prosperous furniture store. "Nana," he said sharply, "I was going to the tent in front of the royal palace early this morning to make a donation to you, but Kwame Lumpopo was waiting on the path and said I should give my donation to him, and not to the person under the tent. Did you get the two million cedis I gave him?"

Two million cedis was about $140, and Kwame Lumpopo had never mentioned it to her or given her a dime. Perhaps with all the commotion and celebration, he hadn't gotten around to it. Perhaps.

"He has not, but I will ask him about it," she said. She sent an auntie to bring him to her, and Kwame Lumpopo with his white grin soon swaggered over.

"Kwadwo Boateng over there told me he had given you two million cedis to give me," Peggy said. "Do you have them? I would like them now."

Kwame Lumpopo smiled and shook his head. "I am sorry, Nana," he said, "but I have changed my trousers since this morning, and the money is in the pocket of my other trousers. I will give it to you tomorrow."

It occurred to Peggy that Kwame Lumpopo's bedroom wasn't more than twenty feet away (she was looking at its door), and if he had changed his trousers they were probably on the other side of that door, stuffed with her money. Or perhaps he had left his trousers somewhere else and walked home with a bare behind? She was tempted to say this, but it was, after all, her coronation, so perhaps it was better not to make a fuss.

The fact was that Peggy needed that $140; she had already run out of all the hundred-dollar bills that she had stuffed down her bra. Kwame Lumpopo asked her for money every day to buy food and drinks for the household and all the many visitors, and the food had cost her a lot more than she had expected. So when it came time to pay the photographer for photos of her enstoolment, she had to borrow $125 from a family friend, Kwesi Cooper. Kwadwo Boateng's $140 could have more than paid back Kwesi Cooper. Otherwise, when she got home she would have to send it to him by Western Union.

It seemed to Peggy a strange twist of fate that on her coronation day, the most important, exhilarating day of her life, she learned that her elders were probably stealing from the town and that Kwame Lumpopo had neglected to mention the money he should have given her. Her mother's last words to her had been "Always remain humble." There was much to keep her humble today.

And then Kwame Lumpopo added, "I got a call from William a while ago. He can't come because his car broke down."

Peggy drooped with disappointment. She wasn't sure if a broken-down car was the real reason William hadn't come. It was probably the crowds that kept him away. Or had he changed his mind about seeing her? Did he still feel guilty? Was that why he hadn't had the nerve to call her directly and called Kwame Lumpopo instead? With so much love, guilt, and hurt swirling around their relationship, it seemed impossible to figure out why he hadn't come.

But he had told her he wanted to be there, and part of him must have meant it or he wouldn't have said it. William never said things he didn't mean. *If we had had a child, she thought again, if I had just kept one of those three longed-for pregnancies, just one, William would be here with me now. Our child would also be here, a boy or girl, the genetic combination of the two of us grafted equally into one human being—*

Suddenly she heard a crash of broken glass. Ekow fled the parlor with a guilty look on his face, raced out the front door, and disappeared into the bush. Peggy hoped he hadn't ruined all of the Other Cousin Comfort's china displayed so proudly in her bookcase. She suspected that Ekow had been drinking. He had promised he wouldn't drink during his visit, but perhaps the liquor-infused enstoolment celebrations had been too great a temptation for him.

Her suspicions were confirmed that night after Peggy chastised Ekow severely for indeed breaking the porcelain. Instead of going to sleep, he paced the house and banged on the walls, muttering to himself loudly and keeping everyone up. Finally, Peggy forced him to take his sleeping mat to the front porch and barred the front door securely.

Peggy sank into bed, too tired to move, as images from the day swam before her: the cheering crowds, the sacred stools, Nana Kwesi's serious face, Kwame Lumpopo's glib smile, and a drunken Ekow banging on the walls. It was an exhausting end to an exhausting day.

10

Even before the chickens and goats blasted forth their four a.m. cacophony the next day, Peggy had been lying awake on her bed worrying about her little stool. Having a stool was a great responsibility, not just to keep your people happy, but also to keep the stool itself happy. Nana Kwesi would soon put on a new roof, which would keep her stool dry, and it would surely like that. But she couldn't get out of her mind the image of Tsiami heading into the dark stool room to pour libations and sloshing the schnapps over all the stools there because that was what he had done for forty years. Would he remember that her stool hated hard liquor and only wanted Coke?

Somehow she doubted it, especially after Tsiami had first drunk a good portion of the bottle himself. Pouring schnapps on her teetotaling stool would insult it after it had made very clear its choice of libation, and it might get mad and do something bad to Peggy or Otuam. As a precaution, she decided it would be better to move the stool to its own nonalcoholic room, which would make it harder for Tsiami to get confused no matter how drunk he was.

Before the sun rose, Peggy sent Aggie to fetch Tsiami, who came with a machete in his belt, ready to attack his pineapple fields. When she explained the problem to him, Tsiami agreed that he might not always be too certain which stools received the schnapps. He promised to clear out a closet in the palace hallway to use as a private room for her stool and put red and white strips of cloth on the door, colors that would remind him of the Coke logo.

An hour later, as the aunties were wrapping Peggy in her cloth, she looked outside at the line of children carrying buckets on their heads and saw among them an elegant white-robed creature with the profile of Nefertiti, gliding majestically down the sandy path, seeming to float despite the heavy load on her head.

Peggy squinted in disbelief as the figure disappeared behind the house. "Oh . . . my . . . God," she said to her aunties. "Was that the queen mother I just saw with a bucket on her head?"

Cousin Comfort hadn't seen her, but Auntie Esi nodded. "It looked like her to me. Not many girls look like that."

Now that took the cake. The queen mother of Otuam going around with a bucket of water on her head, a clear insult to the dignity of the stool. Didn't royalty count for *anything*?

"Is that customary in Otuam?" Peggy asked. "For royalty to be hauling water? Perhaps I should put a bucket on my head and traipse up to the borehole in my royal robes?"

Auntie Esi laughed. "Usually the queen mother isn't a girl, Nana. Usually it's a dignified woman who would never be sent to fetch water, which is what children do. Sometimes her mother sends Paulina to fetch water when her other children are busy."

"This is not acceptable," Peggy said. "I want the people of Otuam to respect their town, to respect their royal family. You must let her mother know this cannot happen again or I will make her slaughter a cow to feed the elders as punishment for this disrespect."

How could Paulina's mother have thought it was appropriate for a queen to haul water on her head? True, Paulina was the queen mother of an African fishing town, not of Great Britain. Peggy suddenly had a vision of Queen Elizabeth opening Parliament in her ermine robes of state, dripping with diamonds, holding her royal scepter, and wearing on her head not a glittering diamond crown but an old tin bucket.

"Otuam has a long way to go," Peggy said sadly, and the five aunties nodded vigorously.

A few minutes later, her phone rang. It was William, apologizing for not coming to her enstoolment party. His car had broken down before he even got out of Accra, he said, and though he could have had a friend drive him, he felt this was a sign that the ancestors didn't want him to go. Perhaps they felt that this was her day, and he didn't belong there, and if he tried again to get to Otuam something worse would happen to him. Would she, perhaps, be able to stop by on her way to the airport?

But Peggy didn't want to wait until the day of her flight. She would visit him the following day when she drove with Cousin Comfort to her home in Tema, which, though twenty miles away from Accra, was considered a suburb of the sprawling capital. Tema had been a sleepy fishing village until the government dug a gigantic man-made harbor in 1960. Now it was a bustling port, through which almost all of Ghana's cocoa was shipped. Oil refineries had opened nearby, along with large factories producing steel, aluminum, and construction materials. Ringing the city were modern apartment buildings and elegant housing developments. Most Temans were fully employed and enjoyed an income well above the average annual income in Ghana, $2,200 per person. Some, including top government officials, factory owners, and successful merchants, enjoyed a lifestyle to rival that of wealthy Americans.

Settling into the taxi the next day with Cousin Comfort, Peggy grew apprehensive about seeing William. Certainly she wanted him to see her now that she was king, a person on a more equal footing than an abandoned, childless wife. Come to think of it, her social standing was now far above his own. But would her old feelings of bruised love and wretched abandonment come rolling back? She had folded them neatly into a drawer and closed it, but they were still there. Would he perhaps, now that he had children and she was a king, suggest they try again to be together? Not immediately, of course; William was never one to rush into a life-changing decision. But eventually?

As if reading her thoughts, Cousin Comfort said, "He is a good, kind man. But don't get your hopes up."

"Hopes?" Peggy said, surprised by the shrillness of her voice. "What hopes? I don't have any hopes."

"Ummm-hmmm," Cousin Comfort replied.

Peggy's heart was pounding as the taxi rolled up to a beautiful, modern house with a gated garden out front. The family hospital bed business was evidently going well. As Peggy and Comfort emerged from the cab, William was standing in the door, waving. Her heart skipped a beat.

William. The one she had loved, and married, and lost. For six years she had learned to live without him, struggled to put the fractured pieces of her life back together into something resembling happiness. For six years the lack of William had been as real a presence in her life as William himself had ever been. Now here he was, in front of her, smiling.

He looked the same, even though it had been so long. His hair was still black, his face youthful, his physique athletic. He greeted Peggy and Cousin Comfort politely and invited them into his living room, where he served them beer. The furniture was comfortable and new and included a wide-screen television.

They chatted a bit about Otuam and Peggy's enstoolment. "I always knew there was something very strange about you," William said. "But I couldn't put my finger on it. Now I know what it was. You were destined to be a king. Now you can use all your energy and your strong sense of justice for something truly meaningful, to help others." He looked at her with pride. "My wife, the king," he said. "Not many men can say that."

Peggy's heart fluttered as if she were a schoolgirl. "Perhaps your firm can help us with hospital beds," she suggested brightly. "Our clinic's beds are forty years old, rusty and broken. Sometimes women have to give birth on the floor."

William looked into his beer and frowned. "I would have to ask my brother about that," he said.

Of course. His response reminded her, in one fell swoop, of the end of their marriage. Nothing had changed, she thought. Nothing would ever change with William. A good man, but ruled by his family. Her heart sank. She had been foolish to hope for anything else. Peggy noticed that Cousin Comfort was looking at her, her large dark eyes shining in compassion.

Peggy couldn't let them see her disappointment. She roused herself and asked, a bit too cheerfully, about his children. He flipped open his wallet and showed her a picture of a tiny boy and she laughed for real. It was as if someone had pasted William's serious round face on an infant. The children, he explained, spent weekends with him.

It was good to see him so happy, even if it wasn't the kind of happiness she had hoped for, their happiness living together as man and wife. But he was obviously prosperous, and healthy, and a loving father. It was clear that he enjoyed being back in Ghana, his homeland, and working with his brother and sisters in the family business. Since the last time she had seen him, at the airport in Washington, William had obtained everything he wanted, and she . . . Well, at least her life had a purpose now.

Life has so many surprises in store for us, she thought, as she sipped her beer while Cousin Comfort and William chatted. You never know what it is going to throw at you. Sometimes it hurts you dreadfully. But God is good and has a special plan for everyone. Maybe she would find out it was all for the best.

But today, looking at William, Peggy felt terribly, terribly sad.

The morning of her flight back to Washington, Peggy took Auntie Esi and Cousin Comfort aside in her bedroom and told them about Nana Kwesi's investigations into the town funds, a subject that she would address most sternly in the final council meeting to be held that afternoon. The evidence of apparent corruption among Peggy's elders was news to Cousin Comfort, who shook her head in such vehement disapproval her long gold earrings flailed in agitation and her huge purple head wrap and glossy black wig threatened to fall off. But Auntie Esi just sighed.

"Quicksand in the bush is dangerous because it looks like solid ground," she said.

As Peggy took that in, she continued, "Nana, I didn't want to frighten you before, but there are some things I think you should know about Otuam."

"Things about the council misusing the funds?" Peggy asked.

Auntie Esi thought a moment before replying. "Yes, it has to do with that. But there's more to it. There are some bad things that run right below the peaceful surface of this little town, things that as the new king you should know about."

"Bad things that you didn't tell me before," Peggy pointed out.

"Otuam needs you, Nana. I didn't want you to get on the next plane to Washington before you were enstooled," she said in evident discomfort. She took a deep breath and added, "You should know that Uncle Moses and the late king truly despised each other."

"But if Uncle Moses was Uncle Joseph's enemy," Peggy said, frowning in puzzlement, "why did he allow him to live rent-free in the two best downstairs rooms of the palace?"

"Oh, he didn't," Auntie Esi replied. "One day several years ago, Uncle Moses just moved his furniture in and told the king that those rooms were his new apartment. He's been living there ever since. The late king was furious about it and tried to get him to leave, but he finally accepted it. He hated conflict of any kind, you know. He would give anybody anything just so they would stop yelling."

Peggy nodded. "I know."

"Do you also know that sometimes even the most generous, forgiving person can get utterly fed up? That's what happened to your uncle at the end. He had turned a blind eye when the elders began to keep the fees and land sales for themselves, refusing to turn them over to him. His palace fell into disrepair, and when Uncle James came by to patch it up this just reminded Joseph that he was a weak, useless king who couldn't even get his elders to turn over taxes so he could buy a bag of cement and a bucket of paint. That was why Joseph chased James off, because he was angry at himself, angry at being reminded of how weak he was."

Ah-henh. That made sense.

"And then one day earlier this year Uncle Moses and his sidekick Isaiah the Treasurer sold several large tracts of land to farmers and refused to give your uncle a penny, even though he was very sick, in a great deal of pain, and needed medicine. That was the moment, after twenty-five years, when the king had had enough. He ordered dozens of stakes with red flags on them, which he was going to have stuck into land that had been bought illegally, land that he was going to reclaim for the stool. And he called the Saltpond police to come and arrest Moses and Isaiah, to cart them away to jail and be tried for fraud."

"Uncle Joseph did that?" Peggy asked in shock. She didn't think he had had it in him.

Auntie Esi nodded. "But it was too late," she said sadly. "He was ninety-two, and his system couldn't stand the stress of it. The day before the police were supposed to come, your uncle had a stroke, went to the hospital, and never came home. The police investigation was dropped. Now, that's all you need to know."

"All I *need to know?*" Peggy squeaked out. "Is there *more?*"

"There's always more," Auntie Esi said cryptically, straightening her head wrap as she made for the bedroom door.

Peggy sat on the bed and watched the door swing shut behind her aunt. She had never heard of the feud between Uncle Moses and Uncle Joseph. None of the many cousins she spoke to periodically on the phone lived in Otuam, so none of them had known about it. Most upsetting was that Auntie Esi had admitted that it was only a fraction of the story, the part of the iceberg you could see. What part was still hidden, jagged and sharp as knives, under Otuam's seemingly placid surface?

Peggy was especially troubled by the news of Uncle Joseph's stroke the day before the police were going to arrest two of his elders. It had certainly been fabulous timing for Uncle Moses and Isaiah the Treasurer, she thought.

Just then Cousin Comfort echoed Peggy's thoughts when she said, "It's so odd, isn't it, that he had his stroke the day before the police were supposed to come. If Uncle Joseph had been a younger man, I might suspect foul play. But at ninety-two?"

"No," Peggy agreed, shaking her head. "He was, after all, ninety-two."

That afternoon, as soon as the elders and aunties had taken their seats on the chairs and bench, Peggy said, "I understand that there are fees paid by fishermen to the stool, as well as land fees paid by all landowners. I want to know who collected them for the late king in the fridge."

Nana Kwesi shot her a long, meaningful look, but the other elders winced or gave her blank stares.

"Who collected the money for the late king?" Peggy pressed. "Someone must have. He wouldn't have done it himself."

Sitting next to each other, Uncle Moses and Isaiah the Treasurer started whispering behind their hands like naughty schoolchildren.

"I can't hear you," Peggy said, feeling like a teacher. "If you have something to say, let us all hear it."

Uncle Moses turned to her and said, "The late king in the fridge hadn't paid attention to financial matters for years. Look at how he let the royal palace run down."

Isaiah the Treasurer added, "He had been unwell for such a long time,

Nana," and here he flashed Peggy a quick nervous smile, "and he was so very old, that he stopped attending to such matters."

"So no one collected the fishing fees for several years?" she asked. "The fishermen have been living on our land and fishing in our waters for free? Not one person who owns a house or farm has paid the annual land tax?"

Silence. "If they haven't paid the fees, and refuse to do so now, I will kick them off Otuam land," Peggy said threateningly. The elders shifted uncomfortably.

"I also want to know who has bought stool land in the past couple of years," she continued. "What plots they own, how much they paid for it, and what happened to the money."

"I don't think anyone has bought stool land," Tsiami said, shrugging. "Probably not for a very long time."

"Nobody has bought land?" Peggy asked sharply. "For the past few years, no one has wanted to clear a field to plant crops or build a house for his children? *No one?*" Just trolling up and down Main Street chatting with people, Nana Kwesi had learned of two land sales in recent months.

"If you dig for bones in the dirt," Uncle Eshun said softly, "you may find a ghost."

Peggy wasn't exactly sure what that meant, but it sounded like a warning to stop meddling. "I am digging for bones in the dirt," she said, "and if there are ghosts I want to meet them. Now, I hear that the late king kept an account book of land records," she said. "Where is it?"

The silence in the room was deafening. Some elders shrugged, others studied the tablecloth or the ceiling. Tsiami was suddenly fascinated by the large orange chickens printed on his bright blue cloth and started plucking at the ones on his lap.

"I WANT THE LAND RECORDS BOOK!" she said so loudly that her elders looked up in alarm. They had probably never in their lives heard a woman speak like that.

"If you want the land records book, go and find it yourself," Tsiami said petulantly. Peggy realized that he had a whininess about him, the whininess of a naughty little boy caught with his hand in the cookie jar. "You shouldn't be asking such questions."

During the silence that followed, there seemed to be a collective intake of breath. Peggy wanted to slap Tsiami, but instead she sat up straight and stared at him hard, a royal stare, the kind imbued with the wisdom of the stool.

The entire room suddenly erupted in a flurry of outrage. "You can't talk to her like that!" cried Aggie, approaching Tsiami with her spatula raised threateningly as if it were a sword. "She's the king!"

"The ancestors will be mad at you, Tsiami! You are disrespectful!" said Baba Kobena, slapping his black hat on the table.

"Such behavior is not kind!" Uncle Eshun admonished, shaking his head in disapproval.

"I bet *you* know where the account book is, Tsiami!" cried Nana Kwesi. Tsiami studied his long, thin fingers in silence.

"In my absence, I want you to find the land records book," Peggy said, glowering at her entire council. "I want you to keep an exact record of all land sales. I want you to collect all fishing fees and keep these funds for me until I tell you what to do with them." There was no bank in Otuam, but someone could hide the money under his bed or in his floor, which is where most people kept their savings.

The council nodded dutifully, but Peggy thought they were very relieved to hustle her into Kwame Lumpopo's car and out of the country. As the car lurched forward, she turned back to wave at them and saw that her elders were grinning a bit too widely, considering they were saying good-bye to their new king. They should have been a bit sadder.

On the way to the airport, once they had passed all the potholes and were on the smooth tarred road to Accra, she remembered what she had wanted to ask Kwame Lumpopo. "Do you have that one hundred and forty dollars that Kwadwo Boateng gave you yesterday as my enstool-ment gift?" she said.

"Oh, Nana!" he cried, looking at her with an apologetic smile. "I forgot to bring it! I am so sorry." Then he looked forward at the road.

Peggy sighed. The $140 had, evidently, disappeared down his trousers.

Part III

WASHINGTON, D.C.

October 2008–September 2009

11

In her first few days back at the embassy, the ambassador treated her a bit stiffly, hesitating before issuing instructions, as if asking himself, *Can I tell a king to get me coffee?* Other employees, too, who needed something from his office, seemed embarrassed to ask Peggy for it, and she found she had less to do. Perhaps they were afraid she would scowl at them and say that kings didn't do office work, which was ridiculous, really, because she was still a secretary. Did they expect her to sit there all day and do nothing but look regal? With the discomfort growing rather than diminishing, and a lack of busyness that bordered on being boring, Peggy realized she would have to put her colleagues at ease.

Finally, one day she told the ambassador, "I'm a king in Ghana, but a secretary here. I'm paid to do this work, so please don't hesitate to ask me to do my job." After she had said this to several people, things went back to the way they had been.

Peggy had returned to Washington at the tail end of September, the height of the U.S. presidential election, which she followed closely. A few weeks later, on election night, November 4, she sat before her television prouder than ever to be an American. Black men had first come to American shores in chains, she thought, stacked next to each other in coffinlike spaces on the slave ships, wallowing in their own filth. Now a black man occupied the highest office in the land, the highest office in the world, actually. *We have come so far,* she thought.

Because President Obama's father had been Kenyan, suddenly Kenya was in all the American newspapers, and many Americans found a new interest in Africa. This pleased Peggy, as she had found that even well-educated Americans were often quite ignorant of the continent. A presidential candidate, Peggy had read, actually thought that Africa was a country, but surely that was an extreme case.

It was true that not even Peggy could name all fifty-three countries, and certainly not a fraction of the two thousand major languages, but it was absurd to think of Africa as having a president you could meet, the president of Africa, living in an enormous presidential palace located in . . . Where would the president of Africa live? Lagos, perhaps. The industrial and commercial center of Nigeria, awash with oil money, sinking in corruption, choked with traffic, devoured by crime, drowning in poverty, it was a microcosm of everything that was wrong with Africa.

But Nigeria was also exemplary of Africa's rich creativity; its art, fashion, and music were enjoyed across the continent, as were its films. Nigeria was the Hollywood of Africa; it was even called Nollywood. Sometimes Peggy watched Nigerian videos she bought at the African food store, dramatic tales of illicit love affairs, babies switched at birth, and mothers-in-law like avenging harpies from hell.

In catering school Peggy had learned to make a reduction sauce, which was simply boiling the water of a particular substance away until you were left with a concentrate. And if you boiled Africa in a pot, sure enough, you would be left with a spicy Nigerian-tasting reduction sauce of crime and creativity, equally mixed. Lagos would, therefore, be a fitting capital of the country of Africa.

Ever since Peggy had lived in the United States, the headlines about Africa had never been very positive, except perhaps when they let Nelson Mandela out of jail to become president. He was probably the only African president who had been in jail *before* he was president rather than afterward, as so many ended up behind bars when their successors incarcerated them for siphoning off billions of dollars into Swiss bank accounts. The jailbird presidents were often joined a few years later by the very successors who had put them there.

Ethiopia had made the headlines in the 1980s because of the famine. There was the genocide in Rwanda in the nineties where they chopped off people's arms with machetes—there had been a popular American movie about that called *Hotel Rwanda*—and the new genocide in Sudan's Darfur region, which the government protested was not an imposed starvation; some tribes were merely going on diets. There was Idi Amin, dictator of Uganda in the 1970s, who killed hundreds of thousands of his own people for no reason other than paranoia, and Hollywood had recently made that, too, into a movie, called *The Last King of Scotland*. Today there was the cholera epidemic and the total collapse of everything in Zimbabwe engineered by a president who was a lunatic.

Peggy sighed. It seemed all the news coming out of Africa and into the American press was bad. As if Africa were indeed one big, bad country that everyone in their right minds should stay away from. *Don't go to Africa! It's very poorly run.*

But that was how the news worked. No one would write or produce a news story that said, "Joshua Ampah gave his last bit of food to his sick neighbor," or "Ruth Gyamfi is working three jobs to send her dead sister's children to school." Hollywood would never film a movie about the beautiful stories happening in Africa every day, small stories of goodness, faith, friendship, and family. One only saw news articles and movies about catastrophes, and heaven knew there were plenty of them in the big awful country of Africa.

In December Ghana's own presidential elections were held. Among the ten contenders, the two most popular were President John Kufuor's candidate, Nana Akufo-Addo, and the challenger, John Atta Mills, who, strangely enough, came from Otuam. Akufo-Addo tallied a few thousand more votes than Mills, but still less than the 50 percent required to win the election. During the runoff between Akufo-Addo and Mills that followed, out of nine million votes cast, Mills won by just fifty thousand.

Many feared that violence might erupt, as had happened a year earlier in a disputed election in Kenya when the results were extremely close. The ruling Kenyan party announced victory despite accusations of fraud made by international observers, and supporters of the opposition rioted, looted, and murdered. Old ethnic rifts ripped open at the seams as tribal groups killed and maimed one another; policemen shot demonstrators on live television, and Kenya's tourism and economy tanked as a result.

But the orderliness and peacefulness of the transition of power in

Ghana showed the world that it had come a long way from the days of the violent coups. It was now a stable democracy. The international press hailed Ghana as a symbol of what other African nations could aspire to.

Though Peggy was delighted at Ghana's increased stature on the world stage, she knew the election results meant that Ambassador Bawuah-Edusei would lose his post. He had been a friend and supporter of President Kufuor, and now President Mills would surely want one of his own supporters in such an important position. It was with great sadness in February that she bid farewell to the ambassador. President Mills didn't announce a replacement right away, and with no ambassador to work for, Peggy was given a new position, in the press office. As Peggy learned her new duties and the gray, cold winter tightened its grip on Washington she became more and more frustrated with her elders. She spoke to them often about what was going on in Otuam, usually in the wee hours of the morning, and each time she also asked them if they had collected the fees from the fishermen, or found the land records book, or if anyone had recently bought land. But she could never get a straight answer.

If she asked Uncle Moses, he would suggest in his blustering walrus way, *Well, I certainly don't know! Why don't you ask Isaiah the Treasurer?* And if she asked Isaiah the Treasurer, he would say, all obsequious toadying, *Nana, my king, your devoted servant—that would be me—respectfully suggests that you ask Tsiami.* And if she asked Tsiami, he would say, *Hell, I don't know. Why don't you ask Uncle Moses?*

She realized that during her visit she should have asked to meet with the major fishing bosses and told them to save their fees for her until she returned. They should have exchanged phone numbers so the fishermen could call her if any elders were bothering them for money. But it had been such a quick visit, with so much excitement, that she hadn't thought of it and had, naïvely, simply told her elders at their last council meeting to collect the fees and hold them for her.

When she called Baba Kobena, he explained in his deep, gravelly voice, "Nana, there is a reason I have nothing to do with town finances. Not that I want to point fingers at others, you understand, but given my religious beliefs I stay out of such things myself."

After a lengthy conversation in which Peggy tried to persuade him to tell her more, she did manage to drag a few bits of financial information out of him. All uninhabited land belonged to the stool, and it could be sold for anywhere between $220 and $1,800 an acre, depending on the quality of soil and its proximity to the beach. For the bill of sale to be legal, the king's signature was required, or the signature of his elders if he was incapacitated or in the village for good. All land in the hands of private owners was taxed at an annual rate of eight dollars to twenty-four dollars an acre, depending on its quality and location.

Peggy continued her investigation by calling Uncle Eshun, who told her that he charged only a few dollars for recording deaths and issuing death certificates. This money he kept until someone came begging for funds to buy a coffin for the deceased, who otherwise would rot in a shed while the family borrowed the money or have to be thrown into the ground without a coffin like an animal. Eshun kept excellent records of these transactions, he said, and would gladly show them to her the next time she came.

This discussion of coffins reminded Peggy that she had been putting off calling Uncle Joseph's sons in Houston to discuss the funeral plans with them. Auntie Esi had said the children hated their father with a passion, though Peggy thought she was wrong about the girls. Perhaps she was wrong about the boys, too, and, being successful American businessmen, they would help her with the palace and funeral. In a surge of hope, she dialed the number of her cousin Wellington.

But Wellington lived up to Auntie Esi's story of lingering resentment. "My brother and I don't want anything to do with our father's funeral," he said, almost spitting the words in anger. "We had to work like dogs to pay our own way through high school and university. We moved to the United States to make something of ourselves, without our father ever lifting a finger to help us. Why should we lift a finger for him now?"

Why, indeed? Because he was one of the two people who gave you life and in death must be forgiven, even as I forgave my erring father. Because he was a human being whose mortal remains need to be buried with dignity. Because he wasn't my father, and I can't do all this on my own.

"Well," Peggy said, trying hard to keep the charm and cheerfulness in her voice, "I know families can be very hurtful, Wellington. I certainly understand that, and in fact my family had a similar situation to your own. It's just that your father left the palace in such terrible condition I have to rebuild it practically from scratch before I can hold the funeral, and I'm not a wealthy woman. Could you and your siblings contribute something, anything really, to renovating the palace?"

There was dead silence on the phone, and for a few moments Peggy thought they had been disconnected. "Hello?" she said.

"I'm still here." After another pause, Wellington said, "We'll pay the fridge fees. That way we won't let the old man rot. They're very expensive in the Accra morgue, you know. And since we'll pay for the fridge, we won't be able to also help you with the palace."

It was something, of course, and something was better than nothing. But that meant that Peggy would have to renovate the palace all by herself.

If that wasn't bad enough, there was the problem of Kwame Lumpopo. He had never given her the $140. That could have been a case of forgetfulness. But then, right after her return to Washington, she had wired him $125 to give to Kwesi Cooper, who had loaned her money for the photographer. Months later Kwesi Cooper called her from Ghana and said, "Nana, it has been so long. Why have you not sent me the money I loaned you?"

Peggy was shocked. "But I wired it to Kwame Lumpopo as soon as I got back," she said, "and he said he would give it to you."

"He never gave it to me," Kwesi Cooper declared.

She called Kwame Lumpopo and asked what he had done with the money. "Oh," he said, "Kwesi Cooper owed me some money so I just kept it to pay his debt." Rather than investigate this matter further, Peggy decided she should just wire another payment directly to Kwesi Cooper. It wasn't fair to make him wait any longer for it, and a king's reputation for honesty was of paramount importance.

Given the fact that Kwame Lumpopo had taken money that didn't belong to him in not one but two instances, Peggy was rapidly coming to the devastating conclusion that he had scammed her. She worried a great deal about it while at the embassy, and at night as she ate while staring blankly at the news, she turned the matter over and over in her head. Was he cheating her? Could it be possible? She had always been so reluctant to trust anyone, and in the exuberance of becoming king she had placed her trust in Kwame Lumpopo despite her misgivings. Had this been an unwise choice?

Then Peggy began receiving reports from relatives that he had behaved strangely at family funerals. In most of Africa, funerals were a common weekend activity; every Friday, Saturday, and Sunday in any town or village you could see dozens of people roaming about or waiting for a *tro-tro* in their distinctive red and black mourning attire, a ragged strip of red cloth tied around the left wrist.

Nor could you help but notice the large funeral tents with red and black stripes. In cities without much open space, like Accra and Cape Coast, funeral tents were often erected in the street of the deceased, blocking traffic for three days. Ghana had a funeral culture; walls were plastered with memorial posters, while some families put the notices on highway billboards; people wore memorial T-shirts and carried memorial key chains.

Ghanaians had such close ties with their large extended families that almost every weekend there was a funeral for an elderly, distant relative who had died, and you would be obligated to travel to his or her village to mourn, feast, and dance. The disadvantage was that many Africans rarely had a weekend to relax and were expected to contribute money to the family of the departed; the advantage was that they had plenty of food and entertainment.

Now Peggy heard that Kwame Lumpopo had attended several family funerals walking under her red royal umbrella, which she had left in his possession, as if he were the king of Otuam, with everybody clapping and bowing down to him. He hadn't asked her permission, which she wouldn't have given anyway. Nor had he ever mentioned it.

The final straw came in one of Peggy's periodic conversations with Nana Tufu, who, as official royal mediator of Otuam and with a concrete palace right in the center portion of Main Street, knew about almost everything that was going on in town as soon as it happened. If the pond was drying up, or the fishing catch was larger than usual, or a government minister was visiting Otuam, Nana Tufu would know about it and tell her. One day Peggy mentioned the lawsuit against the late king who was in the fridge, and his fine of eight hundred dollars, which she had wired Kwame Lumpopo before her enstoolment.

"Eight hundred dollars?" Nana Tufu repeated. "The fine was only three hundred dollars, not eight hundred."

Peggy realized that Kwame Lumpopo had paid off the three-hundred-dollar fine, and the other five hundred dollars had disappeared down his trousers, as so many things did. When she and Nana Tufu hung up, she burst into tears of hurt and shock. She was that most pitiful of creatures, an African woman who had let herself get scammed by an African man. Only she had less excuse than anybody because she was strong, and educated, and American. If she had made such a dumb mistake at the very beginning of her reign, how could she hope to clean up her corrupt council? How could she bring water, medical care, and education to her people? Maybe she couldn't. And to think, she had been considering making him her regent, acting on her behalf when she was in Washington. What a foolish idea that had been. She felt herself sinking down, down to that dark quiet place where pain lived with its Siamese twin, loneliness.

The pain was intensified the next day when Peggy's cousin Florence from Takoradi called and said, "Don't send any money to Kwame Lumpopo. Do you remember during your stay in Otuam how he kept asking you for money so he could buy food for the household and the visitors? Every day you gave him twenty or thirty dollars, and he would bring eggs, bread, rice, and tomatoes. But groceries in Otuam are very cheap, much cheaper than in America, and you gave Kwame Lumpopo way too much money. He kept most of it for himself. After the enstoolment he was seen in bars in Takoradi waving around wads of cash and buying drinks for young women."

Florence continued, "Oh, and if he asks you for money for a chicken or a goat for rituals, don't send him any because none of the Otuam ceremonies needs a chicken or a goat. Kwame Lumpopo will just keep the money and head back to the bar. He's already bragging to his drinking buddies—who told their wives, who told me—that this will be the next way he will scam you."

Bragging to his drinking buddies . . . who told their wives . . . The new king of Otuam was an object of ridicule in some circles, it seemed. After thanking her cousin and hanging up the phone, Peggy crawled into bed, curled herself into a ball, and pulled the blanket over her head. On the little table next to the bed were her Bible, a picture of Jesus, and a framed program from her mother's funeral with her mother's photo on the cover. Periodically Peggy peeked out of the covers and looked at them. God, Jesus, and her mother; clearly, that was all she had in this world. Everyone and everything else were bound to hurt her.

For two days Peggy was in a deep depression. Though she went through the motions of daily life, inside it was as if her soul had been sprained. On the third day her anger began to rise, which was a good thing. Instead of feeling sorry for herself and the injustice of the world, she began to get very, very mad at Kwame Lumpopo. Her mind was no longer benumbed with pain but energized at the need to find a suitable punishment for such a disgraceful con artist.

She soon came up with an idea. She had been ready to send Kwame Lumpopo fifteen hundred dollars to start replacing the roof of the royal palace, but now she certainly wouldn't send the money through him. Nor would she tell him it wasn't coming his way. She would let him wait while she sent the money to Nana Kwesi instead, and one day Kwame Lumpopo would be glad-handing around Otuam, see the workmen crawling all over the roof of the palace, and blow a gasket.

Sure enough, about ten days after she had wired Nana Kwesi the money, Peggy was typing a letter in the press office when Kwame Lumpopo called. She stared at the UNAVAILABLE flashing on the caller ID and chuckled. Now, she said to herself, she had him where she wanted him.

"I was in Otuam today," he said, without even saying hello, and she could hear his voice buckling in barely controlled anger. "And I saw Nana Kwesi and his men ripping off the old roof on the royal palace. I was surprised he had started work on it because you hadn't sent me the money yet. When I asked him why he had already started, he smiled at me and said you had wired him the money directly last week."

Peggy used silence as a weapon. She let Kwame Lumpopo's last words dangle there uncomfortably in the five thousand miles between them.

"Did you wire Nana Kwesi the roof money?" he thundered.

Hmmm, she thought. *That's no way to talk to a king.*

"I did," she replied icily.

"What do you mean sending that money to someone other than me?" he roared. "I was the one to call you with the good news that you were the new king. You agreed that you and I had a special bond and I would help you in Otuam. From now on you must wire all the money through me, and I will need some immediately to buy a chicken and a goat for a priestly ritual."

Even though she was at work, even though she knew a king should keep her cool, Peggy cried, "Go to hell, Kwame Lumpopo!" Though it certainly wasn't regal or ladylike, and her boss had probably heard it through the thin wall, it felt good. She had been wanting to say it for some time.

There was silence on the line, as he must have been shocked by the sudden angry outburst of a woman who he had thought would be meekly subservient to him. "You stole the money Kwadwo Boateng gave you for my enstoolment gift," Peggy continued, "and you stole the money I wired you to give Kwesi Cooper, who loaned me money for the enstoolment photos. You stole most of the food money I gave you in Otuam, and you stole most of the money I sent you to settle the lawsuit of the late king who is in the fridge. Now you are trying to steal the goat and chicken money, and you are very sorry that I prevented you from stealing the roof money."

Peggy paused for a moment to take a deep breath. "I am not sending you any more money because you are a big-time thief!" she said. "Just because you were the one to call me and let me know I was selected king does not mean I have to do what you say. I am king, not you, and you cannot steal my money anymore, not for the roof, the goat, the chicken, or any other thing. And by the way, I am firing you from my council of elders." Then she hung up the phone and glared at it as if it were Kwame Lumpopo himself.

She ran a hand through her hair and tried to collect her thoughts. How did she feel about what had just happened? Rattled, certainly. Exultant, too. What would Kwame Lumpopo do? Run to the council and complain about her? That might be a good thing. That way, the others would begin to learn that they couldn't walk all over her.

About a week after that, Peggy got a four a.m. call from Tsiami, who told her that her stool had been crying in the night, sobbing really. The people who lived in the boys' quarters in the palace courtyard had heard it, crept out of their rooms with flashlights, and tiptoed to the palace. There they discovered that the crying was coming from inside her locked stool room. Some of them wondered if the stool was upset because it had gotten wet when the old palace roof was ripped off.

One of them raced with a flashlight through the bush and over the pineapple fields to tell Tsiami, who as chief priest was the only one able to talk to Peggy's stool to find out why it was crying. A few hours later, as the sun was rising over Otuam, he prayed and poured Coke on the stool. Kwame Lumpopo, the stool told him, had been running around all over Otuam saying bad things about the king. He had said Peggy was a very nasty woman who told lies about him, that she was an ungrateful wretch to treat him so badly after he had been the one to tell her she had been chosen king, and she was uppity because she had lived in the United States for so many years that she thought she was smarter than everyone else. Now the stool spirits, who heard everything people said, were looking for him so they could kill him. But by that time Kwame Lumpopo had already left town and gone back to Takoradi, where the stool had no power to kill anybody.

When Tsiami emerged from the stool room and stepped onto the patio of the royal palace, the other elders were standing there with concerned looks on their faces. A crying stool could portend great hardship for Otuam—storms, droughts, floods, or pestilence. They were relieved when Tsiami told them the stool was crying because it was mad at Kwame Lumpopo for telling people malicious stories about the king. That wasn't frightening news at all, unless your name was Kwame Lumpopo.

The elders went home and told their families about this amazing occurrence, and the family members told their friends, and soon word spread all over town about Peggy's crying stool who wanted to kill Kwame Lumpopo. Someone called Kwame Lumpopo and told him that the stool wanted to kill him, and he was horrified. He immediately stopped talking trash about Peggy because he didn't want to die the next time he set foot in Otuam. He wasn't sure how the stool might kill him, but he knew it could make him have a heart attack and hit the ground dead, or the vengeful tree spirit inside it could ask a tree to fall and crush him.

Peggy laughed heartily at the story. Her stool had put a stop to Kwame Lumpopo's nonsense, and she hadn't had to lift a finger.

She was less glad to hear that Isaiah the Treasurer had suddenly found the money to start his own taxi service. "No one knows where he got the money to do it," Auntie Esi told her. "Suddenly he bought three used taxis, which now sit on Main Street, and he does a good business driving people to the market towns. Some people say he has been selling land that isn't his—that he's been selling *your* land, Nana—and pocketing the money."

Peggy spent a lot of time thinking about this new revelation. And the more she thought about everything happening in Otuam, the madder she got.

Here she was, sending every penny to Otuam to renovate the royal palace, ruining her formerly perfect credit by not paying her own bills, and the elders were stealing the town's funds and selling its stool land. Was she fighting an impossible battle in Otuam? How could she, Peggielene Bartels, a mere secretary, change decades, perhaps centuries of corruption and chauvinism? Had she bitten off more than she could chew? What if she failed, if the only result of her efforts to help Otuam was to devastate her own financial situation in the United States? With her sinking credit rating, she doubted she could even get a car loan when the spirit of her 1992 Honda finally joined the car spirit ancestors.

Peggy believed that her elders would expect womanly weakness, and they would only take her seriously if she was, at times, brash, loud, and strong. She decided to prepare several speeches that she would make to her elders when she returned to Otuam, good speeches that would truly frighten them, and doing this lifted her spirits. Once she had memorized the words, she practiced in front of her mirror, trying to twist her face into the most frightening scowl possible. In the Fante language there was an idiom that she liked—to frown your face like a frog—and now she practiced that frown, the brows knit together, the unblinking eyes bulging out. Then she said her speech:

You have elected a man with breasts! Maybe I don't have balls, but for all that, I am a king, and a man.

That would surprise those elderly men.

She would add:

Why did you people call me at four a.m. and wake me out of a sound sleep and tell me I am king just so you could push me around? If that is all you wanted to do, you should have let me sleep. But it wasn't you who chose me. It was the ancestors. They chose me to straighten this town out and teach you a lesson.

She liked that one, too. Then she came up with another:

If any of you is stealing from me, stealing from the kids and making them walk for hours before school with buckets of water on their heads, you had better watch out.

Then, she might even add:

I am going to squeeze your balls so hard your eyes will pop out.

It would be quite shocking, but it had a nice ring to it. Actually, it was her favorite one.

Peggy decided that when she returned to Otuam she would get to the bottom of the missing money, and if she found the elders had been stealing from her, money she could have used to help the poor people of her town, she might throw them in jail, which would give the chief inspector something to do.

But in debating her strategy, Peggy realized that any truly harsh measures would have to wait until after her gazetting ceremony the following September, during the visit when she hoped to bury her uncle. To be officially recognized by the Ghanaian federal government, at some point after his enstoolment a Ghanaian king had to join the nearest council of chiefs, a group of thirty or forty kings in a particular region who met regularly to discuss matters of concern. The kings consulted one another on how to resolve disputes among their subjects and sometimes even among the kings themselves, how to best work with politicians to bring water, roads, and medical care to their villages, and how to uphold ancient traditions. Any member who failed to honor royal customs, who shamed kingship in any way, would be hauled up before a tribunal and, if found guilty, fined.

The term *gazetting* came from the fact that after the candidate was accepted into the council of chiefs, news of the event would be published in the local gazettes. Once a king was gazetted, if he had any trouble with his elders, the other kings in the group would stand by him, adding huge heft to his—or her—power.

It wasn't easy joining the council, and many enstooled kings weren't accepted. Candidates had to file numerous sets of papers, including lengthy genealogical records. The council looked closely into a king's reputation and moral character and rejected anyone known to be violent, dishonest, lazy, or habitually drunk. And the council of chiefs refused to gazette any king whose rule was disputed by relatives or elders. If Peggy's elders realized she intended to jail them, they could prevent her gazetting by claiming that the rituals of her selection or enstoolment hadn't been conducted properly. Peggy must, therefore, tread carefully until after her gazetting ceremony. She needed her elders to fill out her paperwork; meet with the council of chiefs in Essuehyia, a forty-five-minute drive from Otuam, to plan the ceremony; and assure them that all was harmonious in Otuam.

Because the gazetting was such an important ceremony involving so many kings, it didn't come cheap. On her gazetting day, Peggy would be expected to give $350 in cash to Nana Tufu as a gift for sponsoring her, and she had to give $750 to the council of chiefs itself, along with a goat and several bottles of whiskey. She knew she would have to pay for all this, since her elders had stolen the town funds. She didn't mind, though. These would be the last funds they would ever steal, so they might as well enjoy them as much as they could.

Once she was gazetted, Peggy would use all of her power to investigate Otuam's finances, clean up whatever corruption she found, and make sure the town income went to help her people. She would dilute the council's power by appointing younger, honest elders, if she could find any, and some women.

And she decided to make Nana Kwesi her regent. He was the only possible choice, as all her other elders were completely unsuitable. When she broached the subject in one of their frequent calls, he seemed surprised but quickly accepted. He had the time, he explained, since his construction projects had dried up due to the global recession, which had even affected Ghana. And he shared her outrage over the evident corruption in Otuam.

When Peggy called her elders one by one to let them know her choice of regent, their reaction was predictable. "But he's not from this *town*," they cried.

"That," she replied, "is a good thing."

"And he's too *young*," they said. "Much younger than we are."

"That, too," she said, "is a good thing."

Nana Kwesi had confirmed her trust by using his contractor's contacts to obtain greatly reduced prices on the materials for renovating the palace. In the months since her return to America, she had sent him six thousand dollars in installments to put on the new roof, taking what she could from her salary, along with money some of her art customers had sent in to pay off objects on layaway. It was a lot of money, but a cousin had told her the roof would have cost anyone else ten thousand dollars.

Nana Kwesi suggested that Peggy have a borehole dug on one side of the palace, connected to new plumbing in the kitchens and bathrooms. The late king had had a rain tank on the roof, which sat idly waiting for the bounty of the heavens. But the borehole would have an active spirit, constantly pumping up fresh water to fill the tank so the palace would never go without. Unfortunately, such a luxury was quite expensive— seven thousand dollars, as Nana Kwesi would have to hire a special contractor to dig it. Peggy decided that since she was spending so much money on her own water, she would have the contractor install a pump outside the palace so people living nearby could draw water, too.

Due to its cost, the palace borehole would have to wait, but Peggy sent Nana Kwesi money to buy new pipes for inside the palace, which he purchased and unloaded in the courtyard along with the other building materials. He wanted to start working right away on the interior, but she wasn't able to send more money for his men's salaries. She was getting very late with her own bills and further work would have to wait.

A few weeks later she was greatly saddened to hear that some of the materials had gone missing. It wasn't very much, some bags of cement and several concrete blocks. But over the next few months, other items disappeared: a ladder, a stack of wooden planks, a bucket of nails, and more bags of cement. The problem was that the heaps of material had to be kept close to the palace so the workmen would have them when needed, and there was no place to safely store anything. The tiny houses around the courtyard were crammed with families. Nana Kwesi told the elders and the families in the boys' quarters to be on the lookout for the thief.

The lack of progress on the palace meant that she would not be staying in its spacious, breezy rooms when she returned, but would once more reside in the ovenlike house of her cousin. Except this time, she learned, she and her elders would not be permitted to use the comfortable parlor. Ekow had broken many of her cousin's prized cups and dishes when he had become drunk at Peggy's enstoolment party. To ensure that such a thing would not happen a second time, the Other Cousin Comfort would lock up the parlor.

Nor would Peggy be able to hold the funeral in a partially repaired palace and a courtyard stacked with building materials. She had so hoped she could take the late king out of the fridge and bury him in October, but now he would have to stay there another year. His children would agitate for the royal funeral to be held sooner than that, but she simply did not have the money to pay for it. She just hoped that Uncle Joseph, who had always been kind and forgiving in life, remained so in death. When she poured libations morning and evening, she explained the situation to him and asked him not to haunt her because she was doing the best she could.

————————

Though she was disappointed that work had stopped on the palace, Peggy did get two pieces of good news from Otuam. Her elders and the aunties had evidently spread the word of the new king's tough stance on wife beating because Nana Kwesi told her that it had dried up to the merest trickle. Abusive men were afraid that if they laid a hand on their wives the strict new lady king would race over from America to jail them and then kick them out of town. The only person saddened by this drop in crime was the chief inspector, who now had even less to do.

The second piece of good news came in the form of a phone call from Nana Tufu, who had received a visit in his Main Street palace from a manager of the Rural Agricultural Development Bank. The bank people had noticed at their branches in Winneba and Essuehyia that many customers came all the way from Otuam to deposit money. If they opened a bank in Otuam, right on Main Street, they speculated, many more Otuam citizens would open accounts. Some people in Otuam had substantial amounts of cash by African standards, with their fishing, farming, and selling produce in the Mankessim market and goods in their little shops on Main Street. But there was no place to put their cash in town except for under their beds. When the new bank opened in the fall, Peggy would open up a royal bank account where all the town income would be deposited so no one could steal it.

Peggy chuckled to think about it. What would her elders do when she locked up the fishing and land fees in the bank? It occurred to her that they thought they were smart and crafty like Anansi the Trickster, a beloved character whose exploits Ghanaians had been telling their children about for more than a thousand years. Sometimes he was portrayed as a boy, but usually he was described as a spider, because he wove webs hoping to catch others in them. Anansi the Trickster, in his constant efforts to outsmart others, often got outsmarted himself. One of Peggy's favorite Anansi stories from her childhood went like this:

> Turtle stopped by Anansi's cave just at dinnertime, and Anansi, wanting to eat all the fufu himself, instructed Turtle to wash his hands in the stream before eating. Turtle had to admit his hands were very dirty as he had come crawling through the dirt to Anansi's cave. So Turtle went to the stream and washed his hands and crawled back. In the meantime Anansi was eating the fufu as fast as he could. When Turtle came back, Anansi said, "Oh! Turtle!

Your hands are still dirty!" That was true, as Turtle had crawled back from the stream through the dirt.

So Turtle wandered off to wash his hands again and this time crawled back carefully on the grass. When he arrived at Anansi's cave, Anansi was smacking his lips, having finished the last bit of fufu.

"So sorry, Turtle, that you took so long there is no food left for you!" Anansi cried, thinking he had outsmarted Turtle.

Turtle eyed Anansi slowly and said, "Come to my house for dinner tomorrow and I will serve you a splendid repast."

The next day, Anansi stopped by the pond hoping for a good meal at Turtle's place. Turtle welcomed him and said he had indeed prepared a great feast. Anansi was so excited he did a dance on all his spider legs. But Turtle had set the table on the bottom of the pond, and every time Anansi went down there, he could see a magnificent feast but couldn't stay down long enough to grab anything. He kept popping back up. Turtle continued to eat as Anansi tried to figure out how to remain on the bottom long enough to grab the food. Finally he decided to fill his pockets with pebbles.

This worked. Anansi found himself at the table looking at a delicious meal spread out. As he started to dig in Turtle said, "In my country, people have to take off their jackets before eating." Anansi duly removed his jacket and shot straight back to the top of the pond. Soon after Turtle's head appeared. "Did you like your meal?" he asked, licking the last bit of fufu from his lips.

The way Peggy saw it, her elders were Anansi, thinking they could outsmart anybody and trap him or her in their devious webs. Like Anansi, once they had sent her away, they had eaten all the goods, without leaving even a crumb for anyone else. And Peggy herself was Turtle, plodding along in good faith until she realized she was being taken advantage of. Now, like Turtle, she was plotting how to outsmart the outsmarters. Once she made sure they didn't eat another bite of *fufu*, she would pop her head out of the water and ask them how they had enjoyed their meal.

Part IV

GHANA

September–November 2009

12

Peggy had a month's vacation every year, plus accumulated leave. While it would have been hard to take a long vacation if she had still been the ambassador's secretary, other secretaries could easily fill in for her in the press office. Peggy promptly arranged an absence of seven weeks. She had initially hoped that her brother Papa Warrior could go with her. He had been released from the hospital in August, after a stay of fifteen months, but he was still on crutches and had to go to classes until November to finish his university degree.

She left Washington on September 16, 2009, the same day that *The Washington Post* ran her photo and an article about her on the front page of the Metro Section. A reporter had heard about Peggy's kingship, interviewed her at length, and written an article entitled "Secretary by Day, Royalty by Night," a reference to her many calls to Otuam in the early morning hours. The story began:

> The king folds her own laundry, chauffeurs herself around Washington in a 1992 Honda and answers her own phone. Her boss's phone, too.
> Peggielene Bartels lives in Silver Spring and works as a secretary. When she steps off an airplane in Ghana on Thursday, arriving in the coastal town her family has controlled for half a century, she

will be royalty—with a driver, a chef and an eight-bedroom palace, albeit one in need of repairs she will help finance herself.

The Ebiradze had controlled Otuam for centuries, not half a century, and Aggie wasn't exactly a chef. But Peggy was thrilled with the article—maybe now someone would want to invest in her town—and the author certainly got the palace repairs part right. At Dulles International Airport, several people recognized her, bowed and curtsied, and two of them asked her to autograph the newspaper they were holding.

When she finally landed in Accra, Peggy made her way to the international arrivals area, where she could see Nana Kwesi waiting for her, standing head and shoulders above the others. He was grinning so hard it looked as if his face would break. She threw herself into his arms and screamed. It was good to see him again, this kind man who had helped her so much with the palace. Cousin Charles was standing beside him, thick and solid as ever, and Peggy hugged him, too.

To transport Peggy and her large bags to Otuam, Nana Kwesi had rented a van, which was driven by one of his workmen, Ebenezer, a slender man in his twenties. Peggy and Nana Kwesi piled in while Cousin Charles stowed the luggage in the back. They chatted good-humoredly, catching up on what was happening with family members and news from Otuam as the van crept through traffic out of Accra. Lining the road were political billboards from the December 2008 presidential election and Barack Obama's July 2009 visit, already faded by the African sun.

As they drove along the Accra–Cape Coast Highway, every few miles Peggy saw a red sign with white letters that read "Reduce Speed!! Five persons died here!" or "Twelve persons died here!" One of them indicated that "Seventy Persons Died Here!" and Peggy remembered that a month earlier a car passing another vehicle had crashed headlong into a fuel tanker, causing a massive explosion that incinerated a *tro-tro* and several cars. Despite the dangers of passing slow-moving trucks on the two-lane, winding road at high speeds, almost everyone did it.

As the sun set, they turned left on the little road between the two stands that in the daylight hours sold lemons and pineapples, and for the next half hour bumped over the rutted road through the bush and small villages. As they lurched behind the royal palace, Nana Kwesi pointed to

King Peggy in her royal funeral regalia, leaving the hotel for the funeral ceremony of the late king of Otuam *(Courtesy of Sarah Preston)*

King Peggy (right) and her brother
Papa Warrior as children in Ghana
(Courtesy of Peggielene Bartels)

King Peggy's beloved mother
(Courtesy of Peggielene Bartels)

King Peggy as a young secretary at a
reception at the Ghanaian embassy
(Courtesy of Peggielene Bartels)

Main Street in Otuam *(Courtesy of Eleanor Herman)*

Fishing boats on Otuam's coast *(Courtesy of Eleanor Herman)*

Nana Kwesi, King Peggy's regent
(Courtesy of Eleanor Herman)

Ekow, King Peggy's nephew
(Courtesy of Eleanor Herman)

Moses, King Peggy's uncle and one
of the senior elders in Otuam
(Courtesy of Eleanor Herman)

Papa Warrior
(Courtesy of Peggielene Bartels)

King Peggy and her Soul in the palanquin during her
coronation ceremony *(Courtesy of Peggielene Bartels)*

Pastor Be Louis Colleton (second from right) of Shiloh Baptist Church presents
the covenant with Otuam to King Peggy *(Courtesy of Peggielene Bartels)*

The old palace in ruins before King Peggy restored it
(Courtesy of Eleanor Herman)

The beautiful new palace after renovations *(Courtesy of Eleanor Herman)*
Inset: King Peggy's new golden stool *(Courtesy of Sarah Preston)*

Children fetching water in the dirty stream used by families before Peggy became king *(Photographer Jane Hahn/Getty Images)*

One of King Peggy's new boreholes, which provide free public access to clean water *(Courtesy of Sarah Preston)*

King Peggy's *tsiami* pours libations to bless the water
in the new boreholes *(Courtesy of Eleanor Herman)*

Pastor Be Louis Colleton and members of the Shiloh Baptist Church, dressed in traditional
garb, attend the royal funeral *(Courtesy of Sarah Preston)*

it. "Look!" he cried proudly. "There's the new roof I put on!" But Peggy couldn't see it. There was only one streetlight in Otuam, and it overlooked the bumpy dirt field by the school where kids sometimes played soccer at night. She could see, however, that all the ugly old windows had been removed. She hadn't had the money to buy replacements, and now the windows looked like the empty gaping eye sockets of a skull.

The car bounced to a stop in front of the Other Cousin Comfort's blue house. Aggie ran out and gave Peggy a hug. Peggy noticed that Aggie's turbaned bun had grown larger in the past year; it now looked like a spider's egg sac. As Ebenezer passed Peggy's bags to Cousin Charles, Nana Kwesi bid Peggy good night and climbed back in the van to return to his home in Winneba.

When Peggy walked into the hall, the house felt familiar. Houses, she knew, had spirits, too, and this one seemed to be welcoming her back. She looked down at the worn, tattered sheet of linoleum made to look like pale pink tiles, the concrete floor showing through the torn patches. Ahead was the long dining room table with the ripped pale pink plastic tablecloth, and against the wall was the ancient fridge that belched and rumbled, shuddered and snorted, still going strong, evidently. Above the table was the chandelier with three bulbs, two of them still burned out, though Peggy wasn't sure it was the same two bulbs that had been burned out a year earlier. The smell of Aggie's fried fish hung heavily in the air.

Cousin Charles wheeled Peggy's bags down the long corridor and into the corner bedroom. There was the queen-sized bed and the useless closet with no shelves and no rod. There were the same two beige plastic chairs. But this time, the corners of the room were piled high with crates of Coke and beer, boxes of toilet paper, large bottles of water, and other delicacies that Nana Kwesi had bought at the modern grocery store in Winneba and delivered for her convenience, since you couldn't buy such things in large quantities and at a reasonable price in Otuam. She had asked him, the week before, how much she owed him for these supplies. Nothing, he had said. Nothing at all.

This time there would be no gaggle of aunties to protect her spirit, sprawled out on sleeping mats on the floor. Auntie Esi, who had been so honest about Otuam in Peggy's last days here, had died in the summer and was now one of the ancestors. Another auntie, too, had passed, and two others had family issues they had to attend to in other towns. Only Cousin Comfort would be coming soon as a companion to Peggy. Peggy would miss the other aunties, but Cousin Comfort had always been a particular favorite, and she looked forward to her visit.

Peggy walked into the hallway and flipped on the toilet room light switch, but the room remained dark, the shadow of the toilet outlined by the faint light from the hall. Evidently the bulb was burned out. At night, it wouldn't be hard to find the toilet to sit on, but flinging the bucket of water at it might be tricky. She had never been very good at sports and hoped her aim would prove true.

Next, Peggy flipped on the shower room light. That, at least, still worked. She unpacked her toiletries and took an African bucket bath. Feeling incredibly refreshed, she slipped into her bed. There was nothing like two long international flights to make you sleep well. Peggy immediately sank into a dark place, like the bottom of a deep, murky lagoon, with no dreams or thoughts of any kind.

It was the crowing of the roosters and the baaing of the goats right outside her window that roused her. Ah yes, she said to herself, the Otuam alarm clock, eternally set for four a.m. There was no sleeping late with all that racket. This was followed by the sound of drums from somewhere deep in the bush. *The king is back, the king is back,* they cried in their ancient drum language.

Peggy wrapped herself in her bright blue over-the-shoulder cloth and looked in her hand mirror. Bright blue was quite an attractive color on her. Next she put on all her royal beads, bright red lipstick, and eyeliner, wanting to look her best for the challenges that lay ahead of her that morning. She was planning on starting off her first council meeting briskly.

The rusty iron gate on the front porch squeaked open and clanged shut. This was almost immediately followed by the bump of the screen door. "Oh boy," Peggy said out loud. "Here they come."

As Peggy walked past the parlor, she cast a longing glance through the window of the locked door at the comfortable sofas and overstuffed chairs. She continued to the dining room, where she received a hearty welcome from Tsiami, Uncle Moses, Baba Kobena, Uncle Eshun, and

Isaiah the Treasurer. She sat down at the head of the table, by the window, in the stiff straight-backed chair, and Tsiami took his proper place at her right hand. Nana Kwesi, coming from Winneba, didn't plan on attending any of the four or five a.m. meetings. He would arrive every day around seven or eight.

Aggie served everyone soft drinks, then took up her position leaning against the right side of the kitchen door frame, arms crossed.

Peggy looked around the table. She had had a year to prepare for this very meeting and had practiced her speeches. She cleared her throat and said, "Last year we barely had time to get to know one another due to the shortness of my visit here, and all the rituals for my enstoolment. So I thought I would start this visit off by telling you all a bit about myself so we can all be clear. You may see me as a lady and think that because of my gender I am weak. But you must understand that my thoughts are those of a man. I am as strong as a man. I am as smart as a man. I demand the absolute respect of a man. If you understand this, we will get along well. But if you don't, if you think that because you are men you can misbehave, you will find that you are greatly mistaken."

Her elders nodded and smiled. *Oh boy,* she thought. *This is starting off like last year. They still don't take me seriously.* "It has been a year since my enstoolment," she continued, "and before I left I instructed you to collect the fishing fees. Now, where are they?"

Uncle Moses and Isaiah the Treasurer put their heads together and exchanged a brief nodding whisper, then Uncle Moses pulled a paper from his robe and pushed it across the table to her. "As the elder who deals with all fishing matters, I have written a letter to clear up the situation," he said. Peggy frowned as she took it.

It was in English. At the top was the Ebiradze royal emblem, a spotted tiger on a stool.

LAND TOLLS LETTER

September 13, 2009

To all Drag Fishing Companies: We are directed by Nana Amuah Afenyi VI to inform you that the Land Tolls will not be paid annually again. That the Land Tolls will be paid Daily, that is if you get 10 trays of fish, 1/10 will be collected, again if you get from 4 trays to 9 trays, ½ tray will be collected. Any company or net owner who fails to comply with these rules will be sacked from the beach. These rules take immediate effect. I hope these rules will be abided.

Uncle Moses Acquah

"What is this?" Peggy asked sharply.

Uncle Moses cleared his throat and said, "You are right that we must begin to collect the fishing fees, which we haven't done since the late king in the fridge first went to the village to cure himself. So we issued this letter to try to bring some order to the collection process."

So they were pretending they hadn't been collecting the fees. Peggy felt her blood begin to boil. "Let me get this straight," she said. "You are telling me with a straight face that no one has collected the fishing money since my enstoolment a year ago, despite my clear instructions to do so?"

"Without the king being here, Nana, the process is quite confusing," Isaiah the Treasurer replied smoothly. "So we have taken the liberty to put in place the proper collection measures, and we will start collecting this money now that you have arrived."

Bold-faced lie, Peggy thought. She had been expecting lies about the money, of course, but how dare they issue decrees in her name without her consent? That was infuriating. She grabbed the letter and waved it in the air. "Why did you issue this letter in my royal name without consulting me?"

"You were in America," Tsiami said, shrugging.

"How often do we talk on the phone?" she asked. "And this letter was written four days ago. You knew I was coming! You couldn't have waited until this morning to consult with me? I'm the king, not you!"

Tsiami's long thin fingers made little circles on the tablecloth, which he studied as he said, "Why should we have consulted you when this is obviously the best way to handle the fishing fees? We spent a lot of time discussing it, and you should just go along with it."

"This is a disrespectful way to treat a king!" Peggy roared, slapping the table. "You would not treat me this way if I were a man! And this is not the best way to handle the fishing fees. Who is going to go down to the beach every day and count fish? We will take a percentage of the fish weekly or monthly."

"We have lived here for many years!" Uncle Moses cried, throwing out his arms. "I was born, bred, and buttered in Otuam! I am in charge of disputes in the fishing village! I know more about the fishermen than you. You were born in Cape Coast! You have been in America all this time! What do you know of fish?"

"With all due respect, Nana, I believe this is the best possible method," Isaiah the Treasurer added smoothly.

Without looking up from his lap, Tsiami chimed in petulantly, "Why don't you just do what we say? Why are you making everything so difficult? You just got here a few hours ago and you are already making trouble."

Peggy turned to him. Perhaps now was the time to use one of her speeches, the one she had designed to let them know that she was as strong as they were in terms they could understand. "Maybe I don't have balls, like the rest of you, but I am a man with breasts! I am a man, and a king, and you mustn't forget it!" She slapped herself on the chest for emphasis and waited for the response.

Other than Aggie's burp of a guffaw from the kitchen doorway, this comment was met with a stunned silence. The elders had never heard a woman say such a thing before.

"No, you're not," Tsiami said, shaking his head vigorously, staring at his knees. "You are certainly not a man with breasts. It is well known that you have to have balls to be a man. Having breasts does not qualify a person to be a man."

Apparently Tsiami hadn't understood her point. "I am!" she cried, slapping her chest again with both hands. "I am a man with breasts."

Tsiami had swung his legs to the right side of his chair, and now he seemed to be scrutinizing his royal blue plastic sandals. Shaking his head more slowly, he said, "No, you're not. That is not possible."

"I am! I am!" Peggy cried. "I am a man, like you."

"You're not," Tsiami calmly replied. "Because you don't have balls."

And so it went for a while, Peggy yelling and slapping her chest, insisting she was a man with breasts, and Tsiami feebly but stubbornly protesting and Uncle Moses supporting him. Finally, she launched into her second carefully practiced speech. "Why did you people call me at four a.m. and wake me out of a sound sleep and tell me I am king just so you could push me around? If that is all you wanted to do, you should have let me sleep. But it wasn't even you who chose me. It was the ancestors. They chose me to straighten this town out and teach you a lesson. You think I'm a woman, and you try to treat me like one, but I am actually a man. With breasts, not balls!" Peggy slammed her fist on the table for emphasis, hoping that would make them pay attention. *"Maka!"* she cried, which meant "I'm telling you." *"Maka, maka!"*

Being a peaceful people, most Ghanaians don't like to see a disagreement between friends, and many are willing to jump into the middle of an argument to resolve it amicably, pointing out some middle ground whereby both aggrieved parties could save face. But such an intervention usually just makes the two arguers angry at the peacemaker for interfering in other people's business, and they both start yelling at him until he gets angry too and starts yelling back. Then another peacemaker joins in to break up the fracas among the three, and soon there are four people arguing, and so on until everyone is drawn into the argument.

Such was the case now. Baba Kobena tried to break up the fight among Peggy, Tsiami, and Uncle Moses, who vented their anger at him for interrupting, which made him so angry that he yelled back at them. Eshun, in his wobbly voice, also tried to intervene until Uncle Moses told him to shut up and he, too, started yelling. Isaiah the Treasurer stood and proclaimed grandly, "This council must unite!" to which Tsiami replied, "Oh, for God's sake, Isaiah, shut the hell up."

Within a few minutes, everyone was talking at once. Several times an elder stood up and cried *"Ah-go!"* which meant "May I have your attention, please!" The proper response was *"Ah-meh,"* which meant "Yes, you have my attention," followed by a respectful silence. But no one was crying *Ah-meh.* They were either arguing or crying *Ah-go,* while Peggy was crying *Maka.*

Isaiah the Treasurer stood and hoisted his trousers even farther up his torso before pointing his finger at several elders and yelling. Uncle Eshun started rapping his cane on the table to make up for his weak voice, and Baba Kobena angrily threw his wide-brimmed black hat on the floor.

The interesting thing about a Ghanaian argument is how quickly it ends—often with a chuckle and no lingering grudges. Those who engage in the most vicious verbal altercation in the morning are often seen cheerfully drinking beer together under a tree in the afternoon as if nothing unpleasant had happened. And so, after a time, Baba Kobena,

Eshun, and Isaiah grew tired and, watching stubborn Tsiami and bossy Uncle Moses still fighting with Peggy, started to laugh loudly. Finally, even Peggy and her two angry elders ran out of steam. Suddenly silent, they looked at their mirthful colleagues and started to laugh themselves. It was, Peggy realized, the typical ending to a major Ghanaian argument.

Peggy never expected that she and her elders would come to a decision on the collection of fishing fees in a single meeting. Her people loved to talk, preferably loudly and all at once, so it would be quite impossible to accomplish anything at one sitting, especially if there was any contention. Moreover, such a speedy resolution of an important issue would be an American way of handling matters. In Ghana it would feel shockingly rushed and disrespectful of tradition, which demanded careful consideration of all points of view. But she also knew that in her first meeting she had made her point. Though it had taken a bit of crudeness and a loud argument, she had shown her elders that she was not going to allow them to walk all over her.

Toward six a.m. the elders pushed back their chairs and stood up. "We'll be back later," Tsiami said before ambling off to his pineapple fields. He loved his fields almost as much as he loved being *tsiami,* and he considered his pineapples, though small, the sweetest in the world. He had brought Peggy two of them as a welcome home gift, and now Aggie cut one of them into squares and presented it to Peggy on a plate, next to her bowl of porridge and cup of coffee.

Peggy loved the pineapples, mangos, and coconuts of the Fante region. Their flavors were fresh and true, as if you could taste the very spirit of the plant. In Western countries many fruits and vegetables, she knew, were grown on huge factory farms, sprayed with hormones to make them unnaturally large, tainted with pesticides, picked still sour, and ripened in the truck on the way to market. Ghanaian fruit was carefully tended by loving brown hands, ripened by the golden embrace of the sun, and fed by refreshing seasonal rains.

After finishing her breakfast, Peggy pushed back her chair and walked onto the front porch, where she sat down on the long handmade bench. Though the four a.m. argument with her elders had been upsetting, it had served its purpose and now she suddenly felt exhilarated to be back in her beloved Ghana.

The sun was just starting to rise, and she watched the sky turn slowly from a leaden color to silver, and then to a rose gold. In Ghana there was usually only an hour when the sun was up and the world was still cool, the magical hour between six and seven in the morning. During that time a breeze played around your neck and shoulders like the caresses of a light silk scarf. Suddenly, around seven, the breeze would stop, and the heat would start to rise. By ten the sun became a giant yellow fist, hammering the top of your head into the ground.

As the sun strengthened, Peggy could see pieces of mica twinkling on the red earth. When she was a child and had visited her great-uncle Rockson, Nana Amuah Afenyi IV, she had been fascinated by the shiny flakes, which she picked up and stuffed in her pockets. It was as if eons ago the vaulted mirror of the sky had shattered, hurling a billion tiny glinting shards onto the red-gold earth of Otuam.

Peggy noticed a large brown hen in front of the house, mumbling in chicken self-talk. "Let me see, does that look edible, yes, I think I will eat it, oh no, it wasn't good at all, kaplooey, there, I have spat it out. Where are those chicks, yes, keep close to my tail feathers." The hen's six yellow chicks followed her like a tide, spreading out around her and washing back together again.

A few feet from the chickens, a black goat and a white goat chewed leaves on a bush with fixed determination. Peggy knew that goats, too, had their own language. There was the "Hey, buddy, how's it going?" bleat, which they uttered as they trotted briskly past each other. There was the warning bleat, "Get away from this patch of leaves, you bastard, it's mine." That, of course, was usually from the male goats. The most profoundly disturbing bleat was that of a calf crying passionately for its mother. It was a bloodcurdling, almost human sound, like that of a cat being skinned alive, and it continued unabated until the mother bleated a comforting "Don't worry, little one! I am over here behind this bush."

All around her were the voices of birds—short piping whistles, long shrill tweets, raucous caws, and cheerful chirps. As the sun brightened, the world became even more alive, and the silver stillness, peppered by animal cries, suddenly buzzed with human activity. A fisherman came out from the concrete block house in front of Peggy's, on the other side of a sandy patch and clump of scrubby bushes. Beneath a lean-to, he stretched a fishing net over a vertical frame, took a needle and thread, and started repairing gaps in the net where frantic fish had thrashed their way out. A man walked by Peggy's porch with a heap of long sticks of firewood on his head; some families couldn't afford kerosene burners and collected sticks in the bush for fires to cook food and heat water for laundry.

Peggy noticed a dozen or so clear plastic water baggies, torn open and emptied, on the ground where lazy people had thrown them, and where the breeze rolled them around like large, unsightly dust balls. *I will have to have something done about that,* she thought. *Maybe Mr. Yorke can organize the schoolchildren to clean up the trash.*

From somewhere behind the Other Cousin Comfort's house, Peggy heard the slap of dishwater hitting the dirt, thrown, perhaps, by Aggie. Several young children ran out of the next-door neighbor's house on the left, chasing one another and laughing. One of them had a standard bush toy—an old tin can with rusty nails in it that kids could shake like a loud rattle and dance to the beat. Another had a long stick nailed to an empty spool of fishing line, which he rolled in the dirt. A bedraggled barefoot toddler stood perplexed, her thumb in her mouth. Older children walked home from the borehole in groups of two or three, adeptly balancing large tin buckets of water on their heads and chattering.

Several men walked briskly in front of Peggy into the bush toward their fields. Women from the nearby houses came out holding long dried palm fronds and, bending over at the waist, energetically swept the dirt in front of their houses, making a scraping, swishing sound. Though wealthy Ghanaians cultivated lawns around their gated mansions, swept dirt was the sign of a tidy village house; any sprout of grass would be considered unsightly and immediately plucked.

Friends and neighbors greeted one another cheerfully. Peggy closed her eyes and listened. The voices of Ghanaians had a different timbre entirely from Americans'. Their voices were rich, deep, and reminded her of different kinds of candy—there was the bittersweet chocolate voice of an old man, the caramel and nut voice of a middle-aged woman, the mint chocolate voice of a middle-aged man, the butter cream voice of a young woman.

And Peggy's voice? Someone had once told her it was like hot chocolate, and that her laughter was like boulders of chocolate rolling down a mountain. She had thought the remark was odd at the time but now, listening to the African voices all around her, she understood it.

Behind the human voices were those of chickens, goats, and birds, in trees and thickets, a three-dimensional living grid of speech. She opened her eyes and saw the shimmering gray-green leaves of the trees dance in the breeze, undulate, leap.

Peggy said to herself, *I can sit here and just be. I don't have to do. In the States I am always doing, rarely being.*

Back in Washington, it seemed hard to live in the present. Peggy rushed from the accomplishments of the past headlong into her goals for the future, aided by ever-faster technology. She could have a computer program do her taxes and invest her money and organize her closets, or buy a cell phone that sent e-mails, took pictures, made her coffee, and washed her clothes. She pictured every American holding a remote control, pushing buttons to accomplish what they wanted in life.

In recent years, Americans had invented many new buttons ostensibly to stay connected with people, yet these same buttons actually disconnected them from the people sitting right beside them, or from family members in the next room. Virtual, remote-control connection destroyed human connection, and she sensed that many Americans were, despite their hectic schedules, lonely. She remembered one morning in the elevator of her condo building, when she bid a hearty African *Good morning!* to a man who was inside when the doors opened. He looked at her and snapped, "What's so good about this morning?" She had seen such pain and loneliness in his face that she ached for him. No African would ever say something like that.

She had also seen, on the rare occasions she allowed herself dinner at the Parthenon Restaurant, whole families sitting around a table eating, not speaking to one another, just pushing buttons. Perhaps they had sent text messages to the kitchen, placing their orders without uttering a word to a human being.

Many Africans saw America as a promised land because it was rich in conveniences and gadgets. Americans could make hot air cool and cold air warm. They almost all had running water. They could send men to the moon and cure many cancers. But many of them couldn't loosen their grip on their remote controls enough to sit on a breezy porch with friends and family, talking about nothing in particular, or sitting in contented silence listening to the birds. If some of them were sitting here now on the porch, she thought, with birds singing and children playing and sunshine slanting through the trees, they would nervously whip a remote control out of their pockets and start pushing buttons.

My people have no running water, she thought, and bad schools, and minimal health care, and electricity only part of the time. Most have no cars, no television, and no radio, and the kids don't have games or toys. We are poor in gadgets, but rich in so many other ways. And America, despite all its riches, and despite all the buttons you can push there, is in some respects poor.

Once again she asked herself the question she always asked. *Am I African or American?* And she answered herself with the same reply: *I am both.*

13

Later that morning, a town hall meeting would be held at the royal palace. Tsiami would start off the meeting by pouring libations at the stool rooms, thanking the ancestors for the safe return of the king. But when he arrived at the Other Cousin Comfort's house with several other elders, Peggy took one look at him, swaying slightly, and thought he had already poured some of the libations down his throat.

As they prepared to leave the house, Nana Kwesi's taxi pulled up, grinding to a dusty halt in front of the porch. Nana Kwesi jumped out and bid good morning to Peggy.

The group walked the few hundred feet down the sandy path and through the bushes to the royal courtyard. Peggy immediately noticed that many changes had taken place during her absence. The new white tin palace roof was indeed beautiful, painted sky blue around the edges. The empty windows actually looked better than the old, rusty, louvered ones had.

The three-sided porch on the second floor had temporary columns. Nana Kwesi had been greatly alarmed to find how rotten the old columns were; the fancy Doric pediment above the porch had been likely to collapse at any moment. He immediately removed the old columns, supported the roof with thick clusters of wooden poles, and ordered new Grecian-style columns from a supplier in Cape Coast. Peggy thought she might someday eat her meals on that porch, enjoying the fresh ocean breeze that rolled in over the trees behind the palace. And she would certainly sit there and gaze down on the courtyard to watch royal ceremonies, drumming, and dancing.

Right now the courtyard was littered with building materials—long planks, piles of iron rods, and stacks of concrete blocks, and Peggy was glad to see that there were still large quantities left, despite the mysterious thief. Goats and chickens made good use of the piles as vantage points from which to survey the scene. The large tree in the center of the courtyard spread its thick branches over the building supplies, as well as the usual gaggle of old men, who lounged in rusty patio chairs. Children chased one another around. In front of their little dwellings in the boys' quarters, women washed clothes in large cauldrons of steaming water over open fires, stirring them with sticks, or squatted and pounded cassava into *fufu* with big pestles. As she watched her people perform these basic activities—so simple, ancient, and African—she felt a wave of joy sweep over her to be Ghanaian.

The ceremony would be held on the palace patio. Someone had already set up Peggy's public stool, and benches for the elders had been placed along the edges of the patio.

Uncle Moses unwrapped the royal cow horn from its red flannel cloth and blew it loudly, puffing up his full cheeks. Hearing the summons for a royal meeting, six men appeared carrying plastic chairs and a wooden bench. Peggy sighed. That was only one more than had attended her town meeting the year before. Six. Out of seven thousand.

Tsiami stood up to open the meeting. *"Nana, wonfreye!"* he cried. Let us call all good things to come to us!

"Yemrah," cried the people in the ancient response. Let the good things come!

"Nana, wonfreye!" he cried, louder.

"Yemrah!"

"Nana, wonfreye!" he cried at the top of his lungs.

"Yemrah!"

Tsiami told the group that the king had just arrived from the United States and would be gazetted in two weeks' time. He asked if any townspeople had anything they wanted to say to their king, and all six of them shook their heads and looked at the concrete floor. Peggy felt a bit dejected. They didn't have anything to say to their king.

But this disappointment was soon eclipsed by something far worse.

Peggy saw a figure striding toward her. At first she didn't believe it was him, didn't believe he would have the audacity to show his face. Perhaps it was someone else, the strong morning sun confusing her eyes. She blinked and looked again. No, there was no mistaking him.

Kwame Lumpopo.

Today he was all in white, crisp white shirt, neatly pressed white trousers, and a white straw hat, looking as if he had emerged from the air-conditioned set of a movie shoot. Though it was only shortly past nine a.m., Peggy and her elders were already wilted, dusty, and perspiring. She wondered if he was wearing white as a symbol of purity, honesty, and integrity. She knew that in old American films, the good cowboys wore white, no matter how dusty it was in their frontier towns, and the bad ones wore black, and here was Kwame Lumpopo striding through the dust yet unscathed by it, ludicrously portraying himself as a good cowboy, which he certainly was *not*. He was, without doubt, the bad cowboy who rustled cattle and stole horses and deserved to be shot by the sheriff outside the saloon, or hanged as a public spectacle in the town square.

Kwame Lumpopo even had the nerve to flash Peggy a wide white grin and friendly wave as he carefully picked his way around the piles of building materials in the courtyard. She wondered how the man could walk so jauntily with the stool room just a few feet away. Could he be sure the stool had forgiven him for spreading vicious lies about her? She looked up at the large, three-sided porch overhead. Maybe her angry stool would cause Nana Kwesi's temporary columns to collapse, and the roof would fall on Kwame Lumpopo, burying his starched white clothes in a heap of dust. She didn't think she would mind. She might, in fact, leave him there as a warning to anyone who disrespected the king of Otuam.

He walked around the circle of elders, shaking each one's hand, and then he stood before Peggy with his hand extended. "Nana!" he cried, smiling as if nothing bad had ever passed between them. "Welcome home!"

But Peggy just stared straight ahead, which happened to be at his stomach. It was a flat stomach for a middle-aged man, she had to give him that.

"Why do you not shake my hand?" Kwame Lumpopo asked, horrified to be so humiliated in front of the elders. In Ghana, no matter how mad you were at a relative, you always greeted him politely, especially when others were present. But Peggy would never forget what Kwame Lumpopo had done. *Never.* He had coaxed her into trusting him and then conned her, scammed her, and stolen her money as if she were just a stupid woman.

"You know why, Kwame Lumpopo," she replied icily, still avoiding his eyes. He stepped back to look at her better, and she had a harder time focusing on his midsection.

"Well, I see we have some things to discuss," he said defensively. "I have done nothing wrong. We must meet and have a discussion."

"Nothing wrong?" she cried. "After you stole so much of my money? I never want to talk to you again. Please leave. And bring me back my royal umbrella! Today!"

Stunned, Kwame Lumpopo stumbled backward, then turned and ran. His swagger became a stagger as his tall frame lurched past the piles of wood and stone in the courtyard and disappeared around a corner.

Uncle Moses stood up angrily. "Why did you do that?" he cried, swinging his arms. "You can't treat a family member like that."

"He is a thief," Peggy replied. "He stole my money. He walked under my umbrella at family funerals as if he were the king. Then he told people so many evil lies about me that my stool cried. You are all well aware of that."

"If you are still upset, then we must have a family meeting to iron things out," Baba Kobena advised in his soothing dark voice. "He will give you the umbrella back, and perhaps he can pay you the money back."

"I don't *want* him to pay me back," Peggy snapped. "If he paid me back then he could rejoin the council, and I don't want him back. I do not tolerate thieves." She cast her elders a meaningful glance.

"He has truly treated her disgracefully," Nana Kwesi added. "He wanted to steal the money for the palace roof I put on, but Nana and I went around him. I don't think this palace would have a new roof if the money had gone through his hands."

"But still," Uncle Eshun said, his chin resting on his hands, resting on his cane, "he is a *relative*."

"We must understand Nana's disappointment in Kwame Lumpopo, however," Isaiah the Treasurer pointed out. "And we must unite to find a solution."

There was something about Isaiah's fawning that irritated Peggy even more than Uncle Moses's bossiness and Tsiami's stubbornness. Perhaps this was because the bossiness and stubbornness were sincere, while the fawning was not sincere. It was a coat of fresh paint over a piece of rotten, worm-infested wood.

"I have found the solution," she said, scowling.

Uncle Moses carefully wrapped the royal cow horn up in its red flannel covering and said, "Just remember, when you cook a sea turtle, it stews in its own juices." Peggy wasn't sure what that meant, and she didn't care to ask.

Isaiah the Treasurer cupped his pointed chin in his hand and stared at Nana Kwesi with unblinking eyes as Baba Kobena took off his lozenge-shaped black hat and toyed with it. Tsiami stood up with a bottle of schnapps to perform the libations. He had lost the keys to the stool rooms, he explained, so he would have to pour the libations right outside the doors rather than inside.

Tsiami thanked the ancestors for Peggy's safe return and prayed for her success as king. The ancient gnarled tree in the center of the courtyard was alive with birds singing sweetly, as if in welcome, and its long branches whispered and swayed in the breeze as the elders chanted and prayed. Peggy noticed that the libations sank straight down into the floor, a very good sign that the ancestors were thirsty and had accepted them. They, too, were welcoming their chosen king home.

Throughout the rest of the day, Peggy received visitors who wanted to welcome her back to Otuam. She was glad that many of her guests brought pails of fresh fish or bottles of beer, given how much her council ate and drank. But by midafternoon, jet lag hit her hard, and she longed to lie down. She hoped these visits would be brief, but at the same instant knew such a thing was impossible. Ghanaians weren't always conscious of time passing, particularly when they were enjoying the moment. When they came for a visit they hung around for hours, chatting or just sitting silently drinking beer.

Her guests discussed the price of mackerel on Main Street and Kofi Aswongo's lost goat. How Kwame Ninsin had painted Effi Boateng's yellow-striped chickens green and claimed them as his own until one night she crept out onto Main Street with a bucket of paint and made them yellow again. How the Mankessim—Cape Coast *tro-tro* was so overloaded that it tipped over, injuring several riders and scattering their bags, which had been attached to its roof. One of the bags had opened, revealing very dirty underpants. Several times Peggy wished her guests would leave, but it would have been very rude to suggest it.

Her hopes soared when one group of visitors rose from the table and bid her farewell, but just then another group walked in the door. She forced a smile and welcomed them. She took very seriously the oath she had made at her enstoolment to always be available to meet with her people. And these visits showed that some people, at least, were interested in their new king, despite the poor turnout at the town meeting.

As the sun set, the chief inspector came by with two of his officers to pay his respects. At fifty-two, Kwame Appiah was a tall, slender man with a handsome, lined face. Periodically, his intelligent bright eyes darted around the table, as if he was calculating which of Peggy's visitors had the potential to commit a crime. Sipping his beer, he confirmed what Peggy had heard, that wife beating had indeed stopped since her enstoolment a year earlier. Now all he had to deal with was drunks, and he didn't think any royal order would stop people from drinking.

The policemen and other visitors left around seven p.m., and shortly thereafter Nana Kwesi climbed back in his cab headed for Winneba. Then, before Peggy could catch her breath, the queen mother, Paulina Nyamekyeh, and her cousin, the Soul, Faustina, came by to welcome the king home and join her and Cousin Charles for dinner. They had been in school earlier that day and unable to attend the palace ceremony.

Paulina was now sixteen, and even more beautiful than she had been a year earlier. Peggy studied her. Her flawless skin was dark, the color of bittersweet chocolate. Her long, almond-shaped eyes were set close together. They were very dark, almost black, fringed by thick black lashes. Her nose was long and aquiline, the nostrils perfectly molded. Her mouth was small with plump full lips. She had high cheekbones, a square jaw, and slightly pointed chin. Her teeth were truly marvelous. In a town where many children had rotten, crooked, or dirty teeth, Paulina's were white and even, as if she had endured years of orthodontia like the children of wealthy Washingtonians.

As they ate fried fish on rice with red sauce, Peggy noticed how well behaved the girls were, friendly and respectful, typical Ghanaian children. The dinner was greatly enlivened when Cousin Charles opened the ancient refrigerator to grab a beer and the door came off in his hands and fell to the floor with a crash. He stood there looking at it in surprise, his hand gripping an imaginary handle, while Peggy and the girls howled with laughter. Somehow it struck Peggy so funny she couldn't stop laughing, and she clutched her belly because it started to ache.

To Peggy, the door falling off that ancient machine represented all of Africa in a nutshell. It reminded her of a very famous novel by a Nigerian author named Chinua Achebe, which was still widely read in Africa, Europe, and the United States more than fifty years after its publication, called *Things Fall Apart*. Even though the title referred to a man's life falling apart, it pretty much summed up all of the things that broke every day in Africa. That was why every family had at least one person, usually a man, who could fix anything, whether it was rewiring a lamp, reprogramming a computer, reconditioning an engine and putting it into an ancient car, or hammering a new table leg onto an old table. In Peggy's family, Cousin Charles was the one to call when Things Fall Apart.

Now he tried to pull the door off the floor but it was too heavy, with all the bottles of beer on the inside shelves, so he patiently removed them. Then he lifted the door up and examined its hinge, which seemed all right, but the corresponding hinge on the side of the refrigerator had lost a piece. Cousin Charles looked around the room, saw a wine cork on the table, cut it in half with his dinner knife, and shoved it into the hole in the fridge hinge. He carefully put the door back on, pushing the pin up into the cork, and the door stayed.

"There!" he said, satisfied. He looked at Peggy. "I know that in America you go out and buy new things when something breaks. But this is African engineering at an African price."

Peggy nodded approvingly. "That's what Americans call recycling, Charles," she said, digging her fork into her fried fish and rice.

The one thing Cousin Charles couldn't fix was the light in the toilet room. The problem wasn't the bulb but something in the wiring that he couldn't repair. And so, at night, Peggy blindly flung the bucket of water in the general direction of the toilet.

At five o'clock the next morning, Aggie tapped on Peggy's door to let her know she had a visitor, a cousin of hers who lived in the boys' quarters next to the palace. Peggy had, of course, been up since the chickens and goats started shrieking at four. But she liked to lie on her sheets and feel the silken smoothness of the early morning air against her skin until she absolutely had to get up.

"Tell him to come in," she said, standing up and throwing a cloth around her.

Peggy didn't recognize the man, but it was only members of the Ebiradze clan who lived rent-free in the little cabins surrounding the royal courtyard.

"*Nana, ma akye, woho tsen den?*" the man asked. Good morning. How are you?

"*Woho tsen den?*" Peggy replied, nodding.

"Nana, I saw Tsiami just now," the man said. "He was carrying a flashlight in one hand and the keys to the stool rooms in the other, taking the daughters of the late king into the stool rooms to pour libations. It looked to me that he was sneaking around like a crocodile. They are there now. I wondered if you knew about it."

Peggy certainly had not known about it. And the day before, Tsiami said he had lost the keys so he couldn't open the doors for her welcome home ceremony. What was more, he was always supposed to ask the king's permission before unlocking the stool rooms for a ceremony. Even more disturbing, the children of the late king hadn't come by to pay their respects to Peggy first, nor to ask her permission themselves. Had they simply overlooked this courtesy, or was it an intentional slap in the face of their father's successor?

But right now Peggy needed to deal with her errant *tsiami.* "Tell him I want to see him," she said.

About ten minutes later, Tsiami shuffled into the house and wordlessly slipped into the chair next to Peggy's at the dining room table.

"Tsiami," she said, "I heard you were just in the stool rooms with the children of the late king."

"That is a lie," he replied, suddenly studying the cracks in the ceiling.

"No, the lie occurred yesterday when you said you had lost the stool room keys. You had them the whole time but you didn't want to open the doors. You were mad at me because I had yelled at you about the letter to the fishermen."

Tsiami shrugged. The gesture infuriated Peggy, but she was determined not to show it. She was a king. A calm, regal king.

"I just want you to know," she said firmly, "that if the ancestors are mad at me for not pouring the libations in the proper way, and if they are going to drag me down to hell, I am not going alone. I am taking you with me."

"No, you will not," Tsiami said, shaking his head vigorously. "You will not be taking me down to hell with you. I will not go."

Peggy was having a hard time keeping her temper. "You will go with me, Tsiami, because I will grab hold of you and drag you down! I'm telling you! *Maka, maka!*"

"That is not how it will be," Tsiami said. "I will escape you so you will not drag me down."

Now Peggy felt her eyes bulging from their sockets. "I will not let you escape! If the ancestors are mad at me because you botched the libations, I will tell them to wait a minute before they drag me down to hell, and I will find you and put my two hands around your throat and then I will say, 'Okay, ancestors, I am ready to go now!'"

Tsiami shook his head. "They will not wait for you. It is well known that if the ancestors want to drag you down, they will take you immediately."

"You are disrespecting me because I am a woman! Let me say this, Tsiami. No matter how badly you treat me, there is one thing you must do properly, and that is to pour the libations according to tradition and keep the ancestors happy. If you can't even do that right, I'm going to find another *tsiami*!"

Tsiami stood up bristling with anger and, mustering as much dignity as he could, adjusted his cloth and wordlessly walked out of the house into the darkness, the rusty gate banging shut behind him.

Aggie, who had been leaning against the kitchen door with her arms crossed, burst out laughing. She disappeared into the kitchen and reappeared with a plate of cut pineapple and a bowl of porridge, along with a fork and spoon, which she set down before Peggy.

"Nana, you know better than anyone I've ever met how to tell a man off," she said admiringly. "Is that what they teach women in the USA? Do they have courses there that teach girls how to do it? I would like to take such a course."

Peggy plunged her fork into a chunk of pineapple and thought about it. No, she hadn't learned this particular skill in Washington, or London, for that matter, places where fighting chauvinism was a favorite female pastime. She had learned it well before she ever left Ghana. But how?

Then she recalled that it had to do with the dinner dishes, which she and her siblings were supposed to take turns washing each night. Peggy always dutifully took her turn. But when it came time for her two older half brothers to pitch in, they invariably wandered off, calling over their shoulders that "Peggy should do the dishes because she is a girl." Many times Peggy did their dishes, muttering under her breath about the injustice of it all. Why should her brothers get out of doing the dishes just because they were male? Why should she have to do their work because she was female? It just wasn't fair.

And then one night when she was nine years old, and her brothers went off laughing instead of doing the dishes, Peggy came up with a new idea. She waited until her brothers were fast asleep. Then she crept into their room with stacks of dirty dishes and carefully placed them in her brothers' beds. She returned with two glasses of water and threw them on her sleeping brothers, who woke up wet and angry, surrounded by piles of dirty dishes. "Mother!" the boys wailed. "Look what Peggy did!" Many other African women would have scolded their daughters in such a case, telling them that women were there to serve their fathers, brothers, and husbands without complaint. But her mother only laughed because she wanted Peggy to be strong.

From then on, whenever her brothers tried to make Peggy do the dishes on their night, she would punish them the same way. After several soakings, her brothers wordlessly washed the dishes on their assigned nights. That was when Peggy learned that if a woman stood up for herself against mean-spirited men, she could win and teach them a lesson, and maybe next time they would think twice before stepping all over her.

She popped the pineapple chunk into her mouth, and the taste was incredibly sweet. Still, she couldn't shake the suspicion that her elders and the children of the late king had been doing something behind her back today. What had Auntie Esi said about the children of the late king? *Don't trust any of the children of the late king. There is a terrible hatred there, one that, I fear, has followed Joseph into death.*

Her worries were eased later that morning when the late king's daughters, Perpetual, Dorcas, and Mary Magdalene, came to have a private word with her. *Yes,* Peggy thought, relieved, *they have come to pay their respects after all.* But after the traditional greetings, Perpetual took a sip of her Fanta and said, "Nana, it has been well over a year since our father died, and we want to bury him immediately."

"Immediately," said Dorcas.

Peggy's heart sank. "You must have seen the condition of the palace this morning when you went with Tsiami to pour libations," she pointed out. "It is not yet a dignified backdrop for a royal funeral, with the paint peeling and the empty windows, and the courtyard full of building materials. It is my sincere goal to hold the funeral a year from now, when I return. The palace will be beautiful then, and the courtyard, cleared and landscaped, will be surrounded by funeral tents, a fitting place for the ceremonies."

"We will get him out of the morgue and bury him secretly," Perpetual replied firmly. "Then you can hold the dignified funeral whenever you are ready, using a wooden effigy instead of the body."

Peggy was shocked. What the women were suggesting would dishonor their father and herself. Not to mention, it would dishonor *them.* A deceased king must be interred with drumming, dancing, libations, and other rituals. You couldn't just throw him in the ground, ignoring all the sacred time-honored traditions. Auntie Esi had been right. Obviously these women wanted to punish their father in death for his behavior in life. Their request the year before for a speedy funeral hadn't been out of respect, she now understood, but out of revenge. And perhaps their libation pouring on the stools that morning hadn't been to bless their father, but to beg the ancestors to drag him down to hell for his misdeeds.

"Why would you suggest such a dishonorable thing?" she asked sharply.

Perpetual shrugged. "If you want to hold an expensive funeral, that's your business," she said, a nasty edge to her voice. "But *we* want him buried *now.*"

Peggy shook her head. "I need your father's *body* for the funeral. That is the proper way to have a funeral, after all, with the body. I won't lie to people and tell them we will bury a person who has been buried a year already. He will be buried in a royal tomb in the palace, according to custom."

"He's *our* father," Perpetual growled. "We should decide where and when to bury him, not you." Behind her thick, large glasses, her eyes became small and hard.

"He's *my* predecessor," Peggy barked back. "Each new king owes the last one the dignity of a royal burial. And who do you think you're talking to in that tone of voice? How dare you!"

"That man doesn't deserve a magnificent funeral," Perpetual hissed.

"He doesn't deserve one," Dorcas agreed.

"Well, I intend to give him the best funeral a Fante king ever had!" Peggy snapped, provoked.

The three women stood up and, muttering to one another, left the house. Aggie brought in a glass of just-squeezed orange juice and set it down gently before Peggy. "That was very strange," she said. "They don't want to bury their father as a king. How could you hate somebody so much, after he is *dead,* that you would want to dishonor yourself in order to dishonor him?"

Peggy sipped the juice, so sweet and fresh, and shook her head. "I'm sorry for their family issues, but I can't let them get in the way of my plans for Otuam. I'm going to bring honor and progress to my people, and secretly tossing the former monarch in a ditch will not achieve my goals."

14

The day had started off badly, with Tsiami making such a fool of himself and the late king's daughters' mean-spirited request, but it rapidly got worse. When the sun was at its highest point, and Peggy was eating her fried fish, a taxi careened to a stop in front of the house, spewing sand and pebbles. Holding two suitcases, Ekow barged in the front door.

"Mama, Mama, King Nana Mama, I am here!" he cried.

Peggy stared at him, dismayed. Ekow had, if it was possible, lost weight since she had last seen him a year earlier. His face looked more like a dried prune than ever, and his ears seemed to stick out farther than before.

"Ekow," she said briskly. "How did you know I was coming here?"

"The relatives are all talking about it," he said. "It is nice and very, very fine. I will sleep on the floor in your room. I will help you keep things clean." He bustled down the hall to Peggy's room, dragging his two bags. Peggy looked at his retreating form and groaned.

A few minutes later, Tsiami stopped by to apologize for pretending he had lost the stool room keys, for taking the late king's children into the stool rooms without Peggy's permission, and for lying about it all. "It is quite common for kings and their *tsiamis* to fight frequently," he said, shrugging. "But still, I can't imagine what got into me."

"I know *exactly* what got into you, Tsiami," Peggy retorted. "Alcohol.

Through your mouth. That's what got into you. Do you think I don't know where much of the ancestral libations ends up? If someone gives you a bottle of schnapps to pour to the ancestors, you pour half down your throat and the other half into the ground. Yours is the perfect profession for an alcoholic."

Tsiami said nothing.

"And the next time you pour libations for a ceremony at the palace, I am going to smell your breath first to make sure you are sober. I am going to stick my head inside your mouth and take a deep whiff, so be prepared. I will not have you botch the ancestral libations."

Tsiami considered this. "All right. I will drink afterward, then."

"Fine," Peggy replied. "But if you don't perform your priestly duties correctly, I will fire you, which will be a great dishonor. So bear that in mind."

Tsiami nodded, stood up, and strode out of the house. Gazing at his skinny form retreating into the bush, Peggy was glad that he had apologized. Perhaps her efforts at trying to teach him to respect her would pay off, the way they had paid off with her brothers and the dish duty. Come to think of it, though, her brothers had been very young, and youth is a time when the human mind is flexible and readily accepts new notions. Age, on the other hand, stiffens people, who may become rigidly inflexible, like those trees in California that had petrified and turned to rock. Most likely it wouldn't be so easy to teach her elders anything at all as they, too, had probably already turned to rock.

As Aggie cleared the lunch dishes, Peggy ran a hand through her hair. It occurred to her that she had only been in Otuam two days and had already lost her temper five times. She counted them. Yesterday morning, at her very first council meeting, she had exploded when she saw the fishing fees letter issued in her name and without her permission. She had yelled at Kwame Lumpopo at the palace ceremony. This morning she had threatened to drag Tsiami down to hell for lying about the stool room keys, and she had barked at him again when he came to apologize. She had become infuriated with the disrespect of the late king's daughters.

Peggy tried to remember if she had ever lost her temper five times in two days in her life. She didn't think so. This was a new record.

Should she try to curb her temper, bite her lip, and swallow the retort begging to be heaved into the conversation? Would her elders respect her more if she controlled herself, or would they take her equanimity as permission to run roughshod all over her? Would Tsiami have apologized if she hadn't yelled at him in the first place? She wasn't sure. As a woman, didn't she need to prove that she was tougher than any man, or her elders would never listen to a word she said? It was well known the world over that successful male leaders were called successful leaders, and successful female leaders were called bitches. She mulled this over.

What was more, she was not sure she could control her temper if she tried. What caused her to snap so quickly? Was it the heat? The jet lag? Or were her elders outrageously irritating? She worried that the real reason was that she was just a secretary in over her head who couldn't deal with her many challenges. Taking a deep breath, she cupped her right hand around her mother's little gold bracelet on her left wrist to feel the strength within it.

Well, she decided, *I will take things one day at a time.*

But her equanimity was sorely tested. A new source of irritation was her elders' unceasing attempts to get her to reconcile with Kwame Lumpopo. Peggy wanted to do so much for Otuam in the few weeks she would be there, and here she was mired in quicksand and chained to her nemesis, that disgraceful scam artist. Even though she had fired him from the council, he was still there in spirit, at every council meeting, hovering above her, haunting her. It was so unfair.

The elders were deeply disturbed about the way she had treated him at the palace ceremony. Nothing made Ghanaians more uneasy than a rift in the family, and an African family consisted of cousins so distant you could no longer name a common ancestor but just knew you were related somehow. Sometimes you couldn't have the satisfaction of staying mad at anybody because relatives would come out of the woodwork telling you that you were, in fact, distant cousins with your enemy, so you had to make up.

During a very hot midafternoon council meeting, Baba Kobena urged, "You must forgive him," for the umpteenth time, flashing his large lower teeth. "Fishes swim in schools, and we are one big family, swimming together. Moreover, it is unseemly for a king to be upset at her cousin, and in public, too. Ghanaians don't act that way."

Peggy shot him a look. "I'm an American. We Americans drop our misbehaving relatives."

The elders shook their heads and murmured in disapproval.

"Nana, with all due respect, if a chair is missing a leg, it will not balance on only three legs. If you throw one leg out because you don't like it, the chair will be useless," Isaiah the Treasurer said firmly.

"I'm throwing the Kwame Lumpopo leg out," Peggy quipped.

"And he is a thief," Nana Kwesi added. "I agree that she should speak to him pleasantly in public because he is a family member, but she cannot have him back on her council."

Peggy's elders tended to ignore Nana Kwesi. They knew they were going to have a hard time ignoring him once Peggy was back in Washington and he acted for her as regent, but for now they could ignore him.

"What if he agrees to pay you the money back?" Uncle Eshun asked Peggy.

"I don't want it," Peggy replied. "First of all, how is he going to pay back two thousand dollars? The man doesn't work. I think he gets all his money by cheating people, mostly female people, and think how many innocent people he would have to cheat in order to pay me back."

Just then the discussion was punctuated by a crash of shattering crockery in the kitchen, followed by male and female shrieks and curses. Peggy pushed herself up from her chair, marched to the kitchen, and swung open the door to see Aggie wielding a butcher knife as Ekow raced out the back door, stick arms above his head, screaming wildly. On the floor were a broken plate and a mess of tomatoes.

"Stop it, both of you!" Peggy cried, pulling a handkerchief out of her bra and mopping her forehead. It was already so hard being king, what with the heat and Kwame Lumpopo and the stealing. The last thing she needed was Aggie going after Ekow with a butcher knife.

She returned to her chair and noticed that her elders' gaze was riveted on something outside of the window behind her. She turned around to see Ekow, still flailing his arms, disappearing into the bush.

"Let us continue," she said.

Ekow truly did his best to be helpful around the house. He swept the floors and helped Aggie wash the dishes in large tubs on the kitchen floor. Outside, with a cigarette dangling from the corner of his mouth, he did the laundry, stirring it in large pans of hot soapy water that had been heated on the kerosene burner in the kitchen, rinsing it with cool clear water, and hanging it carefully on the lines behind the dining room. He made the beds, though sometimes he put the blanket on the bottom and the two sheets on top.

Whenever Peggy came out of the bathroom she found Ekow standing there like a statue, holding a bucket of water, ready to toss it into the toilet. Peggy was embarrassed that he had been standing there listening to everything. In the United States, whenever she used the bathroom and thought people outside might hear, she ran the water in the sink. But here there was no water in the sink. Peggy thought about telling Ekow to stop bringing water for the toilet, but she knew he was saving Aggie the trouble of fetching it from the tank in the kitchen.

Every night, Ekow slept on a mat at the foot of her bed, an unlikely guardian of the king's spirit. Despite Peggy's initial misgivings, the arrangement with Ekow seemed to be working out. Every day she gave him some spare change to run up to Main Street and buy the smallest pack of cigarettes they sold, a slender case with eight cigarettes inside.

But Ekow was tempted by other merchandise, as events were soon to prove. It all started a few days before the gazetting, when several strangers stopped by the house to tell Peggy that Ekow had borrowed money from them on Main Street, saying that he was the king's nephew and Peggy would pay it back as soon as they saw her. He had borrowed only a few hundred cedis from each one, but every time Peggy pulled the money from her bra she grew annoyed at another useless scamming man in the family. When Ekow returned to the house late in the afternoon, Peggy scolded him severely. *What had he wasted her money on,* she wanted to know. Ekow shrugged and went out back to smoke a cigarette and see if the laundry was dry.

But Peggy was soon to find out what Ekow had wasted her money on. It started that evening as she ate her fish. Ekow kept opening and closing the refrigerator door, which Cousin Charles had only recently repaired and was already starting to tilt a bit. When Peggy told him to cut it out, he went into the kitchen and emerged with a bucket of water, which he sloshed across the dining room floor. "I will take a bath," he proclaimed, "and after that I will put on your bra and underwear."

Picturing skinny little Ekow in her underwear, Peggy started to laugh, but then she caught herself and told him to behave. When she went to bed, instead of bedding down on his sleeping mat, Ekow paced up and down, muttering to himself. As he did so, Peggy got a whiff of something pungent and sickeningly sweet.

Her heart sank. "You stink of marijuana, Ekow!" she said with dismay. "You can't sleep in my room. Go into the hall and sleep on the floor." She pushed him out the door, banged it shut, and loudly turned the key.

Ekow didn't go to sleep on the hall floor. He walked up and down outside her room, talking loudly to himself and pounding on the walls. Periodically, Cousin Charles came out of his room down the hall to tell him to shut up, and they started arguing. After about forty minutes of trying to get some sleep, Peggy was wound up tight. She had so much to do for Otuam, so very much, and was so tired from sitting at the table sixteen hours a day in the heat, meeting with council members and visitors. At the very least she needed a good sleep every night.

She turned the large key in her lock, which rattled and scraped, and threw open her door.

"Get out of this house so I can sleep!" she cried. "I'm the king and I need my sleep! Take your sleeping mat and your suitcases and get on the tro-tro tomorrow to Accra!"

When Cousin Charles had ejected Ekow from the house, throwing his suitcases and sleeping mat after him and slamming the door, Peggy said, "Maybe now we can get some sleep."

But almost immediately there was a loud banging on the door, louder than the banging of a fist. Cousin Charles opened it and there stood Ekow, wielding a hammer, which he had evidently retrieved from his suitcase. Cousin Charles closed the door and barred it.

All Peggy could think of was that Ekow was going to damage the house, the way he had broken the Other Cousin Comfort's cherished china cups and bowls during her enstoolment. The Other Cousin Comfort had been kind enough not to send Peggy a bill, though locking up the comfortable parlor was punishment enough. Now, however, Ekow threatened severe damage to the house, which was not Peggy's. As king, how could she allow Ekow to damage someone else's property? Yet as his aunt, how could she send her own nephew to jail? Because that was what was going through her mind at each blow of the hammer. Ekow had to go to jail.

"Charles, go and fetch the police," Peggy said, her mind suddenly made up. "They have to pick him up. He's going to damage the house."

"I'm going with him!" Aggie said.

Cousin Charles opened the front door and pushed Ekow and his hammer out of the way, slapping him hard, clearing a path for Aggie and himself to run to the police. Peggy shut the door, lifted the heavy bar, and slipped it into place.

Almost immediately, Ekow started banging on the door again with his hammer. Peggy figured it was about fifteen minutes on foot to the police station, maybe longer in the dark since Cousin Charles and Aggie had forgotten to take a flashlight. She would, most likely, have to wait at least a half hour for help to come, while Ekow was trying to break the door down. She sat down on a dining room chair and waited, shuddering in sympathy with the door at each blow.

It seemed like an eternity until she heard men's voices on the front porch. She crept to the door and put her ear against it. Then she heard the slapping sound of flesh against flesh. She lifted the heavy bar from the door and opened it slowly. Four policemen were dragging Ekow away, hitting him. Charles and Aggie stood on the porch. Cousin Charles's glasses were askew, and Aggie's turban had fallen off. Her unkempt braids were twisted in different directions like friendly snakes.

"He was resisting arrest," Cousin Charles explained, straightening his glasses. "He wouldn't go peacefully."

"He tore the officer's shirt," Aggie added, smoothing her braids.

For the first time they noticed what Ekow had done to his suitcases— he had opened them and strewn their contents all over the porch. There were car magazines, one black shoe, two videos, torn-out magazine pictures of scantily clad girls, a hammer, a silver bowl, a pack of condoms, a tube of lipstick, a filthy pair of tennis shoes, and a riot of worn T-shirts.

Aggie knelt and started pushing the odd collection of items back into the suitcases. Cousin Charles picked up the hammer. "He won't be getting this back," he said.

Peggy sagged against the balustrade. It hurt her to know that the policemen she had called had dragged off that skinny, pitiful, mentally ill boy—everyone called Ekow a boy even though he was forty-two— and slapped him silly. Though maybe he deserved to be slapped, she thought, after getting high and drunk, and making such scenes, keeping everyone up way past bedtime, and then attacking the house with a hammer. Being slapped might have done Ekow some good, but the whole thing made Peggy very, very sad. When she thought of how much her dead sister had loved him, her heart broke.

I miss my sister, and Ekow needs his mother to take care of him. We all need our mothers to take care of us. Ekow went completely crazy when he lost his mother and I . . . How did I change? Unlike Ekow, I had the strength to go to work and pay my bills and do everything I was supposed to do. But I became sad. A part of me is hopelessly, forever sad. I cover it up with humor and efficiency and righteous anger. But nothing will ever be able to take that sadness away from me, until the day when I, too, become an ancestor, and my mother is waiting for me, hand outstretched, to welcome me to her world. When that day comes it will not be a sad day. It will be a happy one. Though, she added, straightening up a bit, *I don't want it to come anytime soon, now that I have so much to do here.*

Aggie and Cousin Charles zipped up the suitcases and took them inside. They appeared a minute later, Aggie holding a glass of orange juice out to Peggy, who took it and sighed. "You don't know how hard that was for me," she said. "But I had to do it. As king, my authority has to start with my own family or no one will respect my rule. My nephew is in a jail cell tonight, and word will get out as it always does in a small town, and people will know I am a serious king who means business."

Cousin Charles and Aggie sat down on the bench beside her in sympathetic support. "You had to do it," Cousin Charles agreed.

"Yes," Peggy said. "You know, there is an American saying that I never understood. It's this: *I have to do what I have to do.* Americans say it a lot, but something got lost in the translation for me. After tonight I understand it completely. It means you have to do things you don't want to do, sometimes terrible things, because it is right that you do them."

For the first time that evening, there was silence. Peggy sipped the orange juice and listened to the slow, rhythmic pounding of the waves behind the trees. Then she walked off the porch, looked up, and saw brilliant stars like brightly shining diamonds against a black velvet background, stars so bright it seemed you could reach up with your fist and grab them. A gentle, cool breeze caressed her, and in a thicket nearby a goat bleated.

"It's no joke being king," Peggy said to no one in particular.

The following morning Peggy instructed Cousin Charles and Aggie to go to the jail with a large bottle of water and a plate of bread and cheese for Ekow, as well as the tip for the chief inspector. The American side of her thought it was strange to pay for having Ekow in there, as if she were putting him up at a hotel, the Otuam Jail Hotel.

The single jail cell was off a raspberry-colored entrance hall and had a wooden door with a little sliding panel at about the height of a short person's head. Prisoners could open the door for a sliver of light, or to cry out to the policemen that they needed to be taken to the toilet in the courtyard behind the station. As Cousin Charles and Aggie spoke in the hall with the chief inspector, the little door slid back and they saw Ekow's mouth saying, "Please tell Nana that I am very sorry and she must let me out of this cell, which is not nice and not fine."

Jangling his big iron keys, which hung from a metal circle on his belt, the chief inspector opened the cell door with a theatrical flourish to reveal Ekow, sober and contrite, if a bit red eyed. He wasn't alone in the cell. Cousin Charles and Aggie saw a huge, muscular young man sulking in the far corner. The chief inspector proudly stated that he had *two* culprits in his custody, a rare and marvelous occurrence, since he usually had none. Fingering his keys and grinning, he boasted that he had solved one of the most important crime cases in Otuam since the thieves had stolen the MTN phone tower wire back in 1999.

"I have just caught Divine, the big-time fish thief," the chief inspector proclaimed. He slammed the door on Ekow, standing hopefully by the threshold, and Divine, stewing in the corner, and locked it. Then he invited Cousin Charles and Aggie into his comfortable office with its overstuffed sofas and chairs and gestured to a waist-high burlap sack on the floor. When Cousin Charles poked his head inside, he saw hundreds of dead fish with yellow rubbery glazed eyes, and emanating from them was the worst odor he had ever smelled in his life. He hastily pulled his head out of the sack. Cousin Charles had noticed a revolting odor permeating the entire jail and was glad to see that it was coming from the sack of rotten fish, and not from the chief inspector himself.

The chief inspector explained that fish packers knew that sacks of fish had been disappearing from the warehouse of a female fishmonger named Dzadi Yatu and were on the lookout for the thief. Two days earlier, they had seen Divine stealing a sack, tackled him, and brought him and the sack to the police station, which was no small accomplishment, considering he was almost seven feet tall.

"Why are you keeping the fish?" Cousin Charles asked, holding his nose.

"Important evidence!" the chief inspector replied. "This matter will go to the court in Saltpond, and the prosecutor will have to pick up Divine and the fish and keep the fish in his office until the trial."

Cousin Charles made a face. "To really punish Divine, maybe you should keep the fish in the cell with him," he suggested.

Peggy laughed when they told her the story. The worst crime in a decade was the theft of a sack of fish. Otuam was truly a safe place to live. She tried to picture Washington, D.C., with a corresponding lack of crime. *The Washington Post* would run a headline on page one, "Divine, Big-Time Fish Thief, Captured," illustrated by a photo of the chief inspector standing pompously next to the burlap sack of rotting mackerel.

"The chief inspector is waiting for your instructions about Ekow," Cousin Charles continued. "And Ekow is begging for your forgiveness. Do you want him to stay in jail a few more days to teach him a lesson?"

Peggy sighed. "I forgive Ekow. But I can't have him here making trouble for us all. I certainly don't want him to attend my gazetting on Friday, where he could upset the sacred rituals. And after my gazetting, I have a lot to do for Otuam. I need my sleep so I can concentrate. Ekow must return to Accra today and not come back."

She swatted at a rivulet of sweat trickling down her cheek and reached into her bra. "Charles, take Ekow's suitcases to the jail along with this money, which should be enough for him to take the *tro-tro* to Accra. Tell him that if I see his face here again I will put him back in jail."

Peggy had heard from her relatives that Ekow was a human boomerang who would surely come flying back. And no matter how passionately you vowed never to let him visit again, when he showed up with his prune face, big ears, and sticklike body, begging to wash your floor and clean your toilet in return for a meal and a place to sleep on the floor, you let him stay. And lived to regret it, as you always knew you would.

15

There were several council meetings to discuss preparations for Peggy's gazetting the following week. Who should purchase the goat and bottle of whiskey to give to the council of chiefs? Who should rent the van to carry the king and her council to the Hall of Chiefs in Essuehyia, where the ceremony would be held? What food should be served at the party held afterward at the house? How many crates of beer and minerals should be purchased, and how many bottles of expensive Johnnie Walker Red, reserved for the elders and the most distinguished guests?

The question of alcohol supplies occasioned hours of debate because everyone at the council table had his own opinion. Some preferred to err on the side of generosity; a lack of refreshments would dishonor the stool, and what was left over would surely be drunk in the near future. Others pushed for a more restrained purchase; extravagance, too, would upset the stool given the void where the royal treasury was supposed to be. Many of her elders discoursed at length on the amounts drunk at parties past, as Peggy felt the sweat trickling beneath her robes.

A king must be patient, she knew, but even the most boring, long-winded embassy meetings she had attended produced snap decisions compared to these Otuam debates. Her elders, in their quaint Fante laced with old sayings of lions and fish, birds and harvests and crocodiles, went around and around and finally spiraled back to where they had started, with nothing resolved.

"A squirrel hides many nuts to keep him fed during lean times," Uncle Moses said. "He never knows exactly how many nuts he will need, but he knows it is better to have too many nuts than too few."

"But a bird does not hide food and always has enough," Uncle Eshun replied.

"A fish never starves," added Baba Kobena. And so it went.

In the end, as for the goat and bottle of whiskey for the kings, it was decided that Uncle Moses would buy them with Peggy's money. Nana Kwesi would rent the van with Peggy's money. The food would be chicken and rice, purchased with Peggy's money. Consensus was finally reached on the amount of alcohol to be purchased for the party. No one said that Peggy was expected to pay for the alcohol, and Peggy assumed it would be the contribution of her elders. Their very first. Finally.

It seemed to Peggy that corruption was everywhere. Yes, other African countries pointed to Ghana as the kind of country they were striving to become. Just look at the recent close elections, where nobody killed anyone else and there were no accusations of voter fraud. Even the most scandalmongering journalists agreed that Ghanaian officials probably stole less than those in other countries, having the good taste to slip millions instead of billions into their Swiss bank accounts. But corruption was still deeply woven into the fabric of everyday life, from high government officials to the people of Otuam.

Peggy had read in her morning perusals of African websites that many well-respected Western economists believed corruption was the cause of Africa's poverty. It certainly wasn't due to Africa's lack of natural resources, with all its gold, silver, diamonds, oil, iron, cobalt, uranium, copper, bauxite, lumber, and agricultural riches. Yet somehow this wealth rarely trickled down to the average people in towns and villages. Somehow with all their resources most African governments couldn't provide the basics of human life: clean water, education, and decent medical care.

The African Union estimated that corruption cost African economies $150 billion annually, which was about 25 percent of the continent's gross domestic product, and increased the cost of goods by as much as 20 percent. Some $30 billion in foreign aid for Africa ended up not digging wells or opening clinics or schools, but in the foreign bank accounts of public officials, while 50 percent of tax revenue disappeared.

The Centre for Democracy and Development had recently conducted a survey on the effects of corruption in Ghana. It was hard to make an accurate survey because not a single government official admitted to taking bribes or embezzling funds. But average Ghanaian citizens were more willing to respond. Some 75 percent of households surveyed saw corruption as a serious problem, with 66 percent paying 10 percent of their incomes in bribes to public officials. Forty-four percent admitted to making unofficial payments.

If a handsome bribe was paid, the clerk issuing driver's licenses might simply hand one over to an applicant, allowing him to avoid the driving test altogether. (Judging from the standard of driving and the countless horrific car crashes, this happened all too often.) Doctors might claim there wasn't a single bed in the hospital for you, until you offered them a wad of cash, and suddenly one opened up. If your power was out, the clerk at the power company might not put your address on the list of repairs until you offered him a bottle of whiskey. If your sick child missed a test, the teacher might insist on an expensive bottle of perfume for letting the student take it.

In societies so rife with corruption, perhaps it was understandable why those at the bottom of the pyramid, when offered the first opportunity to accept bribes, gladly took it. Everyone else was doing it, and the "tips" they received went to helping their families get clean water, education, and decent medical care.

Someone was even collecting tips from the palace courtyard. Peggy had learned from Nana Kwesi that more building supplies had gone missing. The piles of boards and metal bars that the goats had been standing on during her welcome ritual were now only half as high, even though he and his men hadn't done any work since then.

During the day, the courtyard was abuzz with activity, with old men lounging, women pounding *fufu*, and children playing; if anyone had tried to slide a board off the pile and drag it away, he would have been tackled to the ground while someone ran to notify Peggy. Therefore, the thief must be coming at night. Peggy was furious at the thief who was taking supplies she had purchased with her tiny salary, to the ruination of her formerly perfect credit.

More important, whoever was stealing the materials was harming all Otuam. The royal palace was the physical representation of the entire town, and no one could have pride in a place with its major government building in such a derelict state. How would Americans feel to see the White House peeling and dingy, the columns tottering, the roof leaking, and birds flying in and out of broken windows? Or the dome of the U.S. Capitol, cracked open by lightning, the melted statue of Freedom stuck to the side and left to remain that way for years? They would be ashamed, would insist that the buildings be repaired because Americans were proud of their great country. In Otuam, a renovated palace would give the people new pride, new energy, and new hope for the future.

The thief must know he was running a very great risk of death or illness. Surely Uncle Joseph was getting very cold, being in the fridge all that time, and wanted to be buried after a glorious funeral so he could finally be at peace. The more building materials that were stolen, the longer it would take Peggy to bury him. Also, the palace was the home of the stools, and the stools wanted to live in a beautiful home, not a rotten one. No matter how quietly he snuck around at night, the thief couldn't keep his existence secret from Uncle Joseph and the stools, who would most certainly punish him. All she could do was wait.

Meanwhile, Peggy was getting ready for her gazetting, and corruption even followed her on her trip to buy new beads and sandals for the ceremony. At her enstoolment the year before, protocol had required her to wear the beads and sandals of Uncle Joseph, but now she wanted to buy some of her own. She asked Ebenezer to drive Nana Kwesi and herself to Agona Swedru, a market town about an hour and a half from Otuam, where Peggy's favorite little shop, Nadrass Enterprises, was located. She and her mother had shopped there, years earlier, when life was good because they were together. Out front colorful cloths on hangers flapped in the breeze, and you had to duck and push them aside to enter the shop, where you saw tables heaped with beads and sandals hanging from the walls. Nadrass Enterprises was a tiny place, but with so much merchandise you could spend hours sorting through it.

Peggy was looking forward to getting out of the stiflingly hot dining room, to spend an afternoon without visitors and disputes, with no thought of stolen building supplies or Kwame Lumpopo's scams. She would try on necklaces and bracelets, hold cloths up to her face to see if the colors were flattering, and slip her feet into sandals of silver and gold leather with multicolored pom-poms. She would actually allow herself to indulge in the fun and frivolity of shopping, instead of calling on every ounce of her strength to set things straight in Otuam. Yes, it was going to be a wonderful afternoon.

She leaned back in her seat and relaxed. As the taxi lurched over potholes, she chuckled as she saw quaintly named enterprises that would have provoked roars of laughter in Washington. There was the By the Grace of God Brake and Clutch Center, the Jesus Is Our Savior Beer and Wine Pub, and the Thanks Be to God Toilet Facilities. Ghanaians believed their businesses would have good luck if the owners put something religious in the name. Peggy and Nana Kwesi also passed a restaurant called the Forget Your Wife Chop House, which spoke for itself.

Up ahead there was a police checkpoint, a large wooden blockade painted with red and white stripes that could be loaded onto a truck and moved around. It was impossible in Ghana to drive any distance on the main roads without coming to one. Ostensibly the checkpoint was for officers to make sure that drivers had valid licenses, the car was properly registered, and the safety inspection was current. But in reality checkpoints were earning opportunities for the police, who didn't make much of a salary. Anyone who was lacking proper documentation could avoid a ticket by tipping the officer. Across Africa, many policemen made more money from the checkpoints than they did from their salaries. This kind of corruption helped balance the national budget by allowing the government to keep its employees' salaries low.

The taxi rolled to a halt. One of the officers, a brisk no-nonsense man wearing large black sunglasses and tight pants tucked into high black boots, asked Ebenezer to show his license. In the front passenger seat, Nana Kwesi leaned toward the officer, smiling. "This is the king of Otuam," he said, gesturing to the backseat, where Peggy was wearing the robe of a king. In Ghana the police routinely waved dignitaries through roadblocks and would never ask them for bribes. But this officer, evidently, was an exception. He had shot a look at the king of Otuam and noticed that she was a woman, and a woman certainly wasn't going to stop him from collecting his bribe.

The officer glanced at Ebenezer's license. "This has expired!" he said, waving it. "This is a very serious infraction."

"But it isn't—" said Ebenezer.

"Stop being rude! You should not contradict me," interrupted the officer. He took off his dark sunglasses and glowered at Ebenezer.

Sighing, Ebenezer opened his wallet and pulled out several colorful bills. But Peggy had had enough of this foolishness. She couldn't even do something as simple as going shopping without corrupt officials trying to steal money. She was *surrounded* by them, all men, of course, and she knew exactly what she was going to do. For a moment she summoned the dignity demanded of a king, then leaned forward and snatched the driver's license from the policeman's hand.

She peered at it. "Expiration date 2013!" she said grandly. "What is this nonsense? His license is not expired. You are trying to extort a bribe from him. I am the lady king of Otuam and I will not put up with this. I am going to tell the president of Ghana, who is a subject of mine from Otuam, about your thieving! What is your name? Show me your ID!"

The officer's jaw dropped. "I . . . I . . . I misread the expiration date on the driver's license," he sputtered. He stepped back and saluted her, motioning for Ebenezer to go, hoping Ebenezer would go.

Ebenezer put the car in gear, eager to leave. "Wait," Peggy said. She stuck her head and shoulders out the open window and glared at the officer, frowning her face like a frog. His knees seemed to buckle, but somehow he found the strength to make a quick, awkward bow before he scurried back to the other officers at the barrier.

"All right," she said, pulling herself back in and tapping Ebenezer on the shoulder. The car lurched forward.

"These men really have no idea who they're dealing with," Peggy declared. She had just about held her temper and was glad of it. Though she hadn't been able to see the policeman's eyes behind his dark sunglasses, she had seen a wave of fright pass over his face, and it made her feel she had used her kingship for good. Maybe he wouldn't be in such a hurry to squeeze money from the next hapless driver.

Nana Kwesi and Ebenezer were chuckling, but at first Peggy failed to see the humor in the situation. Corrupt officials hurt innocent people, hurt her beloved Ghana. She would like to line them all up in a

room—it would have to be a very big room—and give them a talking
to. She would then put them in the Otuam jail (though it would have
to be in shifts because the cell only held ten at a time), which would
make the chief inspector very happy what with all those tips. Except . . .
why did the chief inspector accept tips? She looked out the window and
scowled.

"You should have seen the look on his face," Nana Kwesi said, clutching his chest as he guffawed. "I thought the poor man was going to pee
in his pants." He put his hands over his eyes and wagged his head from
side to side.

Both hands gripping the steering wheel as he rolled into a pothole,
Ebenezer opened his mouth and guffawed. Even Peggy started to see the
humor in it, the bullying policeman ready to cringe at one word from
her, the frightening lady king of Otuam. The three of them laughed all
the way to Agona Swedru.

That other crook, Kwame Lumpopo, had at least immediately
returned Peggy's red royal umbrella, which she would need for her
gazetting. Its various pieces were now in a large canvas bag leaning
against the wall near the front door. But returning the red umbrella was
yet another blow to Kwame Lumpopo's fragile ego, and word of it, along
with word of the king's treatment of him outside the palace, spread like
wildfire. The next time he swaggered down Main Street in his spotless
white outfit and white straw hat, many people laughed at him.

"Kwame Lumpopo!" they cried. "How is your good friend, the king?
Why aren't you walking under the red royal umbrella?" Many of those
who made fun of him were the very women Kwame Lumpopo had
scammed.

To salvage what was left of his reputation, Kwame Lumpopo told
everyone who would listen that an evil spirit had entered Peggy to
make her hate him. *Him,* the one who had given her the good news
about becoming king. Such bad behavior, he said, couldn't be the king's
fault (and here he must have been thinking about her crying stool, who
wanted to kill him when he had talked so badly about her), therefore it
must be the fault of the evil spirit. He told this to the seamstress hammering away at her little sewing machine, and the man who sold beer

from a stand. He told it to the women selling fish from buckets on their heads, to the old men playing checkers under a tree, and to the four policemen lounging in front of the blue and white police station.

Peggy received several reports of Kwame Lumpopo's nonsense and just shook her head each time she heard it. It was well known that if an evil spirit entered you, it made you hateful to everyone, not just one particular person, the very person who had lied to you and stolen your money. Besides, she always wore a lot of eyeliner, which deflected evil spirits, and her own spirit was strong and just. Evil spirits only entered the bodies of the weak-minded, and it occurred to her that perhaps this had happened to Ekow. Peggy shook her head. Kwame Lumpopo, who cared so much about his image, was just making himself more and more ridiculous to everyone in town.

Bad behavior walks hand in hand with its own punishment, she thought.

The day before Peggy's gazetting, Cousin Comfort rolled up in front of Peggy's house in a car driven by her son from Tema. She was gorgeous in a royal blue gown and large matching head wrap. Though Peggy had enjoyed sleeping alone the two days before Ekow's arrival and after his departure, it had been against royal etiquette, and now she would have an attendant to watch over her. And this attendant—intelligent, pleasant, polite—would be a highly welcome change from crazy muttering Ekow. The timing of Cousin Comfort's arrival was especially helpful because Peggy wanted her opinion on how to stop the corruption as soon as her gazetting was over.

Cousin Comfort immediately settled back into her role as confidential advisor, pulling a chair over to Peggy's left side for the afternoon council meeting. The purpose of this particular meeting was to go over every detail of the gazetting one more time to make sure that no mistake would dishonor the stool or the ancestors.

The electricity had gone off about an hour earlier, and Peggy wondered how long Cousin Comfort's starched robes and head wrap edged with gold lace would stay crisp, how long her black wig would remain perfectly coiffed, how long her rouge would stay perched on her wide mahogany cheekbones before it slowly glided downward and landed somewhere between her jaw and her chin. It was because of the melting effect the heat had on makeup that Peggy rarely wore foundation or rouge; even her eyeliner had a tendency to slide, making her look like one of those sad Pierrot clowns.

As the elders discussed the ceremony before the council of chiefs, Peggy looked around the table at them, the sweat running down their cheeks in streams. It occurred to her that all of them were, in fact, human muffins in an oven, rising, swelling with the heat. At what point would the timer go off—*bing!*—and they would be taken out to cool down? Nighttime, perhaps. Or sooner, if the electricity came back on.

Suddenly Uncle Moses barked, "We will need five hundred dollars from you, Nana, to purchase the drinks for tomorrow's gazetting party."

Peggy's mouth dropped open. She had agreed to pay for the food and the goat and renting the van. She had assumed, therefore, that the council of elders would contribute the money for the drinks. Within this assumption was the belief that she was finally teaching them the respect due their king. Wrong, wrong, wrong. She had been so wrong.

"Give us the five hundred dollars now," Tsiami said, his weathered brown hand outstretched, as if he really expected her to reach into her bra and meekly hand the money over with a beatific smile.

"What!" Peggy cried in outrage. "You're kidding, of course. I paid for my airline ticket over here. I have been sending money from my measly salary as a secretary to renovate that decrepit royal palace. I alone have to pay for the expensive royal funeral of the late king who is in the fridge. And now I have to buy drinks for everybody, too?"

"We should find the money for you," said Baba Kobena quickly. "Nana is right."

"I agree," Uncle Eshun said. "Nana shouldn't have to buy everything herself. Just because she is American doesn't mean she is a multimillionaire."

"How dreadfully embarrassing that we don't have that kind of money," Isaiah the Treasurer said. "But, Nana, you must remember that Americans are, truly, much richer than we poor Africans are."

"Do what you want," Peggy replied, mustering as much dignity as possible, "but I am not buying any drinks for tomorrow. I have bought all the food, paid three hundred and fifty dollars to Nana Tufu for sponsoring me and seven hundred and fifty dollars to the council of chiefs as my enrollment fee. The elders can buy the drinks or you will all go thirsty. And what is a party where you can't all get rip-roaring drunk? I guess you will have a very boring time."

Muttering to one another, the elders left. Peggy put her head in her hands and shook it. She heard Aggie come in, open the fridge, pop the top off a beer, and plop it down in front of her. She put a hand around the beer just to feel its lovely coolness ripple through her fingers. She could be in her condo in Silver Spring, Maryland, right now, with air-conditioning, and a flush toilet, with a hot shower and television. Instead she was *here,* baking like a muffin, washing in a bucket, flinging water at a toilet, and fighting a battle with her temper that she was losing with distressing frequency.

At least I have someone to argue with, she thought, and the thought was so startling that she raised her head from her hands, wondering where it had come from. But it was true, wasn't it? Back in Silver Spring she had no one to talk with at all. During her sliver of spare time, she sat numbly on her sofa eating dinner on her lap, not watching the news. Was that kind of life better than living in a tangle of friends and family, punctuated by periodic arguments? Suddenly she didn't think so. It might sound like a good thing to have no arguments, but people inevitably brought arguments with them, and a life with no arguments meant a life with no people.

This astonishing conclusion was interrupted by Cousin Comfort, who said, "You did the right thing. They'll come back with the drinks because those men always find money when it comes to alcohol. They can't pitch in and dig a new borehole for the kids, or upgrade the health clinic, or buy some used computers for the schools. But they will always find the cash for whiskey and beer."

That made sense. Cousin Comfort always made sense. Still, Peggy sincerely hoped that self-control was like a muscle, and that as she exercised it, it would grow stronger. She did not enjoy shouting and behaving badly and longed to handle disagreements with regal aplomb. She pulled a handkerchief out of her bra and dabbed at her moist face. "I hope you're right. You know, I'm not sure if I can stand this heat a minute longer."

Suddenly the fan came back on with a grunt followed by a reassuring whir. The two women raised their faces to feel the air coming off the fan's blades.

Two hours later, the elders came back with the drinks.

16

Early the following morning, Uncle Moses brought the goat for the gazetting ceremony and tied it to a tree out front. He had ordered it specially for the ceremony from a goatherd who bred sacrificial goats. Otuam goats were tiny, short-legged creatures, some of them not much larger than the obese cats Peggy had seen in America. Their hair was short and bristly and their stumpy horns unimpressive. This goat was tall and well built, however, with a broad chest and large curling horns. His long golden brown hair had been washed and combed.

Peggy had eaten another anti-urination breakfast of boiled yams, palm oil, and hard-boiled egg. Afterward, Peggy's dresser, Grace, arrived to adorn her for her gazetting. Due to the extreme heat already rising so early in the morning, Grace and Peggy agreed that makeup and jewelry would wait until right before the ceremony.

While Grace was draping her in kente cloth, Peggy thought about the throng of relatives and Otuam citizens who would be attending the ceremony and subsequent party. Sadly, one very important person would not be there. Peggy had called William the week before and invited him to join them. But he had laughed and said, "What? With that big crowd? You know I'm shy with lots of people I don't know." She told him she understood and would try to visit him before she left Ghana.

Nana Kwesi's taxi rolled up, and he emerged fiddling in irritation with his red, white, and black checked cloth. He hated wearing traditional cloths and, unless required by a solemn ceremony such as today's, always wore black or khaki trousers and a short-sleeved shirt. When Peggy walked onto the porch to greet him, she saw him clumsily trying to wrap the material over his left shoulder but dropping it each time. Uncle Moses, adept at draping men's traditional robes, rushed to help him with it.

Peggy and her entourage crammed into the van, driven by Ebenezer, and the goat sat on the floor. They drove first to the royal palace and circled the large tree in the courtyard three times as Uncle Moses leaned out the window and blasted the cow horn to let the ancestors know that today was the day of Peggy's gazetting and ask for their support. Then they drove to Main Street, where taxis and vans carrying other relatives joined the caravan.

Essuehyia was a town much like Otuam, also on the coast, though the thick thatch of trees bordering the beach blocked the ocean breeze. There were concrete block dwellings and mud huts, and chickens and goats wandering the streets. The caravan pulled up outside the Hall of Chiefs, a large airy structure. The council of chiefs had instructed Peggy to be there at nine o'clock sharp, which would give her enough time to prepare for the ceremony, which was scheduled to begin at ten. She and her entourage were told to wait in the courtyard of a building adjoining the hall.

They sat in plastic chairs on the veranda, which shielded them from the sun but not from the heat. Grace Bentil put a wig on the Soul, black yarn with yellow stripes, and jabbed in golden ornaments that looked like ancient Egyptian lotus blossoms. This was a traditional wig for Souls, the yellow stripes representing gold, which in turn stood for innocence. Virgin brides, too, often wore the wigs at their weddings, as did queen mothers at official ceremonies, though Peggy's queen mother preferred a closely cropped hairdo, which was also acceptable. The Soul took her place on a little stool in front of Peggy to start deflecting evil spirits immediately.

Grace next adorned the king with long gold necklaces, bracelets, rings, and anklets. She gently placed a black velvet crown adorned with gold-painted wooden moons and stars on Peggy's head. This wasn't the real gold crown Peggy had worn at her enstoolment, but was much lighter and cooler. Then she ground myrrh and dabbed it on Peggy, the queen mother, and the Soul. Peggy asked Grace for eyeliner, which she applied heavily.

A member of the council of chiefs informed Peggy that another king was being gazetted first, so she and her entourage would have to wait a while. They waited. And waited. They simmered. Then they sweltered. Perspiration rolled down their faces and tickled their armpits. Their makeup, sweat, hair, and clothing melted into a sticky glue. Cousin Comfort's head wrap drooped, and below it the curls of her black wig unfolded. Even the queen mother, usually so cool and crisp in her flawless white robes and long gold necklaces, looked like a sadly wilted flower, a jonquil perhaps, its fragile springtime glory blasted by an early heat wave. Peggy took a swig from her water bottle and found that it was as hot as tea.

Finally, at one o'clock, the ceremony was ready to start. Though this was three hours later than the time Peggy had been given, no one in her entourage complained. In most of Africa time was an amorphous thing, hard to grab on to. Precise time was a fussy, Western concept, which the Europeans had brought with them in the form of sundials, clocks, watches, and church bells. Before their arrival, Africans had understood planting and harvesting time, the dry and rainy seasons, morning, afternoon, evening, and the days of the week. For thousands of years Africans had done quite well without a demanding system of hours and minutes, and its sudden imposition by colonizers had often been met with a shrug and a dismissive wave of the hand.

Now, decades after independence, ancient traditions remained strong. Even in modern offices in the capitals, even in the government ministries themselves, a fixed appointment was actually a vague suggestion to try to meet within two or three hours of the stated time. People expected to wait for hours, and they were especially happy to do so if there was air-conditioning and a magazine. With a wink and a nod, Africans generally explained to baffled Westerners this routine sliding of appointments as "African time."

African time was finally ready for Peggy's big moment, which made her happy, since there was no air-conditioning or magazine on the courtyard porch. Tsiami stood next to Peggy holding his *tsiamiti,* his speaking staff, which all *tsiamis* held during important public functions. On top were the symbols of Otuam—the turtle, the snail, and the gun.

Perhaps I should change those symbols, Peggy thought, *to a bottle of beer, a bottle of whiskey, and a wad of cash.*

Cousin Charles opened the giant red umbrella and held it high over Peggy. But it sagged in a way unlikely to impress the council of chiefs. Peggy's elders tried to fluff it up, but one of its ribs had broken where two long, thin metal pieces were held together by a clip.

Peggy took one look at her lopsided umbrella and huffed. *That's another two hundred dollars Kwame Lumpopo owes me.*

Cousin Charles gently placed the umbrella on the ground, rubbed his chin thoughtfully, and looked around. He snapped a long twig off a nearby tree and jammed it in the clip. Then he ripped a long, thick string hanging off the unhemmed edge of his cloth and tied the twig in place. He raised the umbrella and grunted in approval. African engineering at an African price.

Two younger men held the goat up by its front legs, forcing it to walk on its rear legs, though it balked and baaed angrily. Ahead of them, drummers banged their drums. The entourage walked down the path, entered the Hall of Chiefs, and took their seats in front of the wide platform where thirty kings and five queen mothers sat regally in traditional robes and ornaments. A hundred or so other observers sat in plastic chairs facing the platform. Uncle Moses tied the goat to a pillar on the platform.

Since Nana Tufu was officially sponsoring Peggy, his *tsiami,* little Papa Adama, had to make the introductory address. "The king of Otuam, Nana Amuah Afenyi V, having gone to his village, the elders and the ancestors selected his niece, Peggielene Bartels of the United States of America, to be the king," Papa Adama cried in ringing tones. "She is of greatly virtuous character, as strong as a lion, as patient as a turtle, as wise as an elephant, honest, compassionate, sober . . ."

When Papa Adama finished, Tsiami stood up and cried out, "Our new king, Nana Amuah Afenyi VI, was chosen according to custom with no dispute among the family or witnesses." He walked to the stage and handed over a bottle of the best whiskey and an envelope of money and gestured to the goat. "To show our gratitude to the council of chiefs, we have brought you these gifts."

Both *tsiamis,* as a sign of respect when addressing such an honorable group, wore their cloths around the waist, like a bath towel, exposing the entire chest and shoulders.

Sitting on a thronelike chair in the front of the platform, the president of the council was a handsome man of indeterminate age, lithe muscles, and astonishingly glorious bone structure.

"The candidate will address the council of chiefs," he said in a ringing voice.

Peggy stood and, adjusting her cloth over her left arm, gave a slow and regal smile in return. During those long months in Washington, she had had plenty of time to practice her speech and her intonation—loud enough for all in the large room to hear without straining her voice, full-bodied with confidence and pleasantly courteous.

"It is a great and unexpected honor that I have become a Ghanaian king," she said slowly, for kings should never rush. "I, a woman, the first woman of our family to ever become king. I vowed at my enstoolment, and I make this vow again to you now, to devote myself to the prosperity of my people. I have come all the way from America to be gazetted, and I will use everything I have learned in my thirty years there to rule wisely, with compassion and justice, and to spare no effort in helping Otuam. I thank the council of chiefs for this great honor of my gazetting. Thank you, and may God and your ancestors bless you all."

The president gestured for Peggy and her entourage to walk toward the door through which they had entered. On the side of the door there was something bright red and sticky on the floor. It looked too red to be blood, almost fluorescent. But it was indeed blood, the blood of the goat sacrificed for the king before Peggy. The sacrifice of a goat kept the ancestors happy all day, so Peggy's goat would be spared for now, perhaps used for breeding, or sacrificed for another ceremony. The *tsiamis* chanted and poured an entire bottle of schnapps to the side of the red stuff.

They smeared the schnapps on Peggy's forehead and neck. Suddenly ecstatic, she smiled and nodded in acknowledgment of the pivotal moment of the gazetting ceremony. Now she had real power to rein in the corruption of Otuam. Now, no matter how much her elders complained, they couldn't stop her. Though it had been almost exactly a year since her enstoolment, this was her first moment of complete power, and she was flush with the exciting knowledge of all she could achieve— water, education, medical care, prosperity—for the citizens of Otuam.

Thank you, God, thank you, she said silently. *I promise I won't let you down.*

They went back to their seats. The president of the council congratulated her on joining their hallowed ranks and offered advice on how to be a good king. He enumerated the virtues of a wise ruler on one hand: The thumb represented Peace, the first and foremost virtue of kings. The forefinger stood for Truth, for a king must never tell a lie. The third finger symbolized Carefulness, as a king must take time to make decisions and never act in a hurry. The ring finger stood for Fear of God, which was shown by helping needy people. Listening to these virtues, Peggy thought proudly, *I exemplify all of them.* And then he got to the pinky finger. This one, he said, represented the need for the king to forgive and forget all the wrongs done to her. Peggy almost choked on that one. *Oh,* she thought. *I suppose four out of five isn't bad.*

There were a few more speeches as Tsiami and Papa Adama honored the council of chiefs for its virtue and wisdom, and the council of chiefs honored Tsiami, Papa Adama, Nana Tufu, and Peggy for their virtue and wisdom, and then it was over. Peggy was directed into a tiny office on the side of the council chamber to fill out the official paperwork. She sat down at a small desk and wrote her name, address, date of birth, the name of her kingdom, how she came by the throne (through the death of her uncle), and the date of her enstoolment (September 27, 2008).

Then she came to a line that read *King's Occupation.* She looked up and saw a list on the wall of all the current members of the Essuehyia Council of Chiefs, and by each name was either *Fisherman* or *Farmer.* Many of them, she knew, had been government employees when called to their thrones and, having moved to their villages, managed farms or fishing canoes as a means of support. But there were no secretaries on the list. With a proud little flourish, she wrote *Secretary.*

Although it was the beginning of the dry season, when the Otuam entourage left the Hall of Chiefs they saw towering black thunderclouds rolling toward them. A stiff wind was blowing dozens of little empty plastic water bags up and down in the dust. The trees were thrashing violently, bending at the waist, their long branches sweeping the ground like village women tidying their yards. Peggy's elders closed her huge royal umbrella with difficulty as the first fat drops of rain plopped down. Everyone ran to their cars, Cousin Comfort grabbing her head wrap so it wouldn't blow off.

Peggy, Cousin Comfort, and the elders crammed into the van. As they bounced over the dirt roads, it began to pour. They passed villages where naked children were dancing in the downpour, hopping up and down, swinging their arms and rolling their heads, delighted to feel beautiful cool rain on hot and dusty skin. Their parents were quickly putting out buckets and pans to collect the precious drops.

A lively song was playing on the radio, heavenly African voices singing happily as Peggy and her elders bounced over the potholes, keeping close rhythm to the beat. Ebenezer swerved around the largest ones the size of bathtubs, brimming with water now, bright red from the coppery soil.

The rain tapered off as the caravan approached Otuam. They were on Main Street when Tsiami barked, "Stop the van and let me get out here. I want to see a girlfriend in town to have a quickie."

Sitting between Peggy and the driver in the front seat, Cousin Comfort put her face in her hands and clucked. Peggy's mouth dropped open: Tsiami was seventy-seven. In the United States, some men in their forties had to use Viagra because all the stress and preservatives had turned their private parts to mashed potatoes. But in Otuam, eighty-year-olds walked around with an eternal hard-on. Peggy thought it was the food they ate—fresh fish, fresh vegetables, and fresh fruit with no chemicals—and they were always walking miles and miles every day because they had no cars, or were hauling in heavy nets of fish, or working in the fields. These fit and healthy penises were aided and abetted by tiger nuts, which Tsiami must have been eating quite regularly.

She replied, "Tsiami, you are so old, this is ridiculous. And it hasn't stopped raining. Get back in the van." But he was already halfway out the door, clutching his robes so he wouldn't trip.

"I know those girlfriends of yours are young," she called out the open window, "and they don't do it with an old man for free. It is well known that your pineapple fields don't generate enough for you to pay for all those young women." Tsiami closed the door, turned around, and grinned at her like a naughty boy.

Peggy found his sly smile upsetting. Instead of helping the children, her town's funds had gone to pay for foolish things like this—a few minutes of selfish pleasure with an immoral woman. Here was the very essence of Otuam's problems, staring her in the face with an impish grin. She suddenly felt a crude thing percolating deep down in the place where crude things originated and rising rapidly up her throat. Conscious of the honor so recently accorded her by the council of kings, feeling the weight of the crown on her head, she found the restraint to tone down a bit what she wanted to say.

"If it's your own money you're using, I don't care," she said, shaking her finger at him out the window. "But if you are using the town money to have sex with girls, taking water away from Otuam's children, taking medicine away from the clinic, I will make sure your balls shrivel up to nothing. You know how I'm going to do it? I am going to lock up those fishing fees so you can't get your hands on them anymore, and without them, those girls won't give you the time of day."

All the other elders in the van laughed, and Tsiami laughed, too. But Peggy could tell by the look in his eyes that he was worried. He had been stealing a lot of money, and as soon as she locked up the money, his penis would be dead, despite all the fresh fish in the world. He knew it, and Peggy knew it, and all the elders in her royal council who had probably been doing the same thing knew it, and they were rightly scared that Peggy would force their penises into early retirement.

After dropping Tsiami off on Main Street for his quickie, the van reached the royal palace and swooped around the ancient tree again. Uncle Moses tooted the cow horn out the window to let the ancestors know that the gazetting had been a decided success. Their king had been accepted into the council of chiefs.

They pulled up in front of the house and dashed inside. Peggy had had a local woman cater fifty carryout dinners of rice, chicken, and steamed vegetables in white Styrofoam clamshells, which she had neatly tucked into plastic bags with a paper napkin and plastic fork. Aggie gave these out as visitors arrived, though some turned around to take them home. Most stayed, however, sitting on chairs and benches, drinking beer and minerals, and enjoying a rare dish of juicy, meaty chicken. Otuam chickens were used mostly for laying eggs. Their meat was stringy and dry. But this chicken had been imported from the eastern shore of Maryland, in the United States and was sold in modern grocery stores in Ghana's large cities.

Tsiami ambled in about a half hour later, looking refreshed. It had, indeed, been a quickie. He sat down at the table and poured himself a glass of whiskey, which he downed quickly. But his left hand stayed firmly attached to the bottle, a thin, dried brown claw that warned off any intruders. Peggy cocked an eyebrow. *Tell me,* she said to herself, *that he is not planning on drinking that entire bottle by himself.*

Uncle Moses started to reach for the bottle, but something about Tsiami's possessive grip made him change his mind. He pulled a new bottle out of the crates next to the fridge. Pouring himself a drink, he said to Peggy, "Several of those kings at the Hall of Chiefs said you were very beautiful."

She smiled. Despite the heat, she had felt truly beautiful at the ceremony, lush and strong, in the prime of her life, being honored by kings.

"Although when you first walked into the hall under the umbrella they didn't know if you were a man or a woman," Tsiami chimed in shrilly, pouring himself another drink. "They thought you were probably a man."

If this had been intended as an insult, it didn't bother Peggy. The whole world could think she was a male king, for all she cared. Maybe it would be better that way.

"But when they found out you were a woman, Nana, they said you were beautiful," Isaiah the Treasurer added. "And they said you spoke very well, as indeed you should, being an American."

Little did they know that most Americans didn't speak nearly as well as most Africans.

"They also said they were afraid you were going to fall in love with some man who would take your power away from you and rule for you," Baba Kobena added. Everyone burst out laughing at that.

"Not very likely," Peggy said, chuckling, too, at the image of her meekly handing over her royal power to some ridiculous man. But then a stab of pain sliced through her mirth as she thought of William, who wasn't here to share with her such an important day.

Another man who stayed away from Peggy's gazetting party was Kwame Lumpopo, a sensible decision on his part. Yet he haunted her even there. Several relatives came up to congratulate Peggy on her gazetting and express their concern about her rift with the man who had told her she was king. *Had she divorced him?* they asked.

In Ghana, if the head of a family divorced a family member, it meant no one in the family could ever treat him as a relative again. He would no longer benefit from any family ties, nor would he be invited to family meetings. Being divorced from your family was the worst thing that could happen to a Ghanaian. He became an outcast, an orphan alone on the earth without hundreds of outstretched arms to embrace him.

Nor was such a thing undertaken lightly. The head of the family would call the family elders for discussions, and if they were agreed, the matter would proceed to a trial, where the person to be divorced would be given a chance to defend himself, with witnesses and supporters permitted to testify in his behalf.

"We have not divorced him," Peggy said, and her listeners sighed with relief. "He is still a family member and can attend family meetings. But I have cast him out of my council. He stole a lot of my money and I won't forgive him for that, family member or not."

"You must forgive him!" cried an older cousin of Peggy's whose name she had forgotten. "Families must always resolve their disputes."

But the man's wife shook her head in disagreement. "Nana is right," she said. "He is dishonest and doesn't belong on the council. You men always expect forgiveness for your crimes and get very upset when it doesn't come."

Another woman agreed. "Times are changing. We don't want thieves on the council stealing the town's money." The older man flinched. *Good,* Peggy thought, *the women will be fully behind me on the changes I want to enact.*

By this point 120-pound Tsiami had drunk the better part of the whiskey bottle. He sat in his chair, swaying slightly, eyes almost closed, hand still glued to his glass. Then, as the noble Nana Tufu was discoursing on some aspect of Otuam's history, Tsiami stood up and cried at the top of his lungs for no apparent reason, "Be quiet, Nana Tufu! It is time for you to go home!"

Uncle Moses was furious. "How dare you tell Nana Tufu to be quiet and go home!" he thundered, slamming his whiskey glass down on the table. "When it is time for him to go home, *his tsiami* will tell him. It is not your place to tell him."

Everyone looked at Nana Tufu's *tsiami,* who was swaying slightly from side to side as he stared deep into his empty whiskey glass. Papa Adama didn't seem to be in a condition to tell anybody anything. He opened his mouth as if to speak but belched instead.

But Peggy's *tsiami* was in fighting mode. "You can't tell me what to do, Uncle Moses!" he cried in his ringing *tsiami* voice. "I am *tsiami* of this family."

"I can tell you when your behavior is impolite! I can tell you that!" Uncle Moses replied, banging his hand on the table.

Suddenly everyone was yelling at once, a great chorus of voices, male and female, young and old, arguing or crying *Ah-go* for permission to be heard. Throughout it all, Nana Tufu sat with quiet dignity, pretending nothing untoward was happening as the room descended into chaos around him. Nana Kwesi, sipping his Coke and sober as a judge, finally burst out laughing at all the drunks.

Peggy, too, was amused by the scene, and a smile twitched on her lips. Finally, she put a stop to it. "I am king," she said loudly, and the cacophony quieted. "And I will tell people to be quiet or go home, and no one else will tell them. Enough of this argument. Tsiami, sit down and be quiet. Perhaps it is time for *you* to go home."

Tsiami sat down, his face puckered with irritation. He nursed the remains of his whiskey. The party resumed its cheerful nature. Finally, Tsiami stood up to go but was having difficulty turning around to face the door. Once he managed that, he couldn't seem to put one foot in front of the other. Cousin Charles put his strong arms around him and guided him toward the door. But then Tsiami collapsed entirely, so Cousin Charles had to pick him up like a baby and carry him the rest of the way home in his arms. Tsiami's head, eyes closed and mouth open, rested on Cousin Charles's right shoulder, and his skinny legs hung over his left elbow, flapping up and down with every step.

When it came time for Nana Tufu to leave, his *tsiami* had to be carried to the car by his driver and one of his elders, one holding up Papa Adama's shoulders, the other his feet. Nana Tufu politely pretended not to notice as he swept his own tall form into the front passenger seat of the silver SUV and adjusted his elegant robes around him while Papa Adama was loaded into the backseat like a box.

A relative later told Peggy that Nana Tufu, despite his dignified appearance, had been as drunk as anybody. He had passed out in his throne room with his robes and shoes on and slept on the concrete floor, his face mashed against his royal beads, which left marks for most of the following day. Papa Adama hadn't even made it inside the house; he had collapsed just outside and slept snoring loudly on the patio.

It had been, everyone later agreed, a wonderful gazetting party.

17

The following morning, as the sun was rising, Cousin Charles walked through the bush to Main Street to take a cab to the highway, where he would board the early morning *tro-tro* back to Cape Coast and his job grinding lenses at the optician's. But Cousin Comfort remained, much to Peggy's delight. They had lain in bed most of the early morning hours laughing at how poorly the men had behaved at the gazetting party. None of the women, they agreed, had had to be carried out unconscious.

Now that the gazetting was over, Peggy wondered if she should make plans to visit William. But for the next few days, at least, there were other things to do. One of them was to attend the grand opening of the Rural Agricultural Development Bank, Otuam branch, located in a modern building at the top of Main Street. There, as musicians played, Peggy opened the first account, and Nana Tufu opened the second one. The citizens of Otuam, delighted that a bank had finally opened, pulled wads of cash from under their mattresses and out of holes in the floor and opened their own accounts. Then they danced with joy in the street.

After the bank opening, Peggy's next order of business was asking the chief fishmongers to identify in person the elders who had been collecting the fees so there could be no denying their crimes, and then to force the thieves to confess. She sent word to the four fishing bosses and her elders to attend a mandatory meeting the following morning at six.

The subject: whether any fishing fees had been paid, and if so, to whom. Nana Kwesi volunteered to come to Otuam extra early for the meeting, but Peggy didn't think his presence was a good idea. Some of her elders were already irritated by the young outsider, favored by their lady king, and they might prove more defensive with him there.

But plans were afoot to ensure that *no* elders would attend. While Peggy was eating her fried fish that evening, Baba Kobena called her and said Uncle Moses had instructed all the elders to miss the meeting and play checkers with him under the tree in front of Mr. Yorke's International School, a well-traveled path where many could see their blatant disrespect of their unreasonable king. Peggy, in turn, let all her elders know that anyone who didn't show up for the meeting would find a taxi in front of his house, stuffed with four bored police officers just itching to cart him off to jail.

As the sun rose, the four fishing bosses, three men and a woman, dutifully marched into the house and sat on benches at the far end of the dining room table. Tsiami showed up, sliding wordlessly into his chair on Peggy's right side without looking at Peggy or Cousin Comfort, then sagging unhappily and pouting his lips. He wore the incongruous combination of a traditional robe and a Syracuse University baseball cap, navy blue with orange letters, which he slapped disconsolately onto the table.

A few minutes later, Uncle Moses bustled in the door wearing his neatly pressed brown security guard uniform, evidently on his way to lie under the popo tree and guard the cell phone wire. No sooner had the screen slammed shut than he puffed up his cheeks walrus style and asked angrily, "What is this about? Such a summons! What an insult! Such disrespect!"

At his side was Isaiah the Treasurer, who laid a calming hand on Uncle Moses's arm and said, "Moses, we must listen to what our gracious king has to say before we start any argument. Surely it must be of the utmost significance—"

"Sit down and be quiet," Peggy commanded, and they did.

As Aggie served the visitors water and minerals, her spatula tucked under her arm like a weapon at the ready, she was grinning broadly. "What a lovely day it is," she said to Uncle Moses as she plunked his Coke down so hard it spilled a bit. He shot her a withering glance as she sashayed back into the kitchen, swinging her broad hips in an exaggerated fashion.

Baba Kobena arrived, wearing a long black robe and wide-brimmed black hat, mourning attire for his colleagues, Peggy thought, and Uncle Eshun shuffled in behind him. Both Baba and Eshun looked nervous, but Isaiah the Treasurer seemed not to have a care in the world, complimenting Peggy on the effect of her bright blue cloth on her complexion. She realized that he reminded her of that gold butler robot in *Star Wars*, C-3PO. She never could stand that obsequious character. As Aggie brought more drinks, Uncle Moses grumbled to himself, and Tsiami, typically, ignored everybody while studying the rips in the pale pink plastic tablecloth.

"As you know," Peggy said briskly, turning to the four fishing bosses at the end of the table, "you fish in the king's waters. Your fishermen live on the king's land. And you keep your canoes on the king's beaches. You owe the stool regular fees based on how many fish you bring in. If you refuse to pay these fees, I can kick you out of town and bring in fishermen who will pay them. If you have not paid them, tell me how much you owe and we can make payment arrangements. If you have paid them, tell me whom you paid them to."

The four fishing bosses looked uneasily at the elders and then at one another. It was the woman who stood up first. At forty-seven, Dzadi Yatu, known as Daavi, was Otuam's most successful businessperson, even though she had been born an Ewe, in Eweland, in the eastern coastal area of Ghana. Ewes were known as the best fishermen in Africa, and many left their tribal area to start fishing businesses far from home.

Daavi had come to Otuam at the age of eighteen, a bride with a baby in tow. For many years now she had lived independently of her husband, who ran his own fishing enterprise on Lake Volta. She owned two enormous canoes and employed a total of forty-six people. She sold her fish, fresh and smoked, in Accra, Cape Coast, Mankessim, and Kumasi.

Despite her shrewd business sense, Daavi was known for her kind heart. She readily loaned money to those who needed it to pay a doctor or hold a funeral and allowed the borrowers or their family members to work the loan off by cleaning and selling fish. Everyone in Otuam looked up to Daavi, and many girls wanted to grow up to be just like her. Yet even though Daavi was a decided success and a whiz with numbers, she was illiterate. She had had her name tattooed in huge letters on her left forearm so if anyone asked her how to spell it, she could just show them her arm.

As Otuam's wealthiest entrepreneur, Daavi had a certain image to uphold. Today she was dressed in a beautiful pale green linen gown with puffed sleeves edged with gold lace and a matching head wrap. She wore high-heeled gold sandals and real gold jewelry. Her hair was relaxed into large, neat curls that fell below her bulbous head wrap. A bit on the plump side, she was, nonetheless, a very pretty woman. Men chased her, but she had no time to flirt, and besides, if she chose a boyfriend he would probably just want to move in on her business and steal her fish. Looking at her, Peggy recognized a kindred spirit: a woman who was honest, strong, and smart.

"I owe fees from this season," Daavi said, pushing wads of bills across the table to Peggy. "There is three and a half million cedis." That was about $250. "I was saving it to give to you personally, Nana, because I know what is going on. Your elder Uncle Moses has been going through the fishing village collecting fees with Tsiami at his side. After the old king's death last year, I paid Uncle Moses and Tsiami three and a half million cedis."

Uncle Moses stood up and cried, "You did not! That woman is lying!"

"You know I paid you that money!" Daavi cried. "You are like a fish caught in a net, ready to do anything to escape, including telling a lie!"

"That's ridiculous!" Uncle Moses replied. "When was the last time you heard a fish tell a lie?"

"I don't know whether fish tell lies or not, Uncle Moses, but I'm fairly certain you do," Peggy said.

"What about Tsiami?" Uncle Moses asked, pointing at the figure slouched so low in his chair that his chin was almost level with the table. It was as if Tsiami hoped to slip under the table completely, and that way no one would yell at him. "Why don't you ask him? Daavi mentioned Tsiami, too, not just me. It's not fair for you to pin all the blame on me."

Peggy studied her priest, who seemed to be sliding farther under the table. "Tsiami," she commanded, "sit up!" Grunting, he pushed himself up. "Did you take those fishing fees?"

Tsiami shrugged his skinny shoulders and looked straight ahead. "You know," he said, "I'm so old, I actually can't remember."

"You remember every day to come down to the beach and collect them!" Daavi cried. "Your memory can't be all that bad!" Standing in the doorway of the kitchen, Aggie burst out laughing.

"Stop insulting me, all of you!" Tsiami replied, sitting bolt upright and slapping the table. "It is disrespectful of the ancestors to insult a *tsiami*."

"Disrespectful of the ancestors?" Peggy asked. That was a good one. "My chief priest, who holds the ancestral libations in one hand and steals money from the town with the other! *You* have shown disrespect to the ancestors."

Tsiami shrank back into his chair. "Well, what about Uncle Moses sitting here? He's worse than any of us. Why are you picking on me?"

"Oh, everyone will have his turn, don't worry. Now, Tsiami," Peggy asked, with sweetness in her voice, "do you think you can cheat me because I am a woman? Like you cheated the dead king in the fridge because he was old?"

Tsiami was wounded. "Why are you doing this?" he said petulantly. "You are trying to scrutinize our asses."

"That's right!" Peggy smiled and said with relish, "Big, small, medium-sized, short, and tall asses, I will scrutinize them all! I will stick my head up there with a flashlight! Be prepared!"

Tsiami knew better than to say anything to that. As Peggy spoke with the other three fishing bosses, he sat rigidly in his chair, looking straight ahead, like an ancient mahogany sculpture of a pharaoh, his cloth draped over his left shoulder. Odd, Peggy thought, as she cast a glance in his direction, how absolutely motionless the man could sit and then leap up and stride across the room in a heartbeat while her other elders were still trying to rise from their seats, dealing with aching joints and old bones.

All of the other three fishing bosses said that they, too, had given money to Tsiami, Uncle Moses, and Isaiah the Treasurer, as well as free fish every afternoon when the canoes came in. Peggy clucked in disapproval. "You mean my royal elders wait down at the beach with bowls in their hands begging for free fish?" The bosses nodded solemnly. "That is very undignified," Peggy said.

She turned to Isaiah. "Well," she said, "what do you have to say to the fishermen? Do you, too, accuse them of lying?"

"Nana," Isaiah said smoothly, "I would never call anyone a liar, which is a dreadfully unkind word, after all. But you must realize that if these fishermen want to get out of paying you last year's fees, all they have to say is that they have already paid them and point out some innocent scapegoat as the person accused of taking them. Yes, these fishermen certainly have good reason to accuse us. Perhaps they are the fish looking for the hole in the net."

At this accusation, Daavi and the three fishermen stood up and started yelling and shaking their fists. Peggy interrupted. "Quiet! Now I want to ask the fishmongers if they ever gave fees to Uncle Eshun, sitting there with the cane, or Baba Kobena over here in the black hat."

Baba Kobena and Eshun raised calm eyes to the fishmongers, all of whom shook their heads. "Never," said Daavi. "Neither of them has ever taken fees. The one in the hat buys fish from us sometimes, and the one with the cane used to, before his stroke."

"Very well," Peggy said. "I want to thank you all for leaving your canoes to meet with me this morning. You have been very helpful. Now you may return to work. I wish to speak to my council alone."

The fishmongers seemed relieved to be dismissed and hurried away from the byzantine accusations of the royal council down to the fresh salt air of the beach where the waves, wind, and fish never lied.

Peggy looked at her council and turned solemn. "So the three of you have been stealing from me, and from the seven thousand people of this town. You may think it's just a little here and a little there, but that money, over time, could have provided this town with a certain measure of prosperity. You've been stealing from the kids and making them walk for hours before school with buckets of water on their heads. You've been keeping illiterate those children whose parents can't afford their school fees. You've been stealing from the medical clinic, which needs a doctor, a dentist, and an ambulance. As a result, people have died—women in a difficult labor and those having heart attacks and strokes. You are, in a way, murderers."

Tsiami put his elbows on the table, propped his chin in his hands, and promptly shut his eyes. Was he actually falling asleep right in front of her?

Peggy shook her head and continued, "I have news for you. This corrupt system is going to change!" She banged both fists on the table so hard that their drinks rattled, but Tsiami still didn't open his eyes.

"Change has come to America, and I have come from America to bring change to Otuam! I am the Obama of this place!"

"You have lived in the U.S. so long that you have become a white woman," Uncle Moses scoffed.

"Uncle Moses, I *am* a white woman," Peggy rejoined crisply, knowing that when he used the term *white* he meant Western, sophisticated, educated, all those things that white people were supposed to be. Yet he had meant it as an insult: a daughter of Ghana, a child of Africa, she had forgotten the traditions of her birthplace and adopted new, foreign customs. "And I am also a man and a king. Never forget that."

She had them there, cornered. There would be no cleansing of the old, corrupt ways until they had made a clean breast of it, endured the shame of a confession. Peggy said, "I must insist that everyone who has taken any fishing fees tell me the truth about it. If people confess their crimes, I may be merciful. But if I they don't, I will squeeze their balls so hard their eyes will pop out!" There, she had said it, the most shocking of all the speeches she had practiced in front of the bathroom mirror in Silver Spring. How would her elders react? Would they be surprised? Frightened?

The men broke out into guffaws of laughter, some of them slapping their knees, others hitting the table. Tsiami suddenly opened his eyes and brayed out a loud yawn. He looked around questioningly and asked, "What did she say this time about balls?" and the others threw back their heads and roared.

Their laughter exasperated Peggy. Clearly, her speech had not had the desired effect. She would try another tack. "I will put you all in jail if you don't confess," she said. "My forgiveness depends on your confessions. I will send Aggie to the police station to bring the chief inspector here now if the guilty ones don't confess."

"All right," Uncle Moses said quickly.

Peggy inclined her head and let a long, cruel silence hang in the air as she waited for their confessions. She could wait all day, while her elders squirmed under the crushing weight of it. Beating them up with her bluster had turned out to be a failed strategy that just made them laugh. This silence was more brutal than any words could be, perhaps because there was usually more truth in silence than in words.

Finally, Tsiami said, "We did take that fishing money. All three of us."

"We're afraid you're going to put us in jail," Isaiah the Treasurer said miserably. "We know you have the right to do so, dear Nana, but we are too old to go to jail. We will die there. And we will lose our honor and our good names forever."

Maybe you should have thought of your honor and your good names before you stole the town's money, Peggy thought.

"We simply can't pay you back," said Uncle Moses. "I don't see how we can at our age, without full-time work, and we took so much." The irony was not lost on Peggy that Uncle Moses was confessing to theft while wearing his security guard uniform.

Finally, she spoke. "What did you do with the money?" she asked quietly.

"We spent it on women and liquor," replied Tsiami. Cousin Comfort shrieked and stuffed her napkin into her mouth, while Aggie cried, "Ah-henh!"

At last the truth comes out, Peggy thought. She studied the three elders. Their faces were tense. They knew that at any minute the chief inspector could pick them up in a taxi and throw them in the pitch-black cell where they would sit on the concrete floor crying until Peggy let them out. Yes, as the personification of justice in her town, she would have liked to put them there, punish them for their years of selfish misdeeds. But would it truly be the best thing for Otuam? Their large extended families, she knew, would get involved, claiming innocence, begging for mercy, pulling their friends into the fray. Wouldn't it just keep the town mired in the past, swirling in a maelstrom of accusations and denials, for months if not years into the future?

After all the cruelties committed by both blacks and whites during the years of apartheid in South Africa, Archbishop Desmond Tutu had initiated the Truth and Reconciliation Commission. Those who admitted their crimes, even murder, would find forgiveness. South Africa found it was the best way to bury a disgraceful past and march boldly into a new and promising future.

Perhaps the best thing would be to let the past go. She would pardon them for all fishing fee thefts committed up until that day. A king, especially a female American one, should be above petty retaliation, should think of the greater good of the community instead of her own thirst for punishment. She thought of the fifth virtue of a wise ruler, forgiveness.

"Hmm," Peggy said. "I am glad that you have confessed to me. I will forgive you. I will not make you pay the money back. But be advised, from now on if I get wind of a single cedi going missing, going into your pockets, you will rot in jail. There will be no second forgiveness."

The three of them broke into wide grins. "We are going to be making a lot of changes to the structure of this council and the collection of town fees," she said. "But let me say one thing: your days of theft and corruption are over."

Eager to return to his pineapple fields, Tsiami slapped his Syracuse University baseball cap on his head, stood up, and raced out the door. The others ambled slowly out of the house into the awakening day. The screen door—*slap*—and the gate—*bang*—slammed hard behind them.

"Women and liquor," Cousin Comfort said, after the last elder had departed.

"What else would you expect?" Aggie asked as she collected the empty glasses on her tray. *"Men."*

Peggy leaned back in her chair, exhausted but triumphant. In the global scheme of things, it was a small victory. It wasn't a cure for cancer, or the solution to the Israeli-Palestinian problem, or free democratic elections in Iran. But the lady king of Otuam had convinced three corrupt elders to confess their crimes, and that was surely something, the death knell of the old ways. She felt something fluttering within her, rising, ready to soar. Was it hope?

She picked up her cell phone and called Nana Kwesi. After much discussion, they decided on measures to collect the fishing fees. Every day Daavi, whose reputation was above reproach, would examine the catch as the boats came in, write down how many baskets had been caught, collect the tax, and give it to Nana Kwesi, along with her records, every week or two when he visited Otuam. Nana Kwesi would deposit the fees in the Nana Amuah Afenyi VI royal account of the Rural Agricultural Development Bank where they would stay cedis, rather than magically transforming themselves into bottles of Johnnie Walker Red.

18

Peggy's next task was to tackle the land sales. This, she knew, would be a far thornier issue than the fishing fees because it involved much more money and was a far more emotional subject. It concerned farms, livelihoods, and houses people had built with their own hands.

Though she had repeatedly asked her elders about the sale of stool lands, none admitted to knowing anything about it. And no one admitted to ever having seen a land records book.

"Even if you won't give me the book, I can still find out who bought land," she said at one loud council meeting. "Tsiami, tell the town crier to walk throughout Otuam and cry the message that anyone who bought any land in Otuam since five years before my uncle went to the village for good must bring me the receipts or they will lose their land. And he should also cry that no new land sales will be valid unless Nana Kwesi or I sign them and accept the money. Go now." Tsiami resignedly stood up and slouched out the door.

"Why five years before?" Isaiah the Treasurer asked, shifting uncomfortably.

"Because I have a bad feeling that when he was very ill you people took advantage of him and signed your names to land sales receipts. So I will take a careful look at all receipts that my people bring me."

Within half an hour a tall, muscular man came by holding what looked to be part of a rusty muffler, which he banged loudly with a stick. Kwame Aidoo belonged to a family known for having the loudest voices in Otuam, which is why for centuries they had been the town criers. They were fishermen, and the elders had to catch one of them down at the beach before or after their fishing forays and pay them in advance for several hours of loud crying.

As Kwame Aidoo banged his muffler, people came out of their houses and stood silently, watching him curiously. "People of Otuam!" he bellowed in a ringing voice. "King Nana Amuah Afenyi VI has decreed that anyone knowing anything about the sale of Otuam land since five years before the late king in the fridge went to the village for good must come forward and tell her about it. Tell this to all your family members and friends. All those who have sold land, or bought land, or know of any such transactions must come forward and tell the king! They must bring her their contracts and receipts! If they do not, she will confiscate their land! All new land sales must have the signature of Nana or Nana Kwesi, or they will not be valid!"

Kwame Aidoo then walked down to the next group of houses. He walked up and down Main Street twice, and then farther into the bush so everyone would hear him, or hear from their friends what he had cried.

Throughout the day, men and woman trudged up to the Other Cousin Comfort's house, receipts for land purchases in hand. Peggy carefully looked at each one, thanked the buyer, and tucked it into her notebook. Toward evening, as she and Nana Kwesi drank Cokes, they went over them.

"These don't have sales dates," she said, sighing heavily, leafing through a stack.

"These don't have the name of the person representing the stool who received the money," he said, knitting his eyebrows together.

Peggy shuffled her receipts and said, "This one is dated two years ago, when the late king was still alive, but Uncle Moses and Isaiah the Treasurer signed it, not Uncle Joseph."

"This one, too," Nana Kwesi said, plucking one from his pile.

Peggy rummaged through another stack. "These five all seem to be for the same piece of land, sold to five different people. Isaiah the Treasurer received the money."

"Yes," Nana Kwesi agreed, looking through his stack. "I have four of those, too."

"Now we know where he got the money to buy his three taxis." Peggy pushed all her receipts into a heap, rubbed her tired eyes, and said, "Most of these receipts seem to be illegal. I think it will take time to sort this out."

Nana Kwesi nodded.

Peggy was particularly disturbed by the receipts issued while Uncle Joseph had still been alive. Many of them, for several acres each, had been signed by Uncle Moses and Isaiah the Treasurer. At the next council meeting, she held these receipts in the air.

"Why did the late king in the fridge not sign these?" she asked. "Why did you sign them?"

"The late king was going to the village for a cure," Uncle Moses replied tartly. "He asked us to sign for him."

"What happened to the money?"

"We gave it to the late king."

"The one who needed me to send him money for medicine?"

Uncle Moses shifted uncomfortably. "Why are you blaming Isaiah and me? Tsiami also sold land when the late king was ill. You should question him!"

"I needed that money for a hernia operation!" Tsiami countered. "What about Isaiah the Treasurer!"

"You've had *three* hernia operations!" Uncle Moses cried. "And no scars! Quite a doctor you have!"

Suddenly the three corrupt elders were shouting and pointing fingers at one another. They were standing, yelling at the top of their lungs, slapping the table, and making all kinds of accusations.

"You stole the money that farmer gave you for the land near the road—"

"Yes, but I gave half to you so you could get that fancy cell phone—"

"No, I used that money to bury my cousin—"

Peggy thought, *How quick they are to betray one another. There truly is no honor among thieves.* She sat there quietly, intent on pulling important pieces of conversation out of the great whirlwind of accusations. Periodically she jotted down notes in her little notebook.

Over the next few days, land sales receipts continued to come in. Peggy decided that Nana Kwesi would study them at leisure once she was back in Washington and interview the people who bought the land, or thought they had, as well as the elders who took the money. Peggy would consider each sale and decide what to do about it. Perhaps the purchaser could pay the stool a portion of the sales price again and be permitted to keep the land. If they couldn't, they could try to get the money from the elder who had taken it. Or they could simply leave the land, giving it back to the stool.

A married couple approached Peggy about buying two beachfront lots, which she sold them for the princely sum of three thousand dollars cash, which she put immediately into the royal bank account. She would use this money for the funeral, she decided. But she was saddened to think how many land sales had disappeared into her elders' pockets rather than being used to benefit the town.

Peggy knew it was time to choose her new elders and told the town crier to roam about banging his drum and letting her people know that anyone who wanted to join the council—including women—should show up at the Other Cousin Comfort's house for an interview with the king. When candidates showed up, Peggy planned to pepper them with questions about their vision for an improved Otuam.

One afternoon, as Peggy and Cousin Comfort sat at the dining room table sipping beer in the heat, the front door swung open and a woman stomped into the house in an old field dress and apron, her tatty head wrap askew. In her callused hands she held a machete, the kind housewives used to open coconuts and pineapples.

"Nana!" the woman cried in a husky voice as she approached the table and performed a crooked curtsey. "I have heard that you want strong women on your council." Cousin Comfort eyed the machete with apprehension.

Peggy looked the woman up and down and considered. She certainly had a commanding presence. And her voice was very loud, loud enough to make herself heard in council when the men tried to drown her out, as they certainly would.

"What is your name?" Peggy asked. "How old are you? What are your qualifications? Can you read and write?"

"My name is Mama Amma Ansabah," the woman replied, sheathing the machete in her belt. "I am sixty-seven years old. I was born in Otuam but moved away with my husband for many years. Last year I returned here to take care of my sick sister. I don't know how to read and write, but I can tell wrong from right, which is more important, and I let everybody know if they are doing well or not. I already tell everybody in town if they are misbehaving. My neighbors said that I am so loudmouthed and nosy and bossy that I should put these qualities to good use and join your council."

This was exactly the kind of woman Peggy was looking for.

"Would you care to have a beer with my cousin Comfort and me?" Peggy asked. Aggie, who had been standing against the kitchen door with her arms crossed, grinning, quickly brought Mama Amma a beer.

Mama Amma plunked herself down in the chair, gulped her beer in a long swig, set down the empty bottle, and belched. Then she wiped her mouth with the back of her hand. Cousin Comfort squirmed a bit and played with her gold bangle bracelets. She was a lady, an only child carefully educated by adoring parents, who dressed and spoke with delicacy and refinement. Peggy worried, wondering, *What would Cousin Comfort think of Mama Amma?*

"You have a lot of thieving old men on your council, Nana," Mama Amma said. "Dogs, snakes, and crocodiles. They don't care about the children of Otuam. If you let me join the council, I will keep an eye on them. I will keep them in their place when you are not here and make sure they don't steal another penny."

Peggy told the woman she was accepted and should attend the council meeting at the end of the week.

After she left, Cousin Comfort surprised Peggy by smiling broadly and saying, "Nana, of all the applicants, I like that one best of all."

Peggy had been hoping for a mix of women, some with the wisdom of old age, like Mama Amma, others with the energy of relative youth. But women in their thirties and forties, it seemed, didn't have time for the council. They were raising children, keeping house for their husbands, and working full-time selling fish on Main Street or merchandise in their little shops.

Just three women, including Mama Amma, presented themselves: feisty, firebrand grandmothers known for honesty and for keeping their large families, and even their neighbors, in line. And so, after some private discussion with Nana Kwesi, Peggy added six new elders to her group of six, the three older women and three middle-aged men. Peggy knew from experience that many people who felt a rush of importance by joining a committee dropped out after a few meetings, once the dull reality set in of sitting around a table for hours listening to others ramble. She would be glad if even one strong, honest person stayed on her council.

Her elders' reaction to the new council members varied. Baba Kobena looked forward to younger, energetic elders working to bring prosperity to Otuam. Uncle Eshun, too, said the time had come to start transferring power to the younger generation. Uncle Moses and Isaiah the Treasurer, though, were dead set against the addition of new members, especially that frighteningly unfeminine Mama Amma. Such changes would surely lead to unruly arguments.

To Peggy's surprise, Tsiami grudgingly agreed to the change. "Do what you want," he said, shrugging. "I don't really care, but these young people and women must treat the male elders with respect."

Peggy stifled a laugh. She knew that by *respect* he meant *"look the other way."* That would never happen. She had handpicked these people to make sure of it.

Peggy's hopes quickly became reality. The addition of the new members to the council created a sharp generational and gender-based rift at the very first meeting. The younger men weren't afraid to tell the older ones when they were being stubborn, uncooperative, and corrupt, and neither were the older women.

When Mama Amma asked about recent land sales, for instance, the old elders would accuse her of disrespect.

"Why don't you just answer the question?" Mama Amma said with undisguised contempt.

"Because you are a woman and shouldn't be asking us such questions," Uncle Moses answered quickly.

Turning to Peggy, Mama Amma said, "You see? They disrespect women. They have stolen the town's funds and expect us just to sit here and permit it. I want you to put them all in jail, or at least fire them from the royal council and confiscate all their money."

The meeting quickly erupted into a loud quarrel. *Ah-go!* several male members cried, but Mama Amma just kept talking about the terrible things that should happen to wicked thieving old men, and her voice was louder than those of all the male council members combined. Peggy sat back and watched. She had already made her decision not to punish her elders, but she was glad to see that Mama Amma was more like an American woman, self-confident and unafraid to express her opinions. A generation ago, no woman regardless of her age would have dared to contradict men in their seventies and eighties.

But the worst argument of all occurred when Peggy explained to the council that from now on they would deposit all fishing fees into the royal bank account of the Rural Agricultural Development Bank, and they would be using checks for all town business.

"What's a check?" asked Isaiah the Treasurer.

"It's a piece of paper drawing money on a bank account," Peggy explained. "You write an amount on the check, and the person you are paying takes it to the bank and gets the cash from your account from the money you put in. Between the records of cash deposited and the checks, we will have a written accounting of all money going in and out of the royal bank account. Nothing more can go missing."

There was a moment of stunned silence as the elders considered this. Baba Kobena said, "I thought the bank was a safe place to keep your cash, safer than under your bed, and when you wanted some of your money, you would go to the bank and get your cash back." The other elders nodded.

"But I think this new thing, checks, is a very good idea," he continued. "If we keep a careful record of all the money and where it goes, we will save more, and we can dig more boreholes for the children. We can help pay the school fees for parents who can't afford their kids' books and uniforms so they keep them home from school. It is too late for me to learn, but I want my grandchildren to read and write. It is the most important gift we can bestow on the younger generation."

"It will be a very good thing for the town," Uncle Eshun agreed, pounding the floor with his cane for emphasis. "Sometimes, Nana, as the recorder of funerals, I have people coming to me begging for money for a coffin for a relative who died suddenly. I usually don't have it to spare. But if the town has a bank account, we will have money to help these people, and they can pay it back over time."

"And it will prevent these wicked old men from stealing the town's funds," Mama Amma growled.

Uncle Moses stood up trembling with anger. "It is against all tradition to use these *modern American checks*!" he cried, spitting the last words. He bent forward from the waist and gestured excitedly. "The ancestors will grow angry! They will curse us! There will be drought, famine, floods, illnesses!"

Uncle Moses proceeded to recite all the terrible things that would happen to them if they used checks, though Peggy knew he was really only thinking of the terrible things that would happen to him if he couldn't steal anymore. He was practically listing the ten plagues of Egypt. Blood in the water! Festering boils! Hailstorms! Toads! Swarms of gnats and locusts! The death of the firstborn! But actually he was saying, No whiskey! No beer! No vodka!

He slapped the table. He shook his fist. His big cheeks inflated like he was blowing the royal cow horn, and with his brown bald head and long gray mustache Uncle Moses looked more like a walrus than ever, a very angry walrus, as he ranted and raved. Finally he needed to take a deep breath and collect himself, or he might have had a stroke right then and there, a very dangerous thing to do in a town with no doctor, no ambulance, and no hospital. He sat down and gulped his beer.

Peggy studied him. He had recently confessed his stealing, shame-faced and contrite, begging her not to put him in jail or make him pay back the money. Yet here he was erupting into a tantrum at the news that Peggy was going to prevent future theft. She slumped a bit in her chair. He hadn't learned anything. Nothing.

"I think there's a very good reason you don't want checks, Uncle Moses," Peggy said, sitting up straight. "The angriest people, you know, have the most to hide." She glared at her elders sitting around the table.

Tsiami shook his head. "He's right that the ancestors won't like these checks," he said. "They will tell me so next time I talk to them."

Peggy was exasperated. "The ancestors want what's best for the future of Otuam," she said. "The ancestors want clean water for the kids, good schools, and a better health clinic. The ancestors *do not* want the elders to steal the town funds and waste them on *women* and *liquor*."

At the top of her voice, she cried, "There will be No. More. Cash." After each word she pounded her fist down on the wobbly table so hard all the beers teetered and her elders had to grab them to prevent them from falling over.

She continued in a milder tone, "As you know, Nana Kwesi, the most honest person in my family, will be my regent when I am back in Washington, and he will have oversight of the royal bank account."

Nana Kwesi cast a calm glance around the council table. "That's right. I will make sure that not a penny goes missing."

Now it was Tsiami's turn to grow irritated. He had, evidently, drunk some of the ancestral libations, because when he stood up he swayed a bit as he cried, "You think you know everything, Nana Kwesi! You think you do, and you want to tell everybody what they should do, but how can you when you are not even from this town?"

"You are an evil, nasty old man, Tsiami," Nana Kwesi said. His angelic smile had evaporated and his lower lip and jaw, which jutted out from his face, were tense with anger. His eyes, usually sparkling with happiness, had become small and cold. Peggy had never seen him like this before.

She turned to Tsiami. "You are acting like a child, Tsiami!" she said. "Sit down."

Tsiami did not sit down. "Nana Kwesi is the child. He is too young to be telling the elders what to do!"

"He's fifty-three."

"See what I mean? A child. I am"—and here he puffed up his skinny chest—"eighty."

Peggy corrected him. "You are not eighty. You are seventy-seven. And even if you were a hundred and fifty, you are not the king of this place. I am. So be quiet. You are being ridiculous. Now sit down."

Tsiami wobbled and sat down.

Aggie, who had been leaning against the kitchen door holding her spatula, took two strides toward Tsiami and loomed over him, pointing at him threateningly with the long hand-carved implement. "Tsiami is not nice!" she cried. "He has stolen money from Otuam, and he disrespects Nana Kwesi!"

Tsiami cast her a look of loathing. "You are being disrespectful of the ancestors to insult a *tsiami*," he said, almost spitting the words. "They will punish you."

Peggy waved her hands. "Enough!" she cried. Tsiami and Aggie stopped bickering and looked at her.

Mama Amma, who had been silently smoldering, stood up from her bench, her square face tense with anger. "You should put them all in jail,

Nana! Put the thieves in jail and throw away the key! Let them rot there with no liquor and no women! I speak for the honest people of Otuam. I speak for the future of Otuam. We stand behind our lady king! We want everyone to use these new checks. No more cash! These selfish old men have been stealing money from Otuam's children for years. Of course you don't want to stop. How else will you be able to afford all the booze you drink?" She turned to Peggy and said, "You should have no expectations that these crooks will ever learn to be honest. It is well known that you cannot change a donkey into an elephant."

Uncle Moses popped up from his seat like a jack-in-the-box waving his arms and turned to Mama Amma in a fury. "Who are you to speak in this manner to a male elder? I am not a donkey!" he said.

"Yes, you are," Mama Amma countered. "You are a donkey, but you think you are an elephant."

"*You* are a donkey!" he cried, then launched into another rant about ancestral traditions and plagues and the shameless, disrespectful, loud-mouthed old women of Otuam.

When he paused to take a breath, Peggy said pleasantly, "Times are changing, Uncle Moses. Women speak their mind these days. Get used to it."

"And *you*!" Uncle Moses cried. "*You* are just a woman! *You* are supposed to listen to men, to do what we say! Why do you think we chose you as king?"

Peggy could feel her heart stop for a beat. There it was, finally. Confirmation of the suspicion she had had ever since that four a.m. phone call, that Uncle Moses had orchestrated her kingship for his own purposes. That he had seen her not as his king, but as a tool to be used. She felt stunned, as if he had slapped her in the face. But then something occurred to her. Kingship, she knew, was divine. Therefore, Uncle Moses must have been the tool of higher powers to make sure that the candidate they wanted, Peggy, was chosen.

She felt a warm sense of calm spread over her and said, "But *you* didn't choose me as king, Uncle Moses. God and the ancestors chose me as king. They just used you. You thought you were being so smart and crafty, choosing a woman who lived thousands of miles away who would do what you say and let you keep on stealing. But you were just a tool the spirit world used to put me in this position to help the people of Otuam. God wanted me here, and here I am, and you had better get used to it."

"She's right, Moses," Tsiami said, suddenly rousing himself from his usual catatonic state. "I knew you wanted the new king to be a woman who lived far away because you thought she would never look into the town finances, let alone threaten to put you in jail. You've always thought I made the schnapps steam up so that your candidate would be chosen, but I didn't, because really what do I care who becomes the new king? Plus, I wouldn't know how to make it steam up. It was the ancestors who chose her, Moses, not you. And frankly I think they picked the worst possible person on that list in terms of doing what you want the king to do, which is to leave you alone to steal all the money."

Tsiami started to laugh, something so rare that everyone stared at him. His face, usually as expressive as a plank of mahogany, broke into creases and folds they had never seen before. "What are you going to do now, Moses," he guffawed, "kill this king, too?"

"I didn't kill him!" Moses shot back. "At least, I didn't mean to. Besides, he died months after that episode!"

Silence descended heavily on the table.

"After what episode, Uncle Moses?" Peggy asked, shocked. Had she heard correctly? Was Uncle Moses really responsible for the late king's death?

Moses calmly sipped his beer as if he hadn't heard.

"Tsiami, what did you mean when you said that about Moses killing the late king?" Peggy persisted.

Scratching his ear and gazing straight ahead, Tsiami said, "Toward the end of his reign, the late king in the fridge realized how Uncle Moses and Isaiah the Treasurer were stealing the land sales. He called in the Saltpond police to investigate. He was going to put them both in jail." He stopped.

"I know about this," Peggy said. "But why did you say that Uncle Moses *killed* the late king?"

"Uncle Moses was very angry at the late king in the fridge and very afraid of going to jail, so he got out his old military shotgun and took it upstairs in the palace, into the bathroom where the king was standing in the tub bathing with his bucket, and pointed it at him and said he would kill him if the police tried to put Uncle Moses in jail."

Peggy was horrified. "And then?"

"And then the king had a stroke, on the spot, and fell into the bathtub unconscious."

"I knew it!" Mama Amma bellowed, hand on her machete. "You're all murderers."

Uncle Moses cried, "I'm not a murderer! That gun wasn't even loaded!"

"If you push a fisherman off his canoe into the sea and he drowns, is it his fault for not swimming well enough or yours for pushing him in the first place?" Mama Amma asked heatedly. She had a good point, Peggy had to admit.

"He recovered from that stroke and died months later," Uncle Moses insisted.

Tsiami just shook his head. "He never came back from the hospital. He stayed there a few months and died. And you must admit that you were glad he was in no condition to meet with the police. I think it's safe to say you killed him."

Uncle Moses rolled his eyes. "That's what *you* say, Tsiami."

"That's right, that's what I say. And that's what the stools say, too, because they told me you killed him and you would have a heavy price to pay. They say you are going to die horribly and that the late king will come back for you a month after his burial. Anyway, I'd say the joke is on you because the weak lady king you wanted is much younger and stronger than the one you killed, and I don't think you can make her have a stroke by taking a gun into the bathroom to scare her." Tsiami broke into a broad grin, revealing perfect white teeth.

Peggy turned her unblinking gaze toward Uncle Moses, whose cheeks were sagging now, no air in them at all. "Well, Uncle Moses, what do you have to say for yourself? I think your murder of the late king is something that should be discussed."

Uncle Moses seemed about to speak and then closed his mouth. Finally, he said, "All right. I will go outside to pee and when I return we can discuss it."

Peggy nodded. "Go ahead," she said. "I'll be waiting."

Uncle Moses ambled out the door and into the bushes.

Scanning the table, Peggy saw her elders' downcast faces. Isaiah the Treasurer, of course, would never have revealed anything unflattering of his mentor Uncle Moses, but why hadn't Baba Kobena and Eshun ever told her this story?

"Baba, Eshun, did you know about this?"

They nodded sadly.

"Then why didn't you tell me?"

"We didn't want to upset you, Nana," Baba Kobena said.

"Or frighten you," Eshun added, "especially when you were taking a shower."

"To give him some credit," Baba Kobena continued, "after Uncle Moses made the king have a stroke, he came running into the courtyard still holding his shotgun, which we thought was odd, and asked us to get a cab to take the king to the hospital, as he had fallen down in the shower and was having a fit. We had to prop him up unconscious in the taxi between Uncle Moses and Isaiah. Later I asked Uncle Moses about the shotgun, and he told me what had really happened."

Peggy nodded. So Uncle Moses had, at least, immediately called for help. Or had he waited a while before doing so? How would anyone ever know?

"It was a terrible thing," Isaiah the Treasurer said. "Ever since then, Uncle Moses has felt just awful about it." Somehow Peggy doubted that.

The fan swirled around and around over their heads, making a clicking, whirring sound, and outside a goat bleated. Peggy's royal robes were airing on the laundry line strung out right behind the dining room, like colorful tablecloths, flapping in the breeze. Nana Kwesi stared vacantly at them, his lips in a half smile, shaking his head slowly. Tsiami studied his fingernails as if all the mysteries of the world would be revealed in his cuticles.

"It's been a long time," Cousin Comfort said after several minutes, tapping her long red fingernails gently on the table. "Do you think Uncle Moses is all right?"

"Who cares," said Mama Amma, taking a deep swig of beer.

Peggy replied, "Oh, he's all right. I think the coward went home. Perhaps he's coming back with his blunderbuss."

But Uncle Moses didn't come back.

19

Peggy had much to think about. What Uncle Moses had done was far worse than theft; he had killed the late king. Or had he really? Had Uncle Joseph been on the verge of a stroke that would have felled him at some point during that day or the next? Weren't strokes caused by blood clots, which formed over a period of time? Perhaps the shock of seeing Uncle Moses run into his bathroom with a gun, while Joseph was standing there naked with his bucket, pushed the blood clot into a major artery and caused his stroke a few hours or days earlier than otherwise would have occurred.

Uncle Moses couldn't have known that his behavior would make the king have a stroke. Perhaps she could best describe it as an accidental death, though come to think of it, there was nothing accidental about taking a gun into a bathroom and pointing it at a ninety-two-year-old. Should she put Uncle Moses in jail for helping to push the late king into the village for good? Should she mitigate his punishment because he had arranged to get the king to the hospital? She discussed it with Cousin Comfort and Nana Kwesi.

"The important thing is that Uncle Moses knows that you know what he did," Cousin Comfort replied, after much consideration. "I think that alone will take a lot of the wind out of his sails. If he ever acts up with you, all you have to do is mention the words *gun* and *bathtub,* and I bet he will be quiet."

Nana Kwesi said, "Nana, I think Comfort is right. You need to start off your reign fresh, a new beginning. But I also think you should watch out for yourself."

"Watch out?"

"Well, what's to prevent Moses or his partner in crime, Isaiah the Treasurer, from trying to harm you in some other way?"

"You think I'm in danger?"

Nana Kwesi shook his head. "I don't know. But from now on when you are drinking or eating something and your elders are around, don't ever take your eyes off your glass and plate. And regarding the borehole for the palace, I know you wanted pipes outside with a tap for people living in the boys' quarters to get water. But I think I'll keep the pipes inside the palace, so no one can get near them."

Peggy stared at him. "You mean my elders might try to poison me?"

Nana Kwesi looked out the window. "If they did, with no doctor here and no ambulance, you wouldn't get any medical care for at least an hour."

Cousin Comfort said, "They've had an easy lifestyle for several years now, Nana, and you have taken that away from them. They can't get their hands on fishing fees anymore, and everyone in Otuam knows that no land sales will be legal unless they bear the signature of you or Nana Kwesi. So I imagine there is more resentment than you know."

"And there are the daughters of the late king," Aggie piped up from the kitchen door. "My brother here in Otuam tells me they're planning something because Nana won't let them bury their father now and wants to give him a royal funeral. But no one knows what."

Peggy was stunned. Could her life possibly be in danger? Was she surrounded by enemies plotting against her for trying to help her town? But then she shook off the thought. No one was ever going to frighten her out of doing her duty.

Fear, she knew, would paralyze her ability to rule. She had had plenty of experience with fear, especially after William left, living in dread of being hurt again. The fear had slowly boxed her into a smaller and smaller life, until her life was so tiny she could barely turn around in it. It had been the best she could do at the time, but it had still been a mistake. It was not a mistake she would repeat in her kingship.

Angry elders, vengeful daughters, shotguns and poison and plots. She would not be afraid. Not this time. "Bring it on," she said calmly.

For weeks now, Nana Tufu had come almost every day with his *tsiami* to visit. Peggy always welcomed him and gave him and Papa Adama beer and whiskey, and more beer and more whiskey, but it seemed they never wanted to leave. When these visits had started shortly after her arrival in Otuam, she thought Nana Tufu wanted to discuss preparations for her gazetting ceremony, which he was sponsoring. But after making a couple of remarks about it, they stayed, either chatting about nothing in particular or drinking in silence. Now that the gazetting was over, they still came and sat there drinking. As they discussed the fishing fees, or the land sales, or Uncle Moses's killing of the late king—whatever was the main topic of the day—Peggy couldn't help but notice that Nana Tufu often cast fearful glances at the front door.

One day, Peggy finally asked, "What's the matter? Why do you keep looking at the door?"

Nana Tufu slumped in the chair. "My cousin came back," he said. A tall and robust man, he now looked deflated, as if he had once been a big happy birthday balloon but the air had seeped out of him, and he had become a sad and shriveled thing.

"Cousin?"

"Well, Nana, you know that the Nana Tufu, the official mediator of Otuam, has a stool of his own, has kingly status. But I was never actually enstooled since my cousin was in line for the throne, and five years ago he asked me to fill in for him temporarily until he came back. I thought he would be gone a year or so. But it has been five years, and I have worked hard to learn the role of mediator, and I have given much. I don't want to leave."

And maybe you like the palace and the tsiami, *the gifts of whiskey and the bowing and scraping of townsfolk in the street?* Peggy asked silently. *Maybe you don't want to give that up either.* Peggy was fond of Nana Tufu, but she wasn't blind to the appeal of being a king.

Nana Tufu looked at the door again.

"Are you expecting him to show up here?" she asked.

"No. But I told him he couldn't ask me to leave now, after all these years, and that I wasn't going to stop being the Nana Tufu. As a result, he hired the Asafo to follow me around and harass me."

The term *Asafo* meant "company of warriors." In the past, the Asafo was the people's militia, formed to defend the community against aggressors. But there weren't any aggressors these days, so throughout Ghana the Asafo groups, wearing leopard-print army uniforms and red kerchiefs on their heads, sang traditional songs, danced, and beat drums at festivals, funerals, and other town events. More recently, the Asafo had permitted women to join, tough women who enjoyed marching up and down the street chanting and carrying old guns with black powder but no bullets.

For seventy years, the Otuam Asafo had been led by Uncle Fitter, whose name reflected his decades of work as a mechanic fitting together pieces of metal. In his nineties, he was several inches shy of five feet tall and without a single tooth in his head, which gave him a spitting, whistling speech. He wore an ancient khaki hat with a huge hole in the center, as if a mortar had ripped straight through it.

The Asafo had performed on Main Street during Peggy's enstoolment the year before and at the recent opening of the Otuam bank. But they had a role in addition to their musical performances. You could hire them to harass people you didn't like. For some cash and a bottle of whiskey, they would walk down Main Street in uniform, banging on drums and singing loudly—"Kwame Sowah is a jackass" or "Pearl Brempong stole her sister's necklace"—until the harassed person either resolved the dispute or paid the Asafo more money and whiskey to keep silent than the aggrieved person had paid them to sing. Either way, singing or silent, the Asafo made a lot of money and drank a lot of whiskey.

"What are they saying about you?" Peggy asked.

Nana Tufu sighed and ran a hand over his grizzled, close-cropped gray hair. "They are running through the town and standing outside my house banging their drums and crying, 'We don't want Nana Tufu to be the royal mediator! He has stolen the stool from his cousin. Nana Tufu is a thief!' Things like that. Wherever I go they follow me. It's horrible. Especially that hundred-year-old little man without teeth who whistles and spits when he talks."

"Uncle Fitter?" Peggy asked.

"Yes, their leader. He sprays all over me when he calls me liar and thief."

"Why don't you pay them to stop?" Peggy knew that Nana Tufu was rather well off. She had heard that he had a good-sized house on a busy street in Winneba, over a prosperous pharmacy, where his sister was the pharmacist.

He shook his head. "They want a lot of money to stop." He took off his wire-rim glasses, polished them with the edge of his cloth, and glanced at the door.

It was very bad news that the Asafo were after Nana Tufu. They couldn't have harassed him if he had been enstooled—nobody would have dared do that because the ancestors in the stool would kill the harassers or at least give them illness and very bad luck. But since he wasn't enstooled, they could treat him as if he were an average citizen. His stool had been loaned, merely, and he was holding on to it unjustly, his cousin believed.

Peggy realized her house was popular with Nana Tufu because it was the only place in Otuam safe from the harassment of the Asafo as it was the residence of an enstooled king. Poor Nana Tufu was tired of hearing them outside his own house chanting "Nana Tufu is a thief!" She could certainly understand that. But the situation was costing her a lot of money, which wasn't really fair because she hadn't stolen anybody's stool. Maybe it would be cheaper if she paid the Asafo off herself rather than sending Nana Kwesi back and forth to the Winneba liquor store. No, this wasn't her business. Nana Tufu and his family would have to sort out the dispute themselves.

She decided she would have to be blunt. "Nana Tufu, I am sorry for your situation, but I must ask you not to come back here and drink my whiskey every day, unless, of course, you have some Otuam business to discuss. It is getting very expensive, you know, because you and Papa Adama drink a lot." She wanted to add, *You could at least have brought a couple of bottles when you visited me instead of draining me bone-dry,* but she thought that might be a tad rude.

Nana Tufu nodded sadly, and a few minutes later he and Papa Adama stoically walked back through the bush to Main Street, and into the drum-banging, insult-chanting harassment of the Asafo.

Cousin Comfort was right: after the revelation about his shotgun in the bathroom, Uncle Moses was much better behaved in council meetings and far more respectful of Peggy. The shotgun seemed to hang in the air between them; when they looked at each other they both saw it, and it certainly gave Peggy the upper hand.

Uncle Moses's deference came at just the right time because Peggy's next duty was to settle her people's disputes. The king and council were to present a dignified, united front to those citizens who came pleading for justice or mercy.

One case involved the owner of a canoe who had refused to drop his net and meet with Peggy when she called the town's fishermen together to discuss the new tax collection process. Peggy believed this disrespect was because she was a lady king; a fisherman would never have so blatantly disobeyed a male king. To punish him for this insult, she sent word that he was not to cast his nets for three days, not counting Tuesday, which was sacred to the sea god. (Any fisherman out on a Tuesday would likely be pulled beneath the waves by a giant watery fist.) But, not wanting to lose the income, he *still* disrespected her and cast his net anyway. When Peggy heard about this, she sent a message to the chief inspector to arrest the fisherman.

That evening Peggy and the royal council held court in the dining room. She sat at the head of the table, her elders in chairs on the sides, and townsfolk with civil disputes against family members or neighbors sat on handmade benches set against the walls. Peggy noticed a young woman enter the house, pregnant and with a baby strapped to her back, evidenced by a tiny pink sole and five tiny toes that seemed to emerge from each hip.

In the rare case when an offender was already in jail, the court allowed his relatives to plead for leniency and offer surety for future good behavior, usually by paying a fine. When Uncle Moses called the case of the disrespectful fisherman, the woman launched herself from the bench onto the floor. Scrabbling abjectly on her knees before Peggy, she cried out in one long, screeching wail, "Let him out let him out let him out let him out!"

Peggy couldn't bear to see a woman cry. It reminded her of her mother, crying bitterly when she handed Peggy the little gold bracelet, tears of powerlessness and failure, tears that broke the heart. Of her own tears, rivers shed after each miscarriage, at the irrevocable loss of a beating heart, a human soul. It reminded her of the loss of William, the husband she would always love and never again have. Of the loss of her mother, that tower of strength and wisdom, vanished from the earth.

Looking at this young woman, abjectly begging for mercy, Peggy was speechless, crushed into silence by all the losses and all the sadness in the world.

The fisherman's wife made as if to tear her hair, her two clenched fists pulling on her gray cloth head wrap. Then she threw both arms straight up in the air, shaking her head violently from side to side, howling like a wounded animal, as many Ghanaian women did when emotion overcame them.

"Please, Nana! Let him out!" she cried again.

Peggy knew that although words were powerless to bring back her children, or her marriage, or her mother, as king she could utter one word to turn this woman's pain into joy. *I could fix her broken heart,* Peggy thought, *end her grief immediately. But then I would be seen as a weak king, the kind of king people could take advantage of because I am a woman. What should I do? I like to think I'm so tough, so smart. But right now I don't feel tough or smart. I just want to cry and run out of here, run into the bush and not deal with this. I don't mind dealing with corrupt old men, that's easy, but handling this poor woman's husband, how do I do that? Look at her. Her heart is breaking because of something I have done, because of something I can't undo.*

Peggy felt tears stinging her eyes. But it was not permissible to see a king cry. She blinked rapidly and passed a hand across her face. *I can't look at her,* Peggy said to herself. *Poor woman. I don't know what to do.*

Her elders were waiting for a decision, but Peggy was paralyzed, knowing that whatever she did, it would be wrong. Finally, seeing her unwillingness to render judgment, they decreed that the man should be released immediately and pay a monetary fine after he had had a week to bring in fish and sell it. They looked expectantly at Peggy to see if she disagreed, but she said nothing and remained motionless, which was consent in itself.

Then Uncle Moses said, "This is our decision. You may go now to the jail and tell the chief inspector to release your husband."

The woman stood up crying out her thanks, arms high in the air. In this posture she ran from the house. Through the open front door, Peggy could see the shrieking figure disappearing into the trees. She realized the woman was running all the way to the jail to bring home the stupid man whose blatant disrespect of his king had made such trouble for his poor pregnant wife.

Yet it had been handled perfectly. It was her council who had given the order to release the man, not Peggy. The fisherman's wife was happy; her family reunited. The fisherman had been taught a lesson; surely he would never again disrespect his king. And Peggy had done nothing to make herself look weak.

She cleared her throat. "Let's move on to the next case," she said.

Peggy's strict approach had immediate results. From then on, whenever she sent word that she wanted to talk to the fishermen, they dropped their nets, raced to the palace, and respectfully saluted her, so she wouldn't throw them in jail.

The most interesting case Peggy adjudicated involved a fishmonger, Madame Awortor Kokugah, who claimed to be bewitched. Well into her seventies, Madame Kokugah was a large woman with a square dark face, made squarer and darker by the enormous black turban perched on top of it. Peggy asked who she was accusing of witchcraft, and Madame Kokugah gestured to a lithe, muscular man, obviously a fisherman, standing at the end of the table a few feet away from her. Normally his face would have been easy, pleasant, but today it was furrowed into thick brown pleats, and his eyes were bleared with crying. He was wearing baggy black pants and a faded long-sleeved blue cotton shirt that hung limply on his powerful frame. His employer and fellow tribeswoman, Daavi, was there to help negotiate a settlement for him.

Madame Kokugah explained that she was the proud owner of several nets, each one about three hundred feet long. Perhaps the new king, being an American, didn't understand how the Otuam fishermen used their nets? In the middle of the night, she explained, men on a canoe took the net far out into the ocean to catch the schools of fish that would come with the dawn. For the next eight hours, a couple dozen men on the beach would pull the net in, heavy with fish, while a little boy, sitting in the shade of the bushes, would carefully coil it. It took a fisherman years of hard work to save up enough money to buy a net, so the loss of one was no joke. And recently, one of Madame Kokugah's nets had gone missing.

Madame Kokugah looked straight at the fisherman, pointing an accusing finger, but he couldn't return her gaze. "J.J. is *new* in town," she said. "He's been here only a month. He is not Fante like us. He is

Ewe, from *Eweland.*" This seemed to be a damning accusation, and Daavi, resplendent in orange robes and a matching headdress edged with silver lace, stiffened.

Since all the Otuam fishermen knew one another, Madame Kokugah continued, her son thought the thief must be the newcomer and told several people that J.J. had taken the net. One evening, J.J. walked into her house as she was eating dinner, took off his clothes, and uttered a curse, imploring the local fishing god Tantum and the god of Eweland to curse him with death if he took the net and to make whoever stole it suffer unspeakable cruelties.

Peggy tried to picture herself sitting down to a pleasant dinner when a strange man came in, took off his clothes, and jumped up and down with his penis and balls dingle-dangling and bouncing all around, while he uttered a curse. She would have immediately lost her appetite and pushed her plate of fried fish away. In fact, the unexpected sight of such a disgusting thing would have been more disturbing than the curse itself.

Madame Kokugah paused dramatically. "My nephew *died* the next day," she said. "He was twenty-one."

A murmur of shock and fear went around the council table. Peggy shook her head. Dingle-dangling aside, this was very serious business. In the United States, Peggy thought, angry people say *Screw you,* but in Africa they say *You are going to die.* And people die. If she uttered a curse against someone in Silver Spring, would it work? Would the person sicken and die? She didn't think so. Evidently there weren't as many gods and spirits floating around the United States, waiting to hear a curse and act on it. Why was that? Since Americans didn't pour libations to them, maybe they had become so thirsty they went somewhere else, to Africa perhaps, land of liberal libations.

"Your nephew had a fever for four days before he died!" J.J. protested. "He was sick well before I uttered the curse!"

"And the day after you uttered it, he died!" Madame Kokugah retorted. "Maybe he would have recuperated otherwise."

"There will be no curses uttered in Otuam!" Peggy cried. "When you invoke a god, you don't know what you are dealing with. Some gods take the time to fully investigate a dispute before punishing the wrongdoers. But others don't take the time. Madame Kokugah is right.

Mischievous gods dive down as soon as they hear spirits being called and harm anybody associated with the curse."

"Perhaps it won't rain in the next rainy season, and the borehole, the pond, and the crops will dry up," Uncle Moses said.

"Maybe the fish will find new migration paths and the people will have nothing to eat," Isaiah the Treasurer added. "A strange sickness could take Otuam, with people and animals falling over dead."

"And you, J.J., stripped naked to make sure that your curse was doubly effective. Everyone knows a naked curse is the most dangerous kind," Peggy pointed out.

Tears were streaming down J.J.'s face. His eyes darted right and left. "I am so sorry I uttered the curse. But I never touched that net, Nana," he said. "They are just blaming me because I am Ewe. I have worked hard all my life. I am working hard here in Otuam. It was not right to accuse me of theft. Ewes are known to be the most honest tribe in Ghana." Daavi nodded emphatically.

That was true, Peggy knew. Although there were bad apples in every lot, it was widely known that an Ewe couldn't tell a lie if his life depended on it. No matter what you asked them, they opened their mouths and the truth tumbled out, even if it was an awful truth that condemned the speaker. Even now, J.J. could have denied uttering the curse in front of only one witness, and many in his position might have done so. Then the case could have been a he said, she said situation, creating doubt among the judges about what exactly had happened. But J.J., a true Ewe, freely admitted his guilt and stood prepared to take the consequences.

"I know you didn't steal the net," Peggy said, "but you did utter the curse. So there will be consequences for that. I want you all to sit on the porch while my elders and I discuss what is to be done." J.J., Daavi, Madame Kokugah, and her relatives obediently shuffled out to the porch.

After much discussion, it was decided that the elders would sacrifice a goat at the woodland shrine to appease the angry spirit who had killed the fishmonger's nephew, and any other spirits who had been floating around and heard the curse. J.J. would have to pay for the goat, and the bottles of schnapps, and the fee to perform the rituals. The total came to about seventy dollars, a huge amount for a fisherman, which he would have to pay off over several months.

Though J.J. winced at the fine, he agreed to pay it. His spirits improved somewhat when Baba Kobena said consolingly, "And J.J., once the curse has been lifted, we will invoke the spirits to find out who really stole the net. All of us know that you didn't steal it, and we want to make sure we find who did."

It was only after Peggy returned to Silver Spring that Tsiami conducted the rituals to find out who really stole Madame Kokugah's fishing net. The answer he received from the stool was shocking: no one had stolen it. Her son, who disliked J.J., the newcomer from Eweland, had hidden it and blamed J.J. When hauled before the council of elders, the son admitted it. It was no use to call the stool a liar when you knew it was telling the truth about your guilt. If you were foolish enough to do so, it would come and get you. As a fisherman, he knew he would probably be drowned very soon if he continued to lie about it.

Peggy's elders made Madame Kokugah's son pay J.J. back the seventy dollars they had fined him. J.J. was gleeful, his reputation intact. Madame Kokugah hadn't known about her son's lie, and she was very angry with him for making such trouble. In this way J.J.'s curse—that whoever stole the net would suffer greatly—came true, as Madame Kokugah made her son suffer her tirades every day for a very long time.

And so, finally, justice was served.

For almost a month, Peggy had been so busy with cleaning up corruption, appointing new council members, untangling the fishing fees and land sales, and adjudicating civil disputes that no one had said a word to her about Kwame Lumpopo. She was very happy about it. Perhaps that would be the end of it, and she would never have to hear his name again or see him swashbuckling toward her radiating saintliness in white. But no, that was wishful thinking. He was a family member, and this was Ghana.

And, indeed, the day before Peggy returned to Washington, she had one last embarrassing meeting regarding the need to forgive Kwame Lumpopo. The family had sent none other than his ex-wife, Agnes, an attractive woman in her late thirties with a shy smile. Peggy remembered her from some family events in the 1990s.

Agnes sat down at the table and sipped her Coke politely. After the usual chitchat, she nervously cleared her throat and said, "I have heard that you are very angry at Kwame Lumpopo. I am here to ask you to forgive him."

Peggy said, "Hmm. You have divorced him. Why do you seek this favor?"

Agnes replied, "It is not good for families to be divided."

"You divided your family when you divorced him," Peggy pointed out.

Agnes didn't know what to say.

"Did Kwame Lumpopo and his family put you up to this?" Peggy knew they had but felt she should ask.

Agnes nodded.

Peggy stifled a laugh. They must be desperate indeed to put his *ex-wife* up to begging for forgiveness. Poor woman. She was obviously uncomfortable making the request.

"Well, I'll tell you what," Peggy suggested brightly. "There is something you can do that would make me forgive him completely and take him back into my royal council."

The woman's face brightened. This would greatly impress the entire family, if she could pull it off. "There is? What? I will do it!"

"You are right that rifts in families are very bad. Divorce is a very great rift. I want you to marry him again, and then I will take him back as an elder. It is a fair deal. You take Kwame Lumpopo back as your husband, and I take him back as my advisor. Agreed?"

Agnes was horrified. "But . . . but . . . but he stole all my money!" she sputtered.

"And he stole mine, too," Peggy said briskly, nodding. "I think you and I are in the same boat. So let's not hear any more about it."

Agnes quickly finished her Coke and left, afraid perhaps that if she stayed longer the king would force her to remarry Kwame Lumpopo, who had stolen all of her money when they were married and would then be in a position to steal whatever she had amassed since then.

Humming a little tune, Peggy sashayed down the long corridor to her bedroom and returned to packing her bags.

Part V

WASHINGTON, D.C.

November 2009–September 2010

20

Peggy had hoped that her corrupt elders would be grateful she hadn't tossed them in jail and would, with a new sense of sobriety and humility, work closely with her in future, or at the very least not stand in her way. But such was not to be the case.

The elders, already furious at Peggy for taking control of the fishing fees and land sales, were enraged to find that they weren't even allowed to get free fish anymore. Daavi was assigned to chase them away if they came down to the beach with bowls in their hands but no money. This happened only once, a few days after Peggy left Ghana.

"No free fish for you!" Daavi said to Uncle Moses, Tsiami, and Isaiah the Treasurer, who had been hovering hungrily. "Buy your own fish!" She turned to the fishermen unloading their catch, who were grinning at the sight of a woman saying such a thing to the elders. "Nana Amuah Afenyi VI has commanded that anyone seen giving free fish to the elders will be prohibited from casting his net for three days!"

All the fishermen laughed because they had given free fish to the elders for years and were tired of it. It was terribly funny to see the fishless old men with sour looks on their faces scurrying up the rocks on the way back to town, clutching their robes and empty bowls while trying not to slip. They didn't come back.

But this episode was the final straw for two of them. One day Peggy received a call from a female relative in Otuam who reported that Uncle Moses and Isaiah the Treasurer had held a secret midnight meeting with the three daughters of the late king. The subject: how to humiliate Peggy.

To punish both Peggy and the late king with a single blow, it was decided that they would bury Uncle Joseph secretly, in a regular cemetery, and not in a magnificent royal funeral with a tomb in the palace. It was what the daughters had suggested to Peggy during her recent trip, a suggestion she had flatly rejected. Now they were trying to do it behind her back.

At the meeting, Uncle Moses had been particularly vocal in his hatred of Peggy. "I curse her!" he had said, gesturing madly. "I want the gods to make her feet slip out of her sandals, to fall down on the ground and hit her head, and never be the same again. She has taken away the livelihoods of men! She must be punished!"

Peggy was shocked to hear of his curse. But somehow she doubted if it would be effective. If an evil person cursed an innocent one, the gods usually visited the curse upon the curser himself. Uncle Moses should be very careful, with seventy-seven gods living in Otuam.

Perhaps this meeting had been Uncle Moses's way of taking a shotgun into her shower. He had certainly been upset about her opening the bank account and had gone through town spreading the rumor that Peggy hadn't put the elders' names on the account because she planned to use all the money to buy herself nice things. Plus, he had been almost apoplectic when Nana Kwesi kicked him out of his rent-free apartment in the palace so he could renovate it. Grumbling loudly, he moved his things into one of the two-room cottages in the boys' quarters.

Peggy wasn't surprised to hear that Uncle Moses and his protégé Isaiah the Treasurer had been involved. But she was glad that Tsiami hadn't attended, despite his involvement in the corruption and his humiliating grab for free fish. Naturally, neither Baba Kobena nor Uncle Eshun had attended. As far as Peggy had determined, neither one had been involved in stealing fishing fees, or selling land they didn't own, or even making the fishermen give them free fish.

In the months following her second trip to Otuam as king, when Peggy wanted to talk to a council member other than Nana Kwesi, she found herself calling Baba Kobena instead of Tsiami. Though he was illiterate, he was straightforward and reliable, a staunch supporter of family interests, and she certainly trusted him more than she did those who had stolen from the stool. Theirs was an easy, friendly relationship, and she took to calling him almost every day, asking about Otuam news and the health of friends and relatives.

Sometimes she assigned him to mediate with quarreling neighbors or families, as Nana Kwesi wasn't there every day, and with certain family disputes where it was better not to use an outsider. Baba Kobena, with his deep voice, hearty grin, and easy laugh, was as much a part of Otuam as the glittering mica on the red earth and was highly respected.

Though Peggy was glad that she could rely on Baba Kobena, the evil plotted by two of her elders disturbed her. She called the morgue director to make sure that Uncle Joseph hadn't gone anywhere and instructed him to hand over the body only to her representatives shortly before the funeral, which she had scheduled for Saturday, October 9, 2010. Surely this would put the kibosh on the plot. Yet if the late king's daughters and her wicked elders were blocked here, would they find another way to dishonor her? It was a small but irritating worry, which she resolutely pushed to the back of her mind.

Peggy made a list of everything she would have to do for the royal funeral. Almost all Ghanaian funerals, even those for ordinary people, had similar components. There would have to be canopies of thick red and black stripes to shield her guests from the burning African sun during the three days of events. She was expected to provide plastic chairs, either red or black, for her guests, and an area in front of the tents for the drummers, dancers, and acrobats to perform. A sound system, with enormous speakers, would play the music. The corpse was usually laid in a brass bed for the viewing, though in the case of a king an effigy would be placed in the bed, with the real corpse sitting on a royal chair arrayed in royal regalia.

Ghanaian funerals often left families drowning in debt, Peggy knew. Many people squirreled away money for years to pay for the funeral of the next close family member to die, but it was often far from enough. They would have to borrow money, which would take years to pay back, during which time other elderly relatives would die. As a gift to her people Peggy wanted to buy the canopies, chairs, sound system, and bed and allow any resident of Otuam to use them free of charge for their family funerals.

But, looking at her dwindling personal bank account, she decided that she couldn't purchase everything at once. As a start she could buy the brass bed and two hundred of the four hundred chairs required for the funeral and rent the remaining chairs, canopies, and sound system. As fishing fees and land sales piled up in the Otuam bank account, she would make the additional purchases.

She would also have to hire several rent-a-loos for guests to relieve themselves in, as there was nothing suitable near the palace for the seventy or so dignitaries who would attend. These kings, queen mothers, and local government officials would return home at night if they lived nearby or, if they lived farther afield, would stay in or near Otuam with friends and relatives. Peggy would need to cater lunch for these special guests on Saturday and Sunday and drinks for all three days. For dinner, she would provide three cows to be slaughtered on the spot; the dignitaries' families would take the meat and cook it.

Another cow she had vowed to the ancestors, with a portion of its meat going to her elders. Beef was a rare treat in Otuam, as most people ate fish every day, and variety consisted of the occasional goat stew or chicken. Given its expense, some people in Otuam never ate beef in their entire lives. The cost of the four cows was two thousand dollars, which she wired to Nana Kwesi.

Next on the list was royal mourning attire, which she would purchase at a kingship store in Accra. Ghana had so many kings and queen mothers (no one had ever made an official count, but it could be in the thousands) that many stores had sprung up catering to the sartorial needs of traditional royalty. These shops sold royal cloths (multicolored bolts of kente for enstoolments and gazettings and funeral cloths in a variety of black and red patterns), matching sandals for these occasions, palanquins, crowns, red umbrellas, black funeral umbrellas, stools, and royal necklaces and bracelets, which, unlike jewelry for the unroyal, had gold beads strung among the colorful hand-painted beads.

According to tradition, Peggy's funeral invitations to the kings and queen mothers in the region would arrive in the form of bottles of schnapps personally handed over by her elders. They would also deliver bottles to local government officials and the heads of different branches of the Ebiradze family living in other cities. She wired another five hundred dollars via Western Union to Nana Kwesi to buy the drinks to give to the elders.

But the most important, most expensive part of the funeral preparations was the palace itself. Every two weeks, Peggy sent Nana Kwesi as much money as she possibly could to repair the palace, and every day he reported on the progress. The walls were in such bad shape that he had had to gut most of them down to the studs. He hired the contractor to dig a borehole and put a tank on the palace roof, though for security reasons no pump was put outside the palace for local residents. He also put new wiring in every room, new walls, new ceilings, new tiled floors, new windows, and new doors.

Peggy instructed Nana Kwesi to paint the exterior of the palace sky blue with white trim and to cut down the large lopsided tree, since it crowded the courtyard and its roots made walking difficult. Removing this tree would allow the four other trees, which had been dwarfed by its shade, to grow, and would provide an expansive space for the funeral ceremonies and future events.

Though Peggy had spent thirty thousand dollars on the palace, Nana Kwesi still needed about five thousand dollars more for the kitchen and bathroom fixtures and the ceiling lights and fans. Given the money she needed for the funeral itself, Peggy realized she wouldn't be able to complete the palace in time, which was a great disappointment. As the Other Cousin Comfort had rented out her little house, Nana Kwesi offered to find Peggy a suitable hotel in Winneba.

But even if the palace wouldn't be fit to live in, it still had to look good enough for the royal funeral, and Peggy called him daily to urge his work forward. Sometimes she had to remind herself that, as overwhelmed as he was with the palace renovation, Nana Kwesi had additional responsibilities in Otuam. He was supposed to meet every week or two with the elders, yet sometimes when he showed up, after paying for a taxi, he found that only Eshun, Baba Kobena, and Mama Amma Ansabah were waiting. The other new elders were too busy to attend. Tsiami was in his fields dealing with a pineapple emergency. Uncle Moses was nowhere to be found, and Isaiah had been called in to the Methodist church, where he volunteered, to handle some paperwork. Nana Kwesi knew that the absence of the last three was due to their resentment of him.

Nana Kwesi also spent countless days poring over the land sales records, making detailed lists of dubious sales. Many of the sales had been for incredibly low prices, which indicated the corrupt elders were ready to take anything at all for land they didn't own, and the buyer knew very well the sale was illegal and hoped to live there for practically nothing until he was kicked off. Nana Kwesi and Peggy decided in such cases the buyer would be presented with a choice: either to pay the stool the full price of the land or to vacate it so Peggy could sell it to someone else. There was, they knew, no chance of getting any proceeds back from the elders, who had spent it.

Otuam was now Nana Kwesi's full-time job, and one that not only didn't pay very well, but at times actually cost him money. He had accepted the regency and volunteered to renovate the palace out of duty to his family and the belief that the dunderheaded elders might benefit from his steady hand. But even a calm, patient man like Nana Kwesi was often driven to distraction by the problems of Otuam, and the people he dealt with offered little or no recognition for his efforts.

Peggy was glad to see that Nana Kwesi was developing a commanding demeanor and that the bashfulness she had first noticed had disappeared under the landslide of Otuam's irritations. But sometimes he used his new take-charge manner with Peggy herself. One day, for instance, he insisted that he was going to build a new stool room behind the palace, even though Peggy told him you couldn't just move the stools without Tsiami asking them their opinion of the matter. It was a heated argument and Peggy only won by listing all the terrible things that could happen to Nana Kwesi if he did things his way.

She had always known that there was a danger in having a regent, as history has shown that regents often begin to think of themselves as kings and argue with the real kings. This would be particularly true for a female king and male regent in a traditional society like Ghana, where women usually did as the men told them. But Peggy could not rule Otuam from Washington, and given the characters who made up her council, a regent was absolutely necessary. And besides their occasional tiffs, Nana Kwesi was a very good regent.

One day Uncle Moses looked at the freshly spackled, painted, and tiled interior of the palace and grunted in approval. He found Nana

Kwesi in the courtyard and told him that he would be moving back into the downstairs suite, the large rooms Peggy wanted to use as her dining room and council chamber, with the little kitchenette and bathroom on the side.

Nana Kwesi laughed at the suggestion. "I can't imagine Nana would let you move back in," he said. "She didn't pay all that money to fix the rooms for *you*."

"If you don't let me move back in," Uncle Moses growled, shaking his fist, "I will break all the windows and spoil the palace! I will set it on fire! I don't care what the stools might do to me!" Nana Kwesi ignored him and carried a ladder into the palace.

Still in a huff, Uncle Moses went down to the beach to buy a basket of fish from Daavi, which also upset him as he used to get his fish for free. On the little bush path from the beach to his house, he had a fit, fell out of his sandals, and hit his head on the ground. There he lay for hours, the fish all over his head, until someone coming along the path found him and carried him home.

When Uncle Moses regained consciousness, he said that as he had been walking with his fish, it felt as if a giant hand had whacked him over his head and back, causing him to fall senseless to the ground. It sounded ominously like an ancestral hand, and people couldn't help but notice that after that day he didn't seem himself. He lost interest in food, for one thing, and his puffed-up cheeks deflated along with his belly. He fell into long periods of silence. On good days he could still speak sensibly, though it was more quietly than before his fall, with none of his wild gesturing and loud arguing. Sometimes, too, his balance was affected; he cried out in terror that the ground was opening up before him and he would be swallowed up.

Strangest of all, Uncle Moses began wearing his wife's clothes. At one council meeting he showed up in a woman's white lacy blouse over his trousers, and at another one he wore a dress. Peggy heard from Nana Kwesi, Baba Kobena, and Uncle Eshun how odd it was at council meetings to see Uncle Moses, sitting still and quiet, dressed like a woman.

The other elders, who had been friends of Uncle Moses for decades, didn't know whether or not they should ask him why he was wearing women's clothes. Perhaps such a question might offend him, or perhaps he wasn't even aware of it and would be alarmed. Among themselves they decided that if anyone should talk to him about this strange affectation, it should be his wife. After all, it was her clothes that he was wearing, and if she didn't mind, they shouldn't either.

Every week or so Peggy called the morgue to see if anyone had tried to take Uncle Joseph out of the fridge, but no one had. Perhaps those who attended the midnight meeting had come to their senses; clearly such an effort to dishonor her would only dishonor themselves.

Given the unpleasantness of Peggy's last meeting with the king's daughters, she asked a cousin of hers who knew them well to call them up and see if they would at least like to buy their father's coffin. In Ghana people with money ordered special coffins designed to reflect the occupation of the deceased. Tsiami, if he had the cash, might be buried in a giant pineapple coffin, a fisherman in a canoe coffin. Secretaries were buried in typewriters, and kings in effigies of themselves with golden crowns. But such coffins cost thousands of dollars. Peggy decided she would put Uncle Joseph in a normal coffin. Even though the finest of these were only five hundred dollars or so, the daughters' answer was a resounding *no*. Such a refusal was unthinkable in Ghana, where family was everything. How could all three of these women have lost the most important part of themselves as Ghanaians?

At least the sons in Houston were paying the fridge fees, though Wellington called her and asked crossly when she was going to bury his father as the fees had gone up, and he and his brother were tired of paying them. She proudly told him the date and asked if he would like to pay for his father's coffin.

But Wellington said he was doing enough and wouldn't contribute a penny more.

Peggy's mother had often said, "When everything seems dark and hopeless, God will send you a light." One day in her office Peggy received a phone call from the pastor of Shiloh Baptist Church in Landover, Maryland. Founded in 1968, Shiloh was an active, prosperous African American church not far from the D.C. border, with a sanctuary that seated 1,175 and numerous ministries that provided assistance to the local community. In the winter, members donated coats, gloves, and scarves to the needy. Throughout the year, they gave clothing and toiletries to drug rehab centers and women's shelters and children's clothing to an unwed mothers' home. They visited nursing homes, assisted disabled veterans in finding apartments and jobs, and held church services at shelters and in prisons. Homebound seniors could count on Shiloh members to cut their grass and shovel snow, and the needy could rely on food donations. At-risk youth found mentors at the church, which also provided tutors for any children in the area who asked for them. In addition, Shiloh had adopted an elementary school and a high school, where they were on call to provide assistance ranging from buying school supplies to counseling and tutoring. Shiloh members picked up trash from the highway they had adopted and provided a wide array of counseling services to residents of a nearby apartment complex.

Recently, the church, bursting with energy to help still others, had started looking a bit farther afield. It had created a Foreign Missions Ministry and hoped to find a suitable town in Africa to assist. One of the members had read the *Washington Post* article on Peggy and been impressed with her devotion to helping her people. Now the pastor wanted to meet with her at the embassy to learn about the needs of Otuam.

Pastor Be Louis Colleton was a tall, broad-chested man with wide-set eyes, a strong, wide face, a short gray goatee, and a booming voice. His presence commanded attention immediately, which perhaps had something to do with his former position as an army drill sergeant during his twenty-year military career. Yielding to an ardent spiritual calling, he had studied to become an army chaplain, and after his retirement from the army became pastor of Shiloh Baptist Church in 1996.

Arriving at the embassy with some of his foreign mission associates, Pastor Colleton explained to Peggy that for a long time he had wanted to sponsor a community in Africa, even though his local community also had great needs. He felt an intense longing for the places and people his ancestors had left behind.

"Most black people in the United States are blessed, compared to the rest of the world," he explained. "We've had a brutal history here, and we still have problems, but who doesn't have access to clean water? Who can't go to an emergency room for immediate treatment? What child can't learn to read and write? My church feels that the best way to show gratitude to God for our blessings here is to search out the neediest people and help them."

Peggy told the little group about Otuam's many needs, and as she spoke about the water, the schools, and the clinic, Pastor Colleton looked her directly in the eye and studied her face as if he was trying to make up his mind about her. His was a long, probing look, as if he wanted to pierce through her flesh and view nothing less than her immortal soul.

Finally he said, "We could possibly help you with all of that. Naturally, anything we do has to be approved by the church's joint ministry and follow our regulations, but I think all of that might be possible."

Peggy's heart skipped a beat. Really? They might help her with *all* of that?

Two weeks later Pastor Colleton asked to meet with Peggy again for further discussion of Otuam's needs, this time one-on-one. Peggy went into detail about her elders' misuse of the town funds, the opening of the bank, her actions to prevent future thefts, and her reliance on a higher power to help her through her many challenges. "All the town money will go to benefit the town now," she said, "and—"

Suddenly the pastor seemed to make up his mind. "I'm promising you a commitment from Shiloh and its pastor," he said. "My word is binding and trustworthy. You are heartily committed to helping your people, putting yourself second after their needs. You are humble yet strong. You have a sincere relationship with God and are not ashamed to talk about it. You are the one God wants us to help."

Peggy was almost crushed by gratitude and humility. That night as she poured her libations, she said, "Thank you, God. Thank you, ancestors. Thank you, Mother. Maybe I won't have to do this all by myself."

Shiloh Baptist was interested in building a church in Otuam, attached to a school that would run from kindergarten through high school and be administered by Shiloh missionaries. Although the town already had three elementary schools, the church wanted to provide students with a superior education starting at the earliest level.

In February Shiloh Baptist sent two missionaries to tour Otuam and report back to the pastor. Nana Kwesi showed them ten acres of grassy meadows that Peggy was ready to give them for the school and church. Because the land wasn't far from Main Street and the royal palace, many children could walk there, and the church would buy school buses for those living farther away.

The visit to Otuam cemented Shiloh Baptist's commitment to the town. In May, the church held a ceremony in which it made a formal covenant with Peggy to take on the responsibility, to the best of its abilities, for the spiritual and physical well-being of Otuam. Wearing her kente cloth and crown, Peggy stood beside Pastor Colleton in front of the altar as he read the covenant:

> We, Pastor Be Louis Colleton and the congregation of Shiloh Baptist Church of Landover, Maryland, covenant with one another and with the Lord to adopt the people of Otuam, Ghana, West Africa as our spiritual responsibility . . . and to provide care, teaching, and support for continued growth and development.

There it is, in black and white, she said to herself, gasping in wonder as she surveyed the crowd of church members. *I'm truly not alone in this anymore. God has sent me the spiritual and financial help I so sorely need.*

Fund-raising, planning, and building the school would take two or three years, at least. In the meantime, the church wanted to start a program whereby church members could sponsor kids' education. Many Otuam families had difficulties sending their children even to the two free public schools as they had to pay for uniforms, books, and testing fees.

Pastor Colleton decided that the sponsored kids would attend Mr. Yorke's school, the best in town, and would receive breakfast and lunch every school day to alleviate the burden on their families. The cost of tuition, books, testing fees, uniforms, and meals was about three hundred dollars a year, depending on the child's grade. During their visit, the missionaries had taken photos of several poor children who desperately needed scholarships, and though the sponsorship program wouldn't be officially kicked off until later, some members viewed the photos, fell in love with a crooked smile or a pair of big brown eyes, and agreed to sponsor them. Peggy wired the money to Nana Kwesi, who informed the ecstatic parents and gave the money to Mr. Yorke.

The church also started meeting with a local fire chief who could advise them on purchasing used ambulances suitable for Otuam's rutted roads (a good used one cost about fifteen thousand dollars, though it would cost a few thousand more for shipping and customs duties). A local businessman pledged to hold fund-raisers to buy two and to send Otuam's nurses to Accra to train on the ambulances' modern medical equipment. He would contribute a portion of the cost himself.

In July Pastor Colleton handed Peggy a check for seven thousand dollars to build a borehole. A Washington-area journalist paid for another one. Nana Kwesi had determined that while many families in outlying areas had to walk very far for water, the greatest number of people would benefit if the two new boreholes were placed along populous Main Street. And these boreholes would be state-of-the-art: electric, so you didn't have to jump up and down on a pump, and filtered against all water-borne contaminants, which often leached into well water.

Next Nana Kwesi hired a reputable firm to test the area for the best places to dig. The contractors found that Otuam had plenty of good water just below the surface almost everywhere, and while underground boulders would prevent drilling boreholes in some small areas, Peggy could, later on, when she obtained more donations, dot the entire town with black water tanks.

But for now there would be two. It was with great relief that Peggy sent off the money the donors had given her for the boreholes. *Water,* she said to herself as she left Western Union. *I am giving them water.* True, it wasn't running water, nor were the two boreholes nearly enough for her entire town, but it was pure, drinkable, free water in busy locations and would mean the saving of several hours of effort every day for hundreds of families. Each borehole took only a week or so to build.

To spur interest in the church's new foreign mission, Shiloh offered its members a trip to Ghana and Togo with four days in the Otuam area in October. They would visit the great slave castle of Elmina, attend the ceremony inaugurating their borehole, and experience the grand funeral of an African king. Peggy was delighted that her donors would attend the royal funeral.

Another piece of good news was the amount of money piling up in the royal bank account. Within three months of returning home, Peggy had ten thousand dollars, which included land sales and fishing fees, though

Daavi warned her that the coming months would bring in less fish, due to rains and choppy waters. Peggy was happy, of course she was, but she couldn't help thinking of all those years of waste. Ten thousand dollars could purchase one and a half boreholes, or dozens of computers for the schools, or a doctor's salary for half a year, or send twenty kids to high school for a year.

But she shook off these regrets and started thinking of everything she wanted to do for the town after the funeral, improvements she could make as the fishing fees piled up. Main Street desperately needed a large public latrine, maybe six or eight seats each for men and women, kept clean by around-the-clock attendants. She wanted her people to have dignity, which was not afforded by relieving oneself in a bush or against a wall, not to mention the stench and health dangers such activity produced. The latrine would be located near enough to the elementary school without a bathroom that its teachers and students could use it.

Otuam could also benefit from a bakery. Currently, Main Street merchants bought loaves from other towns to sell in their little shops. The bread—which was white, flavorless, and probably without a vestige of nutrition—wasn't fresh, and it cost more than it would if it were baked in Otuam. Peggy could imagine the mouth-watering aroma of fresh-baked bread wafting over Main Street and the long lines of customers eager to buy loaves still warm from the oven. Maybe she would start a bakery herself, which would employ several people.

Many elderly people had also complained to Peggy that they couldn't see well and needed glasses, but the nearest optometrist was in Winneba, and very expensive. Peggy wondered if she could persuade a charitable organization to come to Otuam with eye charts and low-cost glasses.

And she wanted to open a carpentry shop—perhaps this could be in conjunction with the new school—where boys (and girls, come to think of it) would be taught how to make tables, chairs, and cabinets, learning a trade while at the same time providing Otuam with useful household items at a reasonable price. And maybe she could convince the bank to get involved in microfinance—making tiny loans of one hundred or two hundred dollars to help residents expand their businesses, sell more merchandise, and hire more employees.

Then there was the urgent need for a library. The Shiloh Baptist School would have one, but in the meantime Otuam's kids needed to explore the world of books, needed to learn how to use the Internet. Perhaps she could fix up a building on Main Street, obtain donated books and computers, and set up a little library until the school was completed.

Yes, there was much, so very much she could do with the town income. It belonged to her people, not to her council, and she would make sure every last penny benefitted Otuam. Her heart soared with hope when she envisioned the Otuam of the future, where people had dignity, jobs, education, water, and health care, where prosperous little businesses flourished.

Though it wouldn't happen overnight, change was coming to Otuam. She could feel it.

21

Though by tradition Tsiami was supposed to be her right-hand man on the council, Peggy didn't talk to him much anymore, preferring instead to talk to Baba Kobena, and of course her regent, Nana Kwesi. But one day Tsiami called her with amazing news. He had been pouring Coke on Peggy's stool when it piped up and complained that it didn't like Coke anymore. It wanted schnapps, like the big men's stools in the room next door. And it didn't want to be alone anymore; it wanted to be moved into the other stool room and have the male stools for company. Tsiami obediently moved Peggy's stool into the other stool room, never allowing it to touch the ground, and reverently placed it on a shelf. He poured schnapps on it, and it told him it was happy. Then he gently laid a goat-skin over it so it could go to sleep next to its new companions.

Peggy found it fascinating that her stool had, in effect, become a male stool, able to imbibe hard liquor. This must be connected with her own increasing strength as king. As she wielded more and more influence over her community, her stool became stalwart. Perhaps it didn't care anymore if she was a man or woman. After all, kings carried the same burdens. All kings had to be strong.

There was also news—frightening news—about Nana Tufu. One evening he had been sitting with his *tsiami,* Papa Adama, and his elders on the concrete plaza in front of his Main Street palace, enjoying the breeze, which he felt playing around his lower legs and feet. Suddenly, he felt something wet on the back of his right leg, right above his ankle. He looked down and to his horror saw a mouse eating his leg, burrowing its head into the flesh right above his heel. Blood pooled behind his foot.

Nana Tufu jumped up and screamed. His elders, who saw the damage done to his leg and the mouse staring at them with wild eyes and a gore-smeared head, started chasing the creature. It darted around the palace, then inside through the open throne room door. The elders knew they had to kill the mouse because it might not be a mouse at all. It was quite possibly an evil spirit who, at the instructions of a witch, had turned itself into a mouse to attack Nana Tufu while his leg was so bewitched it didn't feel the gnawing. After half an hour they cornered the mouse and beat it to a pulp, then they burned what remained.

Meanwhile, Nana Tufu carefully washed and bandaged his wound. But he and his elders knew that worse was likely to come. Over the course of the next few days, his lower leg and foot swelled. The painful throbbing was almost unbearable. Nana Tufu went first to the clinic in Winneba for antibiotics, and when his whole leg swelled up he went to the hospital in Cape Coast for more antibiotics.

Peggy knew that antibiotics couldn't cure a witch's curse. Supporters of Nana Tufu's cousin, who was fighting him for the position of royal mediator of Otuam, may have hired the witch to curse him as a warning. Or quite possibly there hadn't been any witchcraft involved, and it was simply the ancestors letting Nana Tufu know he should relinquish his position with as much grace as he could at this late date.

When Nana Tufu called her saying he might have to have his leg amputated, she cried, "Nana Tufu! Just let your cousin have the title. If you do that, I am certain your leg will heal. If you cling to your position, you will lose the leg, or even your life."

But Nana Tufu refused to give in. "I will die in this position if I have to," he said. "I am not giving it up."

Stubborn, Peggy thought as she hung up the phone. Why was he so stubborn? She shook her head sadly. Then it occurred to her that the royal mediator of Otuam, known for his fairness and negotiating skills, wasn't very good at mediating his own dispute at all.

When it comes to ourselves, Peggy thought, *we are often blind.*

The dispute between the cousins escalated to a dangerous level. When

Nana Tufu's rival spread the word that he was going to be enstooled one day in July, Nana Tufu's supporters let it be known that they were prepared to prevent the enstoolment at all costs. Both men brought in reinforcements prepared for a battle on Main Street. As the sun rose, perplexed citizens found the street full of police cars from Winneba and Mankessim to keep the peace.

The local court in Saltpond issued an order instructing both men to stop calling themselves the Nana Tufu and to abstain from attending to any official duties until the matter was decided in court. This was a very serious order. If either claimant disobeyed, he would find himself sitting in a real prison in Saltpond, with hard-core criminals for roommates. Peggy was glad that violence had been avoided and the courts had become involved. Although Ghanaian kings resolved many disputes in their jurisdictions, there were some cases where the courts had to step in and help the kings.

So Nana Tufu sat disconsolately in his Main Street palace. Though his elders came by sometimes for beer, it was a solemn little group. They held no council meetings, resolved no disputes, and attended no funerals or weddings in an official capacity. Nana Tufu's *tsiami*, Papa Adama, known for making the loudest, longest speeches of any *tsiami* in the region, suddenly found himself silenced. Perhaps it was saddest of all for him.

Peggy's own *tsiami* was also in the news. Late one night, perhaps at one or two in the morning, Uncle Moses had an upset stomach and left his cottage in the courtyard bearing a flashlight to light his way to the communal outhouse. To his surprise he saw Tsiami's wiry frame loaded up with a dozen two-by-fours balanced precariously over one skinny shoulder as he tiptoed out of the courtyard as quietly as he could.

"Tsiami!" Uncle Moses barked, and Tsiami turned so quickly that he dropped the two-by-fours, which clattered to the ground in a heap. "Are you the thief who has been stealing the palace building materials all these months?"

Tsiami shrugged as he bent down and started collecting the two-by-fours. "I'm building a new house," he explained. "These materials come in handy."

"But you're *stealing*," Uncle Moses said.

"You're a fine one to accuse me of stealing," Tsiami replied, neatly stacking the wood. "I'm just taking a few supplies that nobody will notice missing. I'm a family member so I'm entitled to share in any family wealth."

Tsiami picked up the stack of two-by-fours and started walking out of the royal courtyard.

"Come back!" Uncle Moses pleaded, but Tsiami had disappeared into the bush.

By this time several people, having heard the crash of lumber and subsequent argument, had come out of their houses and seen Tsiami leaving with the wood. Well before the sun rose, Nana Kwesi had received several calls about the theft, and he called Tsiami, ordering him to bring the supplies back immediately. "I'll bring them back later," he said.

"What! After you've built them into your house like you did with all the rest? You bring all those supplies back if you have to yank them out of the ground! You, of all people, should know that the ancestors will punish you and your family if you don't bring them back. The stools must be very mad at you. You drink half of their libations, and now you have stolen part of their house."

Tsiami didn't say anything, but Nana Kwesi thought he could hear a shrug.

Finally Tsiami said, "I'm the one they talk to. I'm the one who feeds them schnapps. They'll never do anything bad to me."

Peggy was livid when she heard the news. Her own chief priest, stealing the paint and nails and wood she had purchased at the expense of her formerly sterling credit in the United States. Peggy was particularly disturbed that Tsiami thought he could get away with anything because he had an insider's edge with the stools, who would indulgently forgive their prodigal son.

But even the ancestors wouldn't protect him from a phone call in which she would give him a piece of her mind. She had prepared a fine speech to lambaste him, but then Nana Kwesi called with sad news. Tsiami's wife had had a seizure and died.

The event was the talk of Otuam. Though the woman had been in her seventies, she had always been strong and healthy, had ten living children, and walked miles every day on the pineapple farm, planting, weeding, and harvesting. The suddenness of her death, coming so soon after the discovery of Tsiami's theft of the palace building materials, was seen as clear proof of the ancestors' anger. It was well known that sometimes the ancestors punished you by killing the person you loved most, making you stay on earth without her, knowing you were responsible for her death.

Peggy received several phone calls from her elders asking her to place a condolence call to Tsiami. Nana Kwesi, Uncle Moses, Baba Kobena, Isaiah the Treasurer, Mama Amma Ansabah, and Uncle Eshun: they all called her begging her to follow the proper etiquette. But Peggy was so mad about the building materials that she hesitated to call Tsiami. She was afraid that her call of condolence might degenerate into abusing the bereaved if she couldn't keep her temper. Perhaps it would be more regal to make no call at all.

But, she told herself, she was a king, and as a king she had to maintain royal etiquette. A *tsiami* was the king's closest advisor, and Peggy was expected by the council of chiefs to uphold Ghanaian royal traditions. A condolence call was certainly necessary, and Peggy steeled herself not to mention Tsiami's thefts.

"Tsiami, I am so very sorry to hear about the sudden death of your wife," she said carefully when he answered his cell phone.

"You know that land you sold last year on the beach?" he asked.

Peggy made a face. Had he heard her? Why was he talking about her land on the beach?

Tsiami continued, "I want you to give me half the money so I can finish the house I'm building. That way, when guests come for my wife's funeral, they can stay in the house."

Peggy was stunned by his reply. No word of thanks for her call, no mention of his grief at the death of his companion of half a century. He just wanted more money.

"I am shocked at you, Tsiami!" she cried. "You already had plenty of help from me building that house because you stole so many of my supplies for the royal palace. And now you want more? You want me to give you cash?"

"Yes," Tsiami said. "I want you to give me cash. I'm your *tsiami* after all, and a family member."

"Let me tell you something, Tsiami," Peggy countered, "you aren't getting a dime out of me. And if you ask me again, I will throw you in jail where you can think about your crimes for a few days!" She hung up the phone panting in anger.

As Peggy had feared, her condolence call hadn't gone very well at all.

In August Peggy reserved her flights. She would leave Washington on September 24 on the new United Airlines direct flight to Accra. That would give her plenty of time to prepare for the official inauguration of the boreholes on October 7, and the funeral on October 9. She would return to Washington on October 21, which would give her almost two weeks after the funeral to take care of other issues and disputes in Otuam.

Peggy was sad to hear that Cousin Comfort wouldn't be coming to Otuam this year. She hadn't been well, and her knees were so sore and swollen that she could barely get out of bed. Peggy would miss Comfort, her confidante and the quintessential African auntie, wise and patient, humorous and kind.

But she was delighted that her brother, Papa Warrior, would be coming from Australia to spend the entire month with her in Ghana, arriving a day after she did. He wanted to attend the royal funeral and hoped to buy some land near Otuam and build a business on it.

"I know that you will need help over there," he told her. "I want you to know that I will be there for you."

It was a new idea, Papa Warrior looking out for Peggy, instead of the other way around, and it felt very strange, not quite right somehow. But the more she thought about it, the more she realized it would be a great relief to have her brother with her in Otuam. Yes, Papa Warrior was impetuous, impatient, and loud, but these very qualities had always helped him get things done quickly in his life while those with greater patience plodded along or stopped moving altogether. When she thought of the hours-long council sessions that awaited her, with her elders going around and around in circles arguing over tiny funeral details, she hoped that Papa Warrior could help guide the conversation forward, if that was at all possible in Otuam.

There was someone else Peggy needed to invite to Otuam. Though she hadn't had time to see William during her last trip to Ghana, Peggy asked him to attend the funeral, knowing he wouldn't come, but courtesy dictated she let him know he would be welcome. They chitchatted about the funeral preparations and family members, and about his toddlers and her elders, who were in many ways quite similar.

And then there was Ekow. A couple of weeks before Peggy left for Ghana, she received a surprising phone call from him. In the midst of her numerous worries about the upcoming royal funeral, there had floated one thin strand of panic that Ekow might make a scene in front of all her important guests. He had made scenes routinely at major family events the past few years, but appearing drunk and belligerent while wielding a hammer at a royal funeral would really be the last straw.

Therefore, she was delighted to hear Ekow say that he had given up drinking altogether, and smoking, too. After his last trip to Otuam—in which he had been jailed and kicked out of town—he had arrived back in his room in Accra and cried. His dearest relatives couldn't stand to be around him. Sure, as family members they helped him out of pity, but Ekow didn't want to be pitied. He wanted to be liked, to be helpful, to be respected even. But how could Ekow ever be respected? He decided then and there, he told Peggy, to change his life, which clearly required total abstinence from alcohol.

Ekow hadn't had a cigarette or a drop to drink since then, he continued. Some days it was unbearably hard, but he had joined the Redeemed Church of Christ, located just across the street from the house where he rented a little room, and he prayed with his fellow church members morning and evening. These church members gave Ekow odd jobs to do—he was incredibly handy with carpentry and painting—and meals when there were no odd jobs and he was hungry.

Now that Ekow had found God and stopped sinning, he wanted to open his own business, a tiny roadside kiosk in Accra where he would sell the staples of Ghanaian life: phone cards, minerals, baggies of water, tins of cookies, Pringles potato chips, matches, kerosene lamps, and bags of rice. He had found a man retiring from his kiosk business with an excellent location, near Ekow's home and church on a busy street. The poor condition of the kiosk—it cried out for repairs and fresh paint—was reflected in its low price, about two hundred dollars. If Ekow had another one hundred dollars or so, he could buy at wholesale the items he wanted to sell and open up shop. And he would have a large group of repeat customers; his fellow church members, those who had so generously helped him in the past, would surely buy snacks from his kiosk.

"Nana," he said softly, "I know that you probably wouldn't trust me with that much money after my behavior last year, and after what I did with the money you sent years ago to my mechanics' school. But I have truly turned over a new leaf. Could you send me fifty dollars as a start? Sometimes I don't have enough food to eat. The church members feed me well when they see I look hungry, but sometimes they don't notice, and I am too embarrassed to tell them. I would like this money to buy some food and repay some money I borrowed."

Peggy thought about the request. A year ago she would have yelled at him and hung up the phone. But something was different now, and it wasn't just Ekow's voice, calm and clear, no longer punctuated by shrieks and whispers. Returning to Ghana had made Peggy more aware than ever before of the concept of African family, of the interlocking layers of support needed to ensure that the weakest do not falter.

She also felt a sense of community that she had never had before, which extended beyond her personal family into the human one. There was Nana Kwesi overseeing the palace repairs in the stifling heat and rushing out in a taxi to Otuam to chair council meetings. There was the amazing generosity of Shiloh Baptist Church, some of whose members had suffered in the recession but still tithed, still wanted to help Otuam.

There was the Washington journalist who said, as she handed over seven thousand dollars for a borehole, "It's not right that I have so many pairs of shoes, and your town's kids don't have water." Or the businessman planning fund-raisers for the ambulance, who said, "Helping to save your people's lives is the most meaningful thing I've ever done."

On her first day back at the embassy, she had been startled to find more than a dozen checks from readers of the *Washington Post* article, small checks mostly, some of them only five and ten dollars. Most donors wrote notes saying they had been deeply impressed by Peggy's desire to help her people, and they were giving her what they could spare. Overcome with gratitude as she had been by these many acts of kindness, who was she to turn a cold shoulder to her own nephew?

Peggy certainly didn't want to be taken advantage of again. Perhaps Ekow had sobered up only long enough to call her to ask for money, which he would promptly spend at the nearest bar. But she had to give him another chance. She formulated a plan to balance practicality with family and forgiveness. She would send Ekow the fifty dollars a week before her arrival in Ghana, and once she was there she would take a good, long look at him to see if her money had ended up in the bags beneath his eyes.

It was with a feeling of tremendous relief that she told Nana Kwesi to call the morgue to let them know that her elders would arrive on Thursday, October 7, to take the late king out of the fridge and drive him to Otuam for his October 9 funeral. Yes, she would finally be rescuing him from that cold place after two and a half years, and the knowledge made her ecstatic.

But Nana Kwesi called her back a few minutes later and said, "Nana, I don't know how to tell you this, but the morgue says no one has been paying the fridge fees. They won't release the body until you give them one hundred and forty million cedis." That was about $9,700.

Peggy couldn't believe it. For two years Wellington had told her he had been paying the morgue, even complained about rising rates. Now she knew why the secret plotters hadn't followed through with the plan hatched at the midnight meeting to bury Uncle Joseph like a commoner: they couldn't afford the morgue fees to take possession of the body. Evidently they hoped that at this late date she wouldn't be able to afford the morgue fees either, and all her vaunted plans for a stunning funeral would be ruined. Her calls to Wellington remained unanswered, probably because he had caller ID.

She couldn't postpone the funeral because the Shiloh Baptist group had already booked their flights to Ghana, and all the kings and dignitaries had been invited. All in all, there would probably be about five hundred people.

But where was she going to find another $9,700 at the last minute, after two years of carefully budgeting the countless funeral expenses? Mulling over the situation, she concluded that everything in Ghana was negotiable, probably even morgue fees, so with charm and skillful persuasion, she might be able to get them reduced. As for what she was still expected to pay, she would have to empty out her Otuam bank account, her Silver Spring bank account, pay some bills late, borrow money from friends, and look under her sofa cushions for spare change. But she would do it.

Part VI

GHANA

September—October 2010

22

The road leading to Otuam was worse than ever. Now, in addition to yawning potholes, long, foot-wide chasms ran down the center of it. It looked like a face pockmarked by deep acne scars then ravaged by wrinkles. As the van dipped into a particularly profound cleft, Ebenezer clenched the steering wheel and cursed under his breath, while Peggy smacked her head on the ceiling and cried, "What happened to the road?"

Nana Kwesi shook his head sadly. "There has been too much rain during this past rainy season," he said. "Often it rained all day, every day, buckets and buckets of rain, and without drainage channels most of the roads are almost impassable. The bridge over the river in the middle of Agona Swedru was washed out in the June flood, and now the town has been cut in half to car traffic. The people built a little metal bridge so they can cross on foot, but they can't take any heavy goods from one side of town to the other. It could be years before the government has enough money to build a new bridge."

Peggy was sorry for the people of Agona Swedru, and sorry that she wouldn't be able to visit her favorite shop, Nadrass Enterprises, for beads, cloths, and sandals, as it was located on the far side of the town, and Peggy was afraid of walking over the jerry-rigged bridge. But most of her thoughts were of Otuam. How on earth was she going to fix the road? How much would it cost? She certainly couldn't do it before the funeral, and the busload of Shiloh Baptist people would rattle up the road cracking their heads.

This was a spur-of-the-moment, unofficial visit to Otuam. No elders or townspeople would be waiting for her. Nana Kwesi had just picked Peggy up from the airport, and on the way to her hotel in Winneba she had asked him to drive her to Otuam for just a few minutes so she could see the palace.

As soon as she had seen Nana Kwesi waiting for her at the arrivals area, she noticed that he was thinner. Gone also was the happy childlike gaze of wonder. Her elders and the pressure of the funeral had been getting to him. Her heart sank. It was because of her that this kind, smiling man had become hardened, harried.

He didn't even seem to want to talk much on the drive. *He's nervous,* Peggy said to herself, *about all the responsibilities of the funeral. That, too, is my fault.*

They rolled onto the beginning of Main Street, which looked the same as she had always known it. There were the same people milling about the little shops and chatting in the street. There were the same well-kept homes next to tottering shacks. There were the same little paths on the left leading down to the fishermen's huts and the sea. And everything was dotted with the same sprinkling of painted chickens and short-legged goats.

But then Ebenezer stopped the car in front of the police station as Nana Kwesi pointed to the other side of the road. "Look!" he cried. "Over there! That's the church borehole!"

Just in from the road Peggy saw a gleaming black six-thousand-gallon tank on top of a whitewashed concrete block building that housed a new borehole, with a state-of-the-art pump in front. Her heart skipped a beat. She had done it! Well, actually, the church had done it, but as king she had obtained the church's support and that was certainly something.

"It's beautiful, Nana Kwesi," she said softly. She composed herself and asked, "Where is the other one?"

Ebenezer put the car in gear as Nana Kwesi said, "The one given by the white woman journalist is down the road, next to the mosque. People have already named them the church borehole and the white borehole. Together they serve thousands of people on both sides of Main Street. The town is very happy to have them."

They drove a few blocks and stopped in front of the mosque. Peggy saw a black tank atop a white building identical to the first one and sighed with pleasure. "You have done well, Nana Kwesi, to go out and get bids from companies, and hire the best firm, and oversee the construction. You have done very well."

For a moment the haggard look lifted from Nana Kwesi's face, and his old smile crept over it, the kind that could light up a room. *We all need recognition,* she thought. *We all need thanks for a job well done. Just a few well-timed kind words can make life go from bitter to very sweet.* She thought of all the times she had called him and pushed and pressed for updates on his progress and felt guilty. *Perhaps I haven't expressed my gratitude to him sufficiently.*

Ebenezer drove down the rest of Main Street then swept to the right, across the sandy field and past the school. And looming in front of her was a place Peggy had never seen before. What was that glorious, azure blue building with the white columns and railings straight ahead? Had they made a wrong turn and ended up in some mysterious corner of Otuam? Hadn't she seen all of Otuam? Peggy's heart lurched a bit in fear as she wondered if they had slipped into another realm, the realm of the ancestors. This building shouldn't be there.

She looked behind her and realized that the new structure sat squarely on the site of the old royal palace. But this was not the royal palace. It looked like a different building entirely. In the United States, she knew, sometimes people put entire houses on trucks and carted them to a new site. She had never heard of this being done in Ghana, but could Nana Kwesi in frustration have knocked down the rotten old palace and trucked in a new, prefabricated one? Maybe that was what had happened, and he had been afraid to tell her.

Spewing sand, the car rolled to a stop in front of the building and Peggy realized that the old tree in the center of the courtyard was gone, as she had ordered, and its absence had confused her. But there were the same little cabins, the boys' quarters, and the children playing tag and women pounding *fufu* and old men lounging in rusted pool chairs. Yes, she thought, relieved, this is the royal palace, a greatly changed royal palace, but the same building underneath.

Still stunned, she slipped out of the car and turned to look at the gleaming mansion. In addition to the new paint, columns, railings, and windows, the palace had a new room in the front. The old patio where she and her elders had met was now part of a much larger enclosed room, with an elegant covered entranceway supported by two pairs of white columns. Peggy rubbed her eyes. It was nothing short of a miracle.

Nana Kwesi's men were still working on it, some on ladders painting the trim or washing the windows in preparation for the funeral. A woman was mopping the step to the new entrance, and when she saw Peggy she bowed low.

Nana Kwesi took Peggy's arm and gently guided her to the entrance. "Now you see why I have become thin," he said. "There is so much pressure to get ready for the funeral. I wanted so much for it to be perfect. It's not perfect, but I think it will not embarrass you in front of your guests."

At the threshold he turned to her and said, smiling shyly, "This new room is a present I built for you. It is not finished yet."

Peggy followed him in and gasped. It was a throne room, a long room with a concrete platform at the end, one level for her elders and the higher, central level for her stool. Here she would adjudicate disputes, issue orders, hold town meetings, and receive dignitaries. The walls were unpainted; the two large window frames held no windows; the cement floor was bare of tiles, and wires hung from the ceiling where the fans and light fixtures would go, but she could tell it was going to be a beautiful room. Uncle Joseph had never had a throne room, but Nana Kwesi had built one for her as a surprise.

She was so overcome with emotion that she couldn't speak or move. "Come see the other rooms!" Nana Kwesi said. "The living rooms and bedrooms are finished, but the kitchen and bathrooms are still lacking fixtures." He gently tugged her elbow but she pulled back, afraid that if she went with him she would degenerate into a blubbering mess of a king.

"No," she said, as her eyes filled with tears. "No. I will see them later. It is getting late. We should go to Winneba. The road will be even harder to navigate in the dark."

For an instant Nana Kwesi seemed offended and opened his mouth as if he were going to say, *You don't even want to see all the work I did for you?* But then his eyes searched her face, and he seemed to understand. "Yes," he said with a smile, "I think you must be very tired after your long flight."

She stumbled outside, turned around, and looked at the palace once more. It was the most beautiful building she had ever seen, far more beautiful to her than Buckingham Palace or Versailles. Now she could see why she had ruined her credit and suffered every day since she had become king. Now she knew it was all worth it.

Because this building wasn't just for her or her elders to enjoy. Nor was it just a dignified backdrop for the funeral. This building was for the people of Otuam. It was a sign, in bricks and mortar, that their new king would bring them schools, jobs, water, and medical care. The palace was a promise of prosperity. And every one of her people who saw it would understand the unspoken covenant she was making with them.

Suddenly she couldn't hold back the tears anymore and she started to sob, heart-wrenching sobs of joy and gratitude. A gaggle of curious children had congregated near the van, and two women holding *fufu* pestles cautiously approached. Peggy was worried that they would see the king cry, which was not allowed and might even be taken for womanly weakness. She threw herself into Nana Kwesi's arms so they couldn't see. "Thank you," she said into his shoulder. "It is beautiful. Thank you."

Suddenly she realized that her effort to avoid public comment by throwing herself into Nana Kwesi's arms might not have been the best choice. She pulled away and walked regally back to the car.

They drove to Winneba, a thriving town of about forty-five thousand halfway between Accra and Cape Coast, known for fishing and pottery, where Peggy would be staying. It had been founded in the late fourteenth century by King Osimpam Bondzie Abe I and later became a major port of call for British traders, who had once operated a huge slave castle there.

It was a pleasant place to live because it had no water problems, like Otuam, which had no running water at all, or Accra, which had so many people using its running water that the government simply turned the overburdened taps off several days a week. A breezy, cheerful town built on a series of gentle hills, Winneba boasted countless bustling, tiny businesses such as the Abundant Grace Wine Shop, the Anointed Holy Hands Hair Salon, and the Christ Is Lord Dressmaking Enterprises. Up and down the streets, vendors sat by little tables selling coconuts, papayas, and pineapples.

Much of Winneba's commerce consisted of providing goods and services to the students and teachers at the prestigious University of Education. The Lagoon Lodge where Peggy, and soon her church donors, would be staying was just past the university, a ten-minute walk from the beach, with a view of marshland, palm trees, and large hills rising majestically in the distance.

The lodge was a U-shaped building, painted beige with blue trim, with eighteen rooms on two levels of balconies. In the center there was a cool, canopied veranda where guests could dine. Peggy and Nana Kwesi sat down and ordered fried snapper.

She tried several topics to engage him in the friendly conversation they used to have, but he seemed tired, unwilling to talk much. He hung his head, and she noticed new lines around his eyes.

Once this funeral is over, she said to herself, *it will be like old times with Nana Kwesi. It has to be.*

Papa Warrior arrived in Winneba the following morning, jaunty in jeans and a jean jacket, a gold hoop earring in his left ear and a gold chain around his neck, with Ekow in tow. Peggy welcomed her brother warmly, fussed over how thin he had become, and advised him not to drink too much during their stay. Then she looked her nephew up and down to see what he had done with the fifty dollars she had wired him. She was relieved to see that he had eaten it rather than drunk it. His face seemed less like a dried prune and had filled out a bit to meet his ears. His legs and arms and chest were fuller, more muscular.

Better yet, there was something clearer, steadier about the gaze that met her eye with warmth and deference. As she and Papa Warrior chatted on the veranda, Ekow listened carefully, without interrupting, and when it came time for him to reply, his comments were sensible, his questions thoughtful. It seemed, indeed, that Ekow had stopped drinking and, moreover, was returning to his right mind. Peggy decided it would be all right to let him sleep on his mat on the floor of her room as the attendant guarding her spirit.

Though Peggy's elders peppered her with calls to come to Otuam, she was in no hurry to get there. During her previous two visits, she had let them fraternize with the king a bit too much, dropping by whenever they felt like it, plopping themselves down in a chair, drinking her liquor and eating her fish.

This year she would be much more difficult to approach. She even told her council she would be staying in Accra, which was such an expensive and arduous journey by their standards that she knew they wouldn't try to find her there. If they had known she was staying in Winneba, they would have pooled money for cab fare and shown up every evening at the Lagoon Lodge for dinner and drinks on her tab.

The following day, Ebenezer drove Nana Kwesi, Papa Warrior, Ekow, and Peggy to the kingship store in Accra to buy funeral cloths, jewelry, and sandals. Peggy was smitten by a glorious shimmering stool with golden disks embedded all over. Her public stool must have been fifty years old, and the white paint on the tiger in the center portion was peeling in some parts, faded in others. As an important king who brought water to her people and provided her predecessor with a sumptuous funeral, she could hardly be seen sitting in her majestic new throne room on a rotten old stool. Though money was tight, she gave in to the temptation to splurge on the golden stool, which she would unveil the day of the borehole ceremony when the Shiloh Baptist group would be there. She also bought a new kente in a pattern of gold, red, green, and purple called *Obama,* created for the president's visit to Ghana the year before.

Two days later, when Peggy, Ekow, Papa Warrior, and Nana Kwesi rolled up in front of the palace for her first official visit, the courtyard was filled with people sitting comfortably in the red and black plastic chairs she had bought for the funeral. There were more than fifty of them waiting, a far cry from the five or six who had attended Peggy's town meetings in the past two years.

Peggy suspected that many people had come because they were impressed with her rebuilding of the palace and the two new boreholes; they were also excited about the magnificent royal funeral she was holding and all the Americans she would be bringing. That was probably why many more people were now willing to take the time to listen to her and to contribute their thoughts during a town meeting.

As Peggy went into the throne room she immediately noticed that the walls had been painted blue since she had first been there a few days earlier. She took her seat on the dais, Papa Warrior nearby, as the elders and townsfolk carried their plastic chairs in behind her. Most of her elders placed their chairs in front of and around Peggy—Nana Kwesi, Baba Kobena, Mama Amma Ansabah, Isaiah the Treasurer, and Tsiami—and the queen mother, looking more beautiful than ever, took her usual seat at Peggy's left side.

But Uncle Moses sat facing Peggy, in the front row. He had lost weight and looked less like a walrus now, she noticed. Or perhaps he looked like a very old, toothless walrus. And he was wearing a purple and blue flowered woman's gown. *Clearly,* Peggy thought, distressed at the sight, *God has done this to him.* It was hard to remain upset at a person whom the ancestors had so completely defeated.

But she couldn't understand what the ancestors were doing when it came to Tsiami. He had stolen the fishing fees, and some of the land sales, and even the palace building supplies. When, only three days after his theft of the two-by-fours had been discovered, his wife had died, Peggy had been certain that this was the beginning of ancestral torments. She expected to see him skinnier than ever, bent with age, his face deeply lined, and relieved of several teeth. Perhaps his mind would have begun to wander and his speech to slur.

Therefore Peggy was shocked to see Tsiami looking at least ten years younger than he had a year ago. He had gained weight, at least fifteen pounds, she reckoned, which he had sorely needed. Gone were the dry stick legs and sinewy arms like braided rope. Now, in addition to bone and muscle, he had flesh. His skin was smooth, with a golden gleam to the mahogany. His chest was broader, though his washboard stomach remained flat as ever. His face shone with health and his white teeth were all still firmly attached to the gums. His hair, which had been gray at the temples, was now a shoe-polish black all over. Why would a man his age, a grieving widower, suddenly start dying his hair?

She wondered if this surprising rejuvenation in a man pushing eighty had to do with the death of his wife of fifty years. Perhaps it hadn't been an ancestral curse after all, but a boon, and Tsiami was dallying with a woman in her twenties, planning to marry her. Baba Kobena had told her that one evening he went to visit Tsiami at his farm and through the window saw a young woman cooking him dinner. Tsiami was sitting like a king in a plastic chair looking very pleased with himself as she fussed over him. Unwilling to interrupt such a scene, Baba Kobena turned around and went home.

Peggy couldn't imagine anyone that young marrying Tsiami now that he couldn't steal any more fishing fees, but perhaps his large pineapple farm was temptation enough. Whatever his matrimonial prospects, she imagined he had been eating a lot of tiger nuts. Yes, the stools must have forgiven Tsiami for all his thefts as he was their favorite son, often indulging in long conversations with them, which no one else could seem to do. That was the only logical explanation for his exuberant good health and improved looks despite his multitude of crimes.

Peggy waited, shifting on her stool, as more people arrived and set up chairs. Soon there was no more space for chairs, and people stood against the walls, or leaned in through the large open windows, as Ekow did. Her elbows on the window ledge beside him, Aggie was barely recognizable, shorn of her braids and hornet-like turban and wearing a long, flat weave. Cousin Charles was on her other side, looking a bit thinner and older. Staying in Winneba with the Shiloh Baptist Church members, making occasional flying visits to Otuam, Peggy would hardly be able to say a word to them this time around.

Others pressed around Aggie and Cousin Charles from behind, hoping to get a view, too, of their new king. How many people were gathered now, she wondered. Eighty? A hundred? And at least half of them were women, who usually stayed away from the affairs of men. There seemed to be a buzzing excitement in the air that she had never noticed before at an Otuam town meeting. One of the older women ambled up to the dais and stood behind Peggy's stool, fanning her with a towel, the kind specially made in Ghana to create a breeze or absorb perspiration.

Tsiami stood up and cried, *"Nana, wonfreye!"* Let's call on the ancestors for good things to come!

"Yemrah," the people said. Let them come!

Three times the ritual call and response were given. Then Tsiami said, "Our king, Nana, has recently returned from America—"

"Tsiami, you shouldn't talk about me until you have poured libations to the ancestors," Peggy interrupted.

Tsiami paused. "Oh," he said, "I don't have the schnapps and I don't have the stool room keys."

Here we go again, Peggy said under her breath in English. "Let me get this straight. You are my *tsiami,* and you have had a year to prepare for this meeting, and you have forgotten to get schnapps and the keys. As I recall, something of a similar nature happened with the keys last year."

"I will go get the schnapps," he said, "but I don't know where the keys are."

A few minutes later, as Peggy waited on her stool, Tsiami returned with the bottle of schnapps. He poured libations on the floor crying, *"Aaaa-bah! Aaa-bah! Ka-kra!"* Mama Ansabah stood beside him and joined in, encouraging God and the ancestors to listen. After every splash of schnapps, a swarm of flies settled on the wet concrete, lapping up the liquor and rubbing their front legs together in drunken delight.

During the prayers, Peggy became aware of the queen mother sitting silently at her left side, stroking her white cloth. Peggy felt sorry for her. She was forced to sit with elderly people and listen to their conversation, which couldn't possibly be interesting for a schoolgirl, and never say a word herself, because a person who didn't know anything shouldn't say anything. A lot of them did, of course, her elders being a case in point, but the queen mother seemed smart enough to know she wasn't yet smart enough and remained silent.

Her beauty and poise certainly made her decorative, Peggy was forced to admit. And perhaps one day, when she was older, the queen mother would become a woman of insight and action, an energetic advocate for Otuam's women and children. The ancestors must have chosen her for a reason.

Just then another elderly woman with a towel shuffled up to the dais to have the honor of fanning the king, and the first one took her seat. Peggy launched into a carefully prepared speech. "I know that some of my elders met secretly at midnight with the children of the late king and discussed how to dishonor me and dishonor the late king at the same time. They talked about burying him privately so that when I went to the morgue to get him for the royal funeral, he wouldn't be there. He would have been dumped into an unmarked grave somewhere, which would have been a disgrace to all Otuam." The people murmured to one another. "Those who attended this meeting should be ashamed of themselves."

Uncle Moses might be forgiven for not looking ashamed, as he sat plucking at the flowers on his dress, but Isaiah the Treasurer held his head high and surveyed the audience as if he had had nothing to do with the meeting.

Peggy continued, "Last year when the bank opened on Main Street,

I opened a bank account in my name alone. Immediately some of my elders started the rumor that I was using the funds for my own personal amusement and not for Otuam, and that was why I refused to put their names on it.

"Now that you can see this palace, I think you have an idea of where the money has gone. I have bought a beautiful brass bed for the late king, which you will see in a few minutes, and two hundred chairs for the funeral guests, some of which you are sitting on. In the near future I will buy a sound system, a tent, and another two hundred chairs. These items are not just for kings, or even the extended royal family. They are for anyone in Otuam who wants to bury a relative with dignity and can't afford the high cost. All you will have to buy for a funeral is food and drinks for your guests. I will take care of the rest. Funerals are a big expense to all families, I know, and this is one way I can help my people move toward economic prosperity." This statement was met with cheers as many jumped to their feet and clapped wildly.

Peggy went on. "If any citizen of Otuam wants to know how much money is in the royal bank account and where it has gone, he should ask me and I will allow him to meet with the bank manager and see the records for himself because I have nothing to hide."

A woman stood up and declared, "It was wise that Nana didn't put any of her elders' names on the bank account. If she had done so, we would have had no bed for the funeral and we would all be sitting on the floor because we would have no chairs! The elders would have stolen the money and spent it on themselves. That is why Nana passes all the good things through Nana Kwesi. She should fire all the other elders except Mama Amma Ansabah, who is the only decent one in the bunch." Sitting next to Peggy on the stool, Mama Amma Ansabah beamed, and Peggy allowed herself a brief smile.

A small, dark man in a black-and-white print shirt popped up near the back of the room. "Everyone here should bless Nana and give her their full support," he said. "Otuam now knows how she will help us. What she says is the truth and is not a lie. We have the proof in this palace and the two new boreholes she has brought us. Anyone here who does not support her, who makes trouble for her, will be punished."

A man in a bright orange cloth stood up. "And Nana is a good woman with a clean heart. She has convinced many Americans to come here, and we are excited about meeting Americans. If Nana had a bad spirit, not a single American would follow her here!" The room erupted into more applause.

Peggy was delighted by her people's response to her efforts. So they had known all these years why Otuam never made any progress, and they realized that she was bringing about the changes they had always hoped for. She looked out over a roomful of bright eyes and eager faces.

"There's another matter I want the town to know about," Peggy said. "The children of the late king haven't helped with the palace, haven't put a penny toward the funeral. They lied about paying the morgue fees, which are over one hundred and forty million cedis, and they even refuse to pay for a coffin for their father to rest in." This last was met with clucks and murmurs of disgust.

"I am prepared to honor the late king all by myself and pay everything necessary, but I don't think it would be appropriate for his children to attend the funeral and sit there accepting condolences and monetary gifts. How do my people feel about this?"

The room erupted into applause.

"That's right!" cried one woman, standing and frantically waving a handkerchief. "We will ask the Asafo to beat them up and throw them out of town!"

"Ungrateful bastards!" brayed another one, shaking her fist.

"Exercise patience!" cried a man in a blue shirt, alarmed at the sudden militancy of Otuam's women.

Nana Kwesi asked the people to follow him down the hall from the throne room and into the council chamber, where the brass bed had been set up, with the coffin beside it that he had picked up from an Accra casket maker the day before. The townsfolk walked around the bed and coffin murmuring in delight and nudging one another. As they reassembled in the throne room, Tsiami stood up and asked, "What do you think of the things Nana has brought us for the funeral?"

They cried out their approval.

"Does anyone have anything else they would like to say?" Peggy asked, then paused. "If there's nothing else, I want to close this town meeting with these words. I'm a woman but I am also a strong king. All of you must know that I have come to help this town, not destroy it. You can see for yourselves all that I have done in two years without even being here most of the time. Just imagine what I will do for you in the future. I want all of you to know that you may talk to me about anything, but please do not hold secret meetings and try to stab me in the back."

The town meeting was adjourned and all but twenty of Peggy's elders and close relatives reluctantly left, many casting longing backward glances at Peggy on the stool. *They want to stay longer,* Peggy marveled. *They are energized by the changes I have made, by the plans for the funeral. My people are solidly behind me.*

It was an astonishing realization. She had been so focused on what she needed to do for her people, writing up a long list and ticking off the first boxes, that she hadn't really thought about changing the relationship between the people of Otuam and herself. Last year almost everyone had ignored her town meeting. What had she sensed this time? Loyalty, support, pride, excitement. Love, even? Yes, the people of Otuam were growing to love their king, a fact that made her feel both humble and ecstatic. Until now, she had focused on her duty. She hadn't put love in the equation.

But something new was undeniably there. She could feel it all around her, not a self-imposed concrete wall of fear, but a warm circle of admiration, respect, and support. Somehow, when she hadn't been paying attention, the one had quietly transmuted into the other.

Her thoughts were interrupted by the scraping of chairs against the concrete floor as those who remained pulled their chairs in a circle around the dais to discuss funeral plans. The first topic was how they could make sure that the funeral chairs didn't walk away. They were comfortable chairs, and many people would probably like to put some in their living room, or even sell them on the Accra–Cape Coast Highway. It was finally decided that a tool and die kit would be used to chisel NAAVI (which stood for Nana Amuah Afenyi VI) into each chair so that anyone who took one would be embarrassed when a visitor noticed the inscription and realized that the chair had been stolen from the king.

They discussed how many drinks would be needed and what kind, always a subject of great debate. They discussed the cow and the distribution of meat; on Sunday evening, the elders would wait near the shrines while the cow was being butchered, and once the butcher called them, they would come in an orderly fashion with trash bags to haul the meat home. They discussed the performers for the funeral: the Asafo, a group of child acrobats, and various drumming and dancing groups. And they discussed the retrieval and preparation of the late king's body. The body would be picked up Thursday night, and on Friday it would be washed, perfumed, dressed, and seated on the golden royal chair by the late king's sister and nephews, to be viewed on Saturday.

It hadn't been easy, but Peggy had found the money to pay the morgue, though she dearly hoped she could get the price reduced when she met with officials there later in the week. She would have liked to go personally to pick up her uncle's body. She, his niece and successor, should be there to take Uncle Joseph home to his new palace. But kings were forbidden to approach a corpse until it had been ritually purified, so she would not be able to see him until the height of the funeral on Saturday.

In African families, everyone has a particular role to play. Some identify relatives' bodies at the morgue, while others counsel unhappy married couples, and yet others help with wills and inheritances. In the Ebiradze clan, the two people designated to bring bodies back from the morgue were Isaiah the Treasurer, because he could read and write and take care of any paperwork, and Baba Kobena, as one of the main elders, even though he was illiterate. Peggy looked at the two men who would retrieve her uncle. Isaiah the Treasurer was sharp as a razor but also the biggest crook in Otuam, now that Uncle Moses was in poor health. She was glad that he would be accompanied by Baba Kobena, who, though he couldn't spell his own name, would let her know if Isaiah the Treasurer started with any shenanigans.

But perhaps she was worrying too much. What kind of shenanigans could a person get up to at a morgue? She would certainly be well advised to worry about sending Isaiah to a bank or a jewelry store, but to a morgue? Yet when it came to her elders, she worried about pretty much everything.

23

The following day, Peggy met with various executives at the morgue in Accra, politely pointing out the impossibly high cost of the fees, a staggering sum to which the king's own children had not contributed a dime. With her sharp secretarial and accounting skills, she showed them how incomprehensible their paperwork was, poorly handwritten, with dates and sums crossed out and written over and figures that didn't add up. After several hours of meetings, it was decided that the price would be reduced to $8,100, which included $400 for the ambulance to take the body from Accra to Otuam.

Peggy had hoped the fee might be reduced further, but she was grateful for any reduction and paid the money personally to the director of the morgue. Frederick Aduako was a trim little man of about fifty with black close-cropped hair and thick glasses who had the calm, consoling manner of the consummate mortician.

After handing over the money, Peggy sighed with relief. "You don't know how happy I will be to get him out of that fridge," she said.

"Your uncle, Nana, is no longer in the fridge," Mr. Aduako explained. "After a year there, the bodies are moved to tanks of a special solution including formaldehyde, which is a better long-term preservative."

Odd, Peggy thought. For so long everyone had been calling him "the late king in the fridge," when they really should have called him "the late king in the tank."

"Who will be coming to pick up the body?" Mr. Aduako asked.

Peggy gave him the names of Baba Kobena and Isaiah the Treasurer.

The borehole ceremony, which would be held on Thursday, October 7, would be a joyous but rather simple affair. Peggy, her elders, the Shiloh visitors, and her townsfolk would gather in the throne room for speeches of gratitude, then go to the boreholes for the ribbon-cutting ceremonies, where there would be more speeches and prayers, and Tsiami would pour schnapps. Peggy instructed Nana Kwesi to buy two large colorful ribbons to tie to the faucets, which Pastor Colleton would cut ceremonially with a large pair of scissors to officially open the new water supply.

But it was the funeral plans that required the greatest energy and, as the big day crept closer, they accelerated in pace. Peggy and Nana Kwesi met with the caterers, the drink vendors, and the funeral program designers. Papa Warrior looked after renting the canopies, the portable toilets, the sound system, and the extra chairs, which was a great help to Peggy. Business owners often raised prices when a woman did the negotiating, and Papa Warrior knew how to get the best price possible, though it was a lengthy process. During the haggling, dickering, and arguing, you had to walk away at least three times as the business owner cried out for you to come back, he was prepared to lower his price.

He had less success in hiring a bulldozer to grade the palace courtyard, which was dotted with holes and mounds of earth after all the construction and the removal of the center tree. One firm had given him a reasonable price and then, when the owner went to Otuam and looked at the ground to be leveled, tripled the price, probably because he saw the first poles of the funeral tents going up, heard that it was a royal funeral, and knew he held Papa Warrior over a barrel.

But Papa Warrior wasn't about to let anybody hold him over a barrel. He sent the man on his way with a volley of epithets. Later that day, he returned to the courtyard to see how bad it really was, and if some visiting king might break his leg by tripping over a mound or falling into a hole. To his surprise, he found about a dozen men with shovels hard at work, using dirt from the mounds to fill in the holes.

He thought perhaps Nana Kwesi had organized the work, but in talking to the men he discovered that they were volunteers. "We heard that the bulldozer man wanted to overcharge you," one man said, leaning on his shovel and wiping the sweat from his face. "And the king needs a nice flat courtyard for the funeral. We want to help her. She does so much for us that we want to do things for her."

The air-conditioned bus containing members of Shiloh Baptist Church arrived at the Lagoon Lodge late Wednesday evening. The group consisted of a dozen middle-aged to elderly African Americans, including the two missionaries who had visited Otuam back in February and planned to move to Otuam.

The Shiloh group was excited to see the land of their ancestors, the funeral of an African king, and the town that would benefit directly from the church's ministry. They had spent a couple of days visiting Togo, a French-speaking splinter of a country on Ghana's eastern border.

Peggy was overjoyed to see them and welcomed each one cordially. These kind people had come so very far and at great cost to see her town and to spread the word back home to help Otuam. Being a gracious host was one of the major components that made a Ghanaian a Ghanaian, but these weren't just any guests. They were very, very special guests.

Pastor Collcton had never been to Africa before. But he had been to New Orleans after Katrina, and Haiti after the earthquake, and his eyes seemed particularly attuned to people in need. When Peggy asked him what he had seen in Togo, he sighed and said, "Poverty, mostly, Nana. Poverty."

Yes, poverty. There was an endless abyss of poverty in Africa. Here she was devoting her life to helping one little bitty place, and even that was a struggle. She could never help the rest of her beloved Ghana, or the deserving people in all the other African countries. But even as she had the thought, she wondered, why couldn't she? If she ever got Otuam up and running the way she wanted, surely she wouldn't just sit on her palace balcony enjoying the breeze? Not when there was so much else to do for others.

Her experience in bringing prosperity to Otuam might be useful in helping other places, in reforming corrupt systems, bringing in good governance, and attracting donors to their communities. She shuddered at the thought of what she really hoped to do because it was big, very, very big. And she was just getting started.

The following morning, the Shiloh bus followed Nana Kwesi's van to Otuam for the borehole celebration. Peggy found the throne room more crowded than ever because her people wanted to see real Americans. They were fascinated to find that these Americans looked much like they did, which made sense, since they were all, in a way, cousins.

Before the meeting started, Baba Kobena took Peggy aside and whispered that Uncle Moses had arrived in a dress, and this time the other elders convinced him to go home and don a cloth so as not to embarrass them all in front of the Americans, and he had obediently returned in a crisp printed cloth. Peggy nodded and proudly took her seat on her shiny, golden new stool.

After Tsiami had poured libations, Peggy introduced her American guests who, among them, had paid for a borehole, were sponsoring kids' school fees, and would build the school. One by one the church members stood and spoke about their hopes for the town as a townsman translated into Fante. Those from Otuam clapped loudly to acknowledge the generosity of every American visitor.

Suddenly Peggy saw something disturbing: Nana Tufu was walking in with his *tsiami,* Papa Adama. Given his ongoing legal dispute with his cousin, she had instructed him to stay away from her, as she couldn't be seen to have a favorite. What was he doing here? True, he wasn't dressed like the Nana Tufu. He wore no beads or regalia, not even a traditional cloth. He had on a lemon yellow linen shirt and trousers as if he were an ordinary citizen. And he seemed to be walking well enough.

Suddenly a gaggle of large, sobbing women rushed in from outside and pushed between the chairs toward the stool crying, "We have offended Nana! Nana, forgive us!"

Peggy recognized them immediately—Perpetual with her huge round glasses and her sisters Mary Magdalene and Dorcas, the selfish children of the late king who had refused to pay a penny for their father's coffin. Now they had the effrontery to push their way in, begging for mercy in front of all the visiting Americans.

"Not now!" Peggy cried in alarm. "It is too late for this!" Wearing red and black mourning clothes for the father they despised, they tumbled toward her feet, chewing her leg, as Ghanaians called it, flailing around and blubbering and crying out. Their tears, which seemed genuine enough but couldn't really be, were running fast and hot down their cheeks.

Peggy tried to be cold, defiant, regal, but the sight of crying women always disturbed her, reminded her of the many reasons she had to be sad. She sat motionless, looking out impassively over the room, seeming to ignore the women thrashing around at her feet as if in the throes of death, but a large shimmering tear started to form in each eye.

It is not permissible to see a king cry. It is not permissible to see a king cry.

Finally, Tsiami and the other elders hustled the women out of the throne room. As they went clucking and sobbing, Peggy thought, *This was planned. They had all week to meet with me, yet they waited until my American donors were here so I wouldn't want to appear vindictive.*

Peggy noticed that her Shiloh guests seemed shocked and concerned by the performance, uncertain of what was going on, whispering to one another. "Those were the children of the late king," she explained. "They want me to forgive them for not paying any of the costs I have borne for their father. They wouldn't even give a penny toward their own father's coffin. That crying is all theater, well-timed theater. They could have talked to me any day before this to ask forgiveness. Now they do it at the last minute in front of you all."

Pastor Colleton rose and said, "We understand, Nana. Do as you see fit."

Peggy sighed. "I will allow my council to advise me."

On her right side, Tsiami, Baba Kobena, Mama Amma, and Isaiah the Treasurer huddled in a circle, speaking in urgent whispers. Finally, Tsiami stood and spoke. "If the children of the late king come with the money Nana paid for the morgue fees," he said, "then we advise Nana to allow them to attend the funeral. Otherwise, they will not be allowed."

Suddenly Papa Adama approached the dais holding three bottles of ancestral schnapps. "Let it be known that the children of the late king do not dare to come empty-handed," he cried. "They most humbly beg Nana to accept these bottles of schnapps as tokens of their sorrow for having offended her." Now Peggy understood why Nana Tufu was there. He had come, still playing the role of Otuam mediator, on behalf of the children of the late king, and it irritated her.

She was further irritated by the cheapness of the gift. A bottle of schnapps cost about $5. So in return for $15 the women expected to get out of the thousands of dollars she was paying for the funeral, the $8,100 for the morgue, and the $30,000 she had paid to renovate the palace. They would have the honor of attending the funeral and set up a table to receive the *nsawa,* the funeral donations, which usually amounted to several hundred dollars or more. They would actually make a good profit on their $15 investment.

She barked at Papa Adama, "Keep the schnapps. I don't want the schnapps. But I do want the morgue money. Tell the daughters that they may fully participate in the funeral if they bring me that."

Papa Adama went outside to speak with the women who had been keening, sobbing, howling as if the world were coming to an end, black shawls pulled over their heads. When he returned, he reported that the daughters would contact relatives in various towns to determine how much money they could raise. They would return to tell Nana what they could pay. But Peggy figured she wouldn't hear from them again about the morgue fees. And she was right.

After the borehole ceremony, the Shiloh guests went to visit Elmina Slave Castle, that sacred place of endings and beginnings so important to African Americans. At least some of their ancestors had probably passed in chains through the Door of No Return, the now-famous portal to the beach and waiting ships. In 1998 the Ghanaian government had created the Door of Return program, asking people of African descent all over the world to come back and honor their dead ancestors who had been imprisoned there. These members of the African diaspora, descendants of the hardy 30 percent who survived out of the estimated ten million who had been shipped to the Americas, were called heroes.

Peggy didn't join them. She had seen the castles before: every Ghanaian schoolchild had. Now sitting on the airy veranda of the Lagoon Lodge, she thought about the floors of the dungeons, which contained gruesome evidence of the appalling conditions forced upon the captives. The stone floor of the women's dungeon in Elmina had never been redone, and it still reeked of feces, urine, sweat, and menstrual blood. There had been so much of it, from so many thousands of women imprisoned there over the centuries, that the smell seeped deep into the rock and wouldn't ever come out. At Cape Coast Slave Castle, a short distance from Elmina, archeologists digging in the main male dungeon had found three feet of compacted human feces where captives had wallowed for months until the slave ships docked to take them away.

Otuam's own castle, Tantumquerry, was one of many. The British had dynamited it in the nineteenth century, after slavery had been outlawed in the British Empire, and there were only a couple of walls left. Even so, the people of Otuam avoided the castle hill at night because untranquil spirits were known to walk there.

So many people are not here in Ghana who should have been because their ancestors were stolen away, Peggy thought. On the other hand, without slavery none of the tens of millions of African Americans living in the United States, who contributed so much to American culture, would exist. What would music be like without jazz, blues, swing, and hip-hop? Sports would consist of short white men bumping into one another and falling down.

Those Africans captured and enslaved had been the unlucky ones, forced to endure the slave dungeons on the Ghana coast and the heinous Middle Passage to the Americas and, if they survived, a lifetime of backbreaking work in the fields feeling the sting of the whip on their backs. The lucky Africans remained in Africa with their homes and families.

But by the second half of the twentieth century that was reversing itself. African Americans, despite their continuing challenges, gradually attained access to the best education and jobs. They had clean water running hot and cold right out of their taps and didn't have to carry it in buckets on their heads, and a significant percentage of their children didn't die before the age of five. It was the cousins left behind who now struggled to survive. Things had shifted, she realized, as things in the world so often did. The descendants of the unlucky ones had become very lucky indeed.

As usual, nothing involving her elders ever went smoothly. When Isaiah the Treasurer and Baba Kobena arrived at the morgue Thursday afternoon, at the section reserved for kings, Mr. Aduako asked them for a few cedis to pay for the pillow and the mat they would place under the body during transport in the ambulance. Her elders didn't have a penny between them, so they had to drive all around Accra in gridlocked, fume-belching traffic to borrow the money from friends. During the several calls to report on the stages of this ridiculous odyssey, Peggy noticed that Baba Kobena and Isaiah seemed to be slurring their words, and she wondered if the friends they visited had been plying them with liquor.

Peggy received updates while sitting with Nana Kwesi, Papa Warrior, and Ekow on the veranda in Winneba, enjoying the breeze and drinking a Star beer. Finally Baba Kobena told her, "Nana, we have brought the king home and will watch him in the council chamber until his family prepares him tomorrow."

Thank you, God, she said silently. *Thank you, Mother, and all the ancestors. After two years of being king of Otuam, I have done my sacred duty and brought the late king home.*

But no sooner had she said this than her phone rang again and she heard Tsiami's raw voice. "Nana, I want to pour libations beside the body of the late king, but Isaiah the Treasurer and Baba have locked the door and won't let me in."

Peggy knew there had been growing resentment between Baba Kobena and Tsiami ever since her last visit to Otuam, when she had discovered Tsiami's crookedness and Baba Kobena's honesty and given more responsibility to Baba Kobena. She had felt confirmed in her choice once she learned that it was Tsiami who had been stealing the palace building supplies.

"Tsiami," she said sharply, "you can pour the libations just outside the door of the room where they have laid him, just as you pour them outside the stool rooms when you are so drunk you have lost the keys. Naturally, they don't want the door open with anyone walking in to see the body undressed and on the floor, which would be a dishonor."

Tsiami grunted and hung up.

Peggy pulled her handkerchief from her bra and blotted the perspiration streaming down her neck and onto her shoulders.

Seconds later, the phone rang again. "Nana," said the raspy voice of Mama Amma Ansabah, so loud that Peggy had to hold the phone away from her ear. "According to tradition, a woman is supposed to be present when they bring in the body. But those dogs Isaiah the Treasurer and Baba have locked themselves in the room with the late king and won't open the door for me."

Naturally, there was resistance on the council to Mama Amma as a loudmouthed woman who had only lived in Otuam for two years. An unlikely friendship had blossomed between Mama Amma and Tsiami, however, which everyone found quite odd since he had never had any close friends other than his bottles of schnapps and his pineapples. Soon after she had joined the council, Mama Amma and Tsiami had begun drinking beer together under the popo tree in the afternoons when the sun was hot. Sometimes Mama Amma would call Tsiami "a thieving, horny old toad" and poke him in the ribs, and he would grin broadly as she stated, "I'm going to marry a twenty-five-year-old, too." They seemed to always agree with each other in council meetings, so of course she would be on Tsiami's side in this dispute.

"Don't worry about it," Peggy advised. "Baba and Isaiah have done the right thing. We can't have any curious person going into the room because the body is not prepared yet."

A few minutes later came a third call. "Nana, this is Kofi Assuman, a nephew of the late king," said a deep male voice. "I have knocked on the door twice and insulted both Isaiah and Baba twice, but they still won't let me in to see my uncle."

"You will see him on Saturday during the viewing," Peggy said irritably. "I can't imagine your insults will make them open the door." She hung up.

"What's the matter now?" Papa Warrior asked, leaning toward her.

"Everyone is mad because they want to see the body, and Isaiah and Baba won't let anyone in," she said.

Nana Kwesi clucked in disapproval. "To make such a scene the day before the funeral."

"Cut off their heads," Papa Warrior advised her solemnly.

Children, little children, Peggy thought. *Mommy! He stole my crayon! Mommy! She ate my cookie! I seem to be in charge of an African kindergarten. All those years I tried so hard for children, and now I have them, and they are very irritating.*

On Friday morning the red and black striped tents were constructed, dozens of them, all around the palace courtyard forming a long rectangle. As the tent men packed their ladders in their trucks, painters slapped the last strokes of blue paint on the front of the two rows of boys' quarters, which now matched the palace and created the image of a unified palace complex. Decades earlier, the boys' quarters had been painted white to match the original color of the palace and over time had faded to a grayish dinge color. Now the sides and back of the quarters remained dinge, as there was no time to paint them, too, before the funeral.

Townspeople, who had eagerly watched the canopies being tied to the tent poles, helped set out the hundreds of red and black funeral chairs beneath them. Then, when that was done, they sat in them, enjoying the shade of the tents, and chatted with each other about the biggest event Otuam had ever seen, given by their amazing new lady king.

Peggy and her entourage wouldn't arrive in Otuam until later in the day. That morning, Pastor Colleton and Nana Kwesi met with the draftsman who was working on the initial plans for the Shiloh Baptist School, which would serve one thousand students drawn from Otuam and nearby communities. While the average class in Ghana had fifty students crammed into a sixteen-by-twenty-foot room, Pastor Colleton wanted to put twenty-five students in the same-sized room. "I want to offer something better than, rather than the same as," he explained to the draftsman.

The Shiloh Baptist Church, Otuam branch, would be located in the school complex and would be used for morning services as well as a school auditorium. Given its dual use, it would have to be big enough to hold the one thousand students and dozens of teachers and other school employees. The entire school complex would be some 24,000 square feet. Pastor Colleton, Nana Kwesi, and the draftsman discussed plans for the cafeteria, library, computer lab, administrative offices, dormitories for students from other areas, and teachers' bungalows, as most teachers would be hired from towns across Ghana and would live on-site.

After the meeting, Peggy and the Shiloh Baptist group drove to Saltpond to meet with the Honorable Henry Kweku Hayfron, chief executive of the Mfantsiman District, which included Otuam. Pastor Colleton explained that they planned to build a high school in Otuam and wanted to find out what they needed to do with local authorities to get things started.

Henry Hayfron was delighted that an American church would build a school in his district. "Write me a letter of intent," he said, "stating that you will fund the construction. We will get you accreditation. We will inspect the facilities and make sure everything meets our requirements."

Then he turned to Peggy and said, "Don't mind my road! We've put the Otuam road in our budget to be repaired within the next year."

Peggy was thrilled to hear that her road was on the schedule to be repaired. Perhaps the government had chosen that road, out of so many rutted roads in the district, because they had heard about the lady king who was bringing American donors to help her town, and the Ghanaian government liked to help those who helped themselves. She knew, however, that many road projects were held up, sometimes for years, as government officials tried to determine which company would get the lucrative paving contract, so she shouldn't get her hopes up for a speedy fix.

Still, one of her fondest daydreams was Nana Kwesi driving her to Otuam in a shiny, air-conditioned SUV, on a road as smooth as marble.

24

Early Saturday morning, Nana Kwesi appeared at the Lagoon Lodge in a long red robe with long, full sleeves and gold embroidery around the collar and a red silk scarf around his neck. "I can't drape a cloth," he explained to Peggy. "I would be constantly fussing with it and then it would fall off and I would be standing in my underpants at the funeral."

Peggy knew that the requirements for royal funeral garments were very strict for kings and their elders, and she hoped the members of the local council of chiefs, who had gazetted her, wouldn't fine her for Nana Kwesi not wearing a traditional cloth. Though perhaps it wasn't a bad decision on his part, considering that the council would definitely fine her if her regent was seen standing at the royal funeral in his underpants with his traditional cloth pooling around his ankles as he bent down to find the end of it.

But Peggy, Papa Warrior, and Ekow could have been fashion models of proper royal funeral attire. They looked resplendent in their fire engine red cloths, the bold color contrasting starkly against their smooth dark brown skin. Papa Warrior and Ekow also wore striking red headbands. Though Papa Warrior's slender form seemed engulfed by the red wave of cloth, he carried it with princely dignity, as Peggy knew he would. She was more surprised by Ekow's appearance. The outfit made him look aristocratic, powerful, an ancient and noble figure, the man Peggy hoped he could someday be. He had certainly behaved himself during her stay in Winneba, keeping her room tidy, running errands for her, and sleeping quietly on his mat on the floor.

Peggy's van could hardly proceed up Main Street, so filled was it with revelers. The Asafo were marching in funeral costumes with hundreds of tiny strips of cloth—white, orange, purple, red, blue, and green—that fluttered like feathers as they danced. Some of them wore Halloween fright masks and multicolored wigs. Some blew trumpets or banged drums, while others danced with umbrellas. Otuam citizens, wearing traditional black and red funeral garb, danced with the Asafo in the street. Peggy noticed that many of the chickens watching the spectacle were appropriately attired for a royal funeral: they had strips of red cloth tied to their wings.

Slowly, the van eased past the parade and down Main Street. Ebenezer parked on the side of the palace, and Peggy, Papa Warrior, Nana Kwesi, and Ekow took their place in the royal funeral tent right in front of the building. Most of her elders were there, the queen mother and the little Soul, as well as several kings and queen mothers and some government officials.

Peggy was upset to see that the caterers hadn't arrived. The drinks had been delivered, so it wouldn't be a total disaster, but it was against all royal etiquette to invite a king over and offer him nothing to eat. Nana Kwesi called the caterers in Winneba, who said the food was waiting for him to pick up. Yes, they had known the funeral would be held in Otuam, but nobody had actually asked them to transport it there, and anyway, they didn't have a truck large enough to do so. Exasperated, Nana Kwesi had to race back to Winneba and hire a truck that was both available immediately and big enough to cart all the food to Otuam. By the time he returned with the food, the visiting kings had been cooling their heels for two hours without anything to eat, a clear breach of royal etiquette. A member of the council of chiefs told a chastened Peggy they would fine her two hundred dollars for the insult.

While Peggy had met most of the nearby kings and queen mothers during her gazetting ceremony at the council of chiefs, there was one she hadn't met, Nana Ameyaw, the queen mother of Elmina. Petite and slender, with the figure of a girl and ramrod straight posture, Nana Ameyaw looked a decade younger than her sixty-three years. She had smooth skin and large, compassionate eyes. Her jaw was slung forward, which should have made her plain, yet had quite the opposite effect. Hers was an exquisite face of unexpected beauty in sleek, dark lines.

"Nana, I was a good friend of your uncle's," Nana Ameyaw said politely. "He was like a father to me. I visited him often in the hospital when he was ill, and I was with him when he died. He spoke of you often in his last days, telling me how proud he was of his niece who had made a life for herself in America. I am so happy you are giving him such a digni- fied burial. I know he is happy, too, and you will receive many blessings."

Just then Peggy saw Uncle Moses shuffle up in a black cloth, which was a great relief because she had been afraid he might appear in a woman's dress, which would have occasioned a huge fine. But then she noticed that he wore gold sandals rather than red or black, another clear breach of royal funeral etiquette. The same man from the council of chiefs took her aside and informed her that this misstep would cost her another hundred dollars. When she protested that Uncle Moses had lost his mind, the man cut her off, saying that she was ultimately responsible for the behavior of her elders. She sighed. The council of chiefs certainly took its duties seriously.

At one end of the courtyard stood Peggy's royal umbrella, like a lonely tree, symbolizing the missing king. It had been patched once more to repair the depredations of Kwame Lumpopo. Peggy supposed her nemesis wouldn't miss this funeral either, and at one point she saw him sauntering into the courtyard in a bright red cloth, glad-handing as only Kwame Lumpopo could. Wisely, he kept away from her.

The sound system cranked up, playing vibrant African melodies, and groups of women started to dance. Some of them had smeared their faces with mud, which was eerily light on their dark skin. It was customary for men to fire black powder from old rifles at all public events, and now several men knelt in the courtyard and fired up at the trees. When the music stopped, bands of drummers marched around the courtyard, as Inkumsah's fetish priests danced and writhed on the ground in a trance. A group of child acrobats performed their stunts for the better part of an hour, and then the visiting kings paraded around the courtyard with their elders and drummers, walking under black funeral umbrellas as the crowd cheered.

Many of the kings from the thirteen little communities surrounding Otuam complimented Peggy on the royal palace, the like of which they had never before seen. They congratulated her on the boreholes and asked if she could build some for them, too, as their people drank stagnant pond water and sometimes got sick. Anyone from outside the villages drinking that water would become immediately and terribly ill, she knew, but apparently most people there had built up immunity to water-borne disease.

She had already determined that these villages—Dogo, Emuna, Agyankwa, Etsibuedu, Gomoa Fomaya, and the others—would be included in the Shiloh Baptist school district, and that her ambulance, when she got one, would also serve these outlying areas. How could she deny them clean water? Especially Gomoa Fomaya; every time she drove to or from Otuam she saw its people dipping buckets into a roadside pond filled with water red as blood. It had been so easy to dig the Otuam boreholes. Of course, given the widespread prevalence of corruption, she couldn't just hand over the cash to the kings and their elders. She and Nana Kwesi would have to raise the money and oversee building the boreholes. She promised the kings that she would help them as soon as she could.

Around noon, the members of Shiloh Baptist and other nonroyal dignitaries were invited into the palace to see the effigy on the brass bed and the late king on the royal chair. The Shiloh people looked splendid in the elegant black and red funeral outfits made by a Winneba seamstress.

Late in the afternoon, when the kings and queen mothers were finally permitted into the chamber, Peggy led them first past the effigy on the brass bed, a shellacked piece of wood painted dark brown and dressed as a king. Then she pushed through the curtains and walked into the other room to view the real body, which was sitting among large vases of orange and yellow flowers. Behind him were two towers of black and red balloons.

She was startled to see that Uncle Joseph, too, looked like an effigy, a hard, painted thing without any indication that a human soul had once inhabited it. *Oh, Uncle Joseph,* she said, her heart lurching as she remembered his bright eyes, kind smile, gentle voice. She wanted to cry, but with all the kings and queen mothers around her, she had to quickly pull herself together.

He wore a gorgeous gold and black cloth over a white silk gown that came down to his elbows, a black velvet crown with gold-painted wooden decorations, and heavy jewelry. In his right hand he held the traditional goat's hair scepter, and his left fingers were slightly curled for visiting kings to give him money to pay the ferryman who would carry him across the river of death to the land of the ancestors. As they did so, the kings and queen mothers would bend down and whisper in his ear prayers they wanted him to take to the other side.

As Peggy approached the throne, she was even more shocked by her uncle's appearance. For one thing, he had been such a big, tall man, larger than life, and now he seemed wizened, shrunken. Naturally, she knew that many people shrank as they grew old, and evidently this had happened to Uncle Joseph in his last years. But even his face had changed in the morgue. In life Uncle Joseph had had a long face, with heavy-lidded eyes. Now his face seemed shorter, his eyes smaller. Whatever they had done to preserve him for two and a half years had truly changed him. Her heart sank. *I'm sorry I couldn't get you out earlier,* she told him.

At least he seemed to be smiling. Peggy was glad that he was happy with the funeral, even if it had been a long time in coming.

"Is everything all right?" asked Queen Mother Ameyaw of Elmina, who had appeared by her side.

Peggy shook her head sadly. "I wish I could have buried him before now," she said. "I barely recognize the man I knew. It makes me sad to see him so changed. I got him out of the fridge as soon as I could, but still, it took too long."

"I know," Queen Ameyaw replied. "But death is all-powerful, Nana. It changes everything, and we must accept it."

Peggy nodded and tried to steady her quivering lower lip. With one more silent apology to Uncle Joseph, she swept out of the palace back to her place under the tent to watch the Asafo drummers.

That evening Peggy sat in the dark tomb with her uncle in the coffin. Now was the time to speak to his spirit, to tell him everything she wanted him to tell the ancestors. Now was the pivotal moment of the entire funeral.

It was well known that most people, terrified of spirits, blocked themselves from seeing and hearing even the most benevolent beings standing right next to them. To make communication between the worlds easier at such a crucial time, therefore, Tsiami had given her a mild hallucinogenic consisting of special herbs, which he placed on her tongue.

Often, in such cases, the living king saw the dead one sitting up in the coffin as if he were alive, and the two of them held a lively conversation, during which the live king gave the dead one messages to take to the ancestors, and the dead one offered the live one words of advice. Then, unburdened of all earthly duties, the deceased would gratefully leave the netherworld between the living and the dead and fully join the ancestors waiting for him, smiling, arms outstretched in gleeful welcome. Once he lay down and became dead again, that was the signal that the conversation was over and the lid should be nailed down. Peggy sat in the dark, wondering whether she would see an apparition, or at least hear a voice, as she had in the past.

But this time, perhaps because she was expecting it, nothing happened. She was just there, in the dark, with the body. After several minutes of waiting, she decided she would speak to him. "Uncle Joseph," she began in a clear voice, "I hope you are pleased with the magnificent funeral I gave you."

Silence. Nothing. Peggy didn't feel as if any spirit was in the room with her. When she was back home praying and pouring libations she sometimes got the feeling that someone was with her, but now she sensed nothing at all.

She cleared her throat and told him about the boreholes, and the high school, and the kids' scholarships. She told him about all her goals for Otuam and asked him to tell the ancestors to keep her strong despite all the obstacles she knew would be in her way.

Then she waited, truly expecting an answer of some sort, a voice, a feeling, a sigh in the darkness. But there was nothing. Only silence. Was he not there?

"Have a good journey, Uncle Joseph," she said. "May you find peace with the ancestors."

Soon after, Tsiami, holding a flashlight, opened the door. The time was up. The beam of white light lit up the body in the coffin, which seemed to be absolutely grinning now. *Well,* she said, *I'm glad you're happy.*

Her official duties were done. She had planned to stay around for the secret royal burial rituals, some of which would be performed by the

Asafo and others by the members of the council of chiefs. But Peggy was so completely exhausted, so drained, that she decided to return to the hotel in Winneba with Nana Kwesi, Papa Warrior, and Ekow, and go to bed early.

As they got into the van, Peggy thought, *Well, it's done now. Tomorrow there's a farewell lunch with my most important guests, and a church service where Pastor Colleton will give the sermon, and a bit of drumming and dancing that we will watch, but not anything truly draining. Everything I've worked so hard for the past two years is, for the most part, over. And it was a huge success.* She went to bed feeling oddly empty when she had expected to be euphoric, but maybe that had to do with exhaustion.

Sunday evening Peggy bid the neighboring kings and queen mothers farewell, except for Queen Ameyaw of Elmina, who would stay in Otuam another week. The three-day extravaganza was over. Yet despite her fatigue, for a second night she couldn't sleep deeply.

The following morning at six she received a phone call from Nana Kwesi.

"Tsiami called me just now to say there was a terrible ruckus in the palace last night," he said. "There were the sounds of doors banging, and dishes being shattered, and angry voices, though no one could make out exactly what they were saying. People in the palace courtyard heard the noises beginning at midnight, even though the palace was empty and dark. Some of them crept in there with flashlights, but they couldn't find anything out of the ordinary. So they believe it was a spiritual fight, that the ancestors weren't happy to receive your Uncle Joseph. After the people left the palace, the noises started up again and continued for several hours."

Peggy frowned. What could the ancestors be upset about? She had followed all the rituals for royal burial with great precision and had spared no expense. So they couldn't be mad about his funeral. But perhaps Uncle Rockson had been yelling at Uncle Joseph for letting the palace go to rack and ruin. Yes, surely that was it. And once the two uncles had had it out, things would be quiet in the palace. She pushed it out of her mind.

"Also, the fetish priests of the god Inkumsah told Tsiami they couldn't go into a real trance for the dancing and had only pretended to. They are worried that the cave god didn't speak through them, which also indicates something is wrong." That, too, was very worrying.

"And last night when they slaughtered the cow to the ancestors at the woodland shrine," Nana Kwesi continued, "the elders were each supposed to take a few pieces and leave the rest behind for the spirits. But they are all complaining that Tsiami stole the entire cow before they could even get there. They have uttered curses against one another, and they want you to come to Otuam today to resolve the issue."

Peggy had hoped to rest that day, but that would be impossible with her elders stealing meat and uttering dangerous curses. After breakfast she bid a fond, sad farewell to the members of Shiloh Baptist, who were off to tour the Ashanti capital of Kumasi before flying back to Washington. Then she drove to Otuam to investigate the mystery of the missing beef.

Sitting on her golden stool, Peggy listened to her elders' complaints against Tsiami. The butcher was supposed to slaughter the cow next to the shrine, chop off some of the best pieces and put them inside the little igloo-like building of concrete blocks. Then he was supposed to tell the elders when it was their turn to come and divide up the rest of the carcass.

"But Tsiami was waiting there with trash bags while they slaughtered the cow," Baba Kobena said accusingly, "and didn't even let them give the ancestors the good pieces. He carted off as much meat as he could carry before anyone else could get a piece. The prime rib, the rump roast, the sirloin, all the best bits went into Tsiami's trash bag and all he left was cow bones. He is like a greedy lion that kills an antelope and doesn't share the meat with his own kin."

Peggy's eyes felt as if they had glazed over. She asked the stool for energy and said, "Tsiami, what do you have to say about this?"

Tsiami stood up with great majesty and began picking at his cloth, draping and redraping the fabric over his left shoulder and arm. Finally he wadded it up in a ball and held it firmly in place with his left elbow. He frowned as he said, "The reason Baba and Uncle Moses came to the shrine before they were called is because they were planning on stealing the entire cow. I just got to it before them, so they are mad. They cursed me for taking the beef, asking the ancestors who didn't get the beef to punish me, and I cursed them with the same curse to make things even."

Tsiami gave his head a vigorous scratching and added, "You know, Nana, you always favor Baba Kobena, so if he had stolen the whole cow you probably wouldn't have said anything. By taking the beef, I only prevented Baba's theft, for which you should thank me. Plus, as your *tsiami,* it is clear that I should receive a larger share. Baba and Uncle Moses are the greedy lions." He sat down.

"Lions!" Mama Amma Ansabah cried, popping up from her plastic chair. "You are giving yourselves too much dignity. You are warthogs rooting around for whatever you can push into your snouts—whiskey, beer, beef, and everything else."

As other elders stood up and cried, *Ah-go!* Peggy called on them to speak with a polite *Ah-me!* Early that morning she had naïvely imagined that it would only take her an hour or so to resolve the beef issue, that she would then be able to return to the hotel to rest after all the funeral activities. But one hour of discussing the beef turned into two, and then five, and then eight. The extended family members of the elders also wanted to be heard; they, too, had been expecting some beef and thought it heinously unfair that Tsiami had stolen it.

Sitting next to Peggy on the dais, Papa Warrior grew increasingly agitated as the time went by. "These people are talking in circles," he said to her in English. "How many things can they say about Tsiami stealing the beef? He freely admits he did it. So why don't you just punish him and let's go back to the hotel? I want a beer."

Peggy shook her head, sending some drops of sweat flying. "I have to have patience, Papa Warrior," she said. "I need to listen to everything everyone has to say before rendering a decision."

"You can get blisters on your butt if you want," he said, "but I'm taking a cab back to the hotel. Otherwise, I might kill them."

She put a hand on his arm. "Stay here with me."

Though a woman was fanning her with a towel, Peggy wondered if she might keel over in the heat and roll down the steps like a ball. She had no idea how she could make Tsiami return the beef, which his large family had probably already devoured, especially knowing that the other elders were hot on their trail. One thing was very clear, however: every elder who had uttered a curse would be required to return to the shrine with a bottle of schnapps and reverse it.

As the sun set, Peggy postponed any further testimony until the following morning. In the van, Papa Warrior said, "You should do like Henry the Eighth and cut off their heads. Except, since they have no brains, they might not miss their heads. The elders' headless bodies would show up in council with just as much intelligence as before their decapitation. I wouldn't mind the bodies showing up for council meetings if the mouths were somewhere else."

Peggy was having a hard time following this reasoning and frowned. "Papa Warrior, what are you talking about? You're talking nonsense."

"*I'm* talking nonsense? You just spent eight hours listening to grown people arguing over a sack of meat and *I'm* talking nonsense? And we're going to go back there tomorrow to continue this discussion about beef that has already been eaten?"

True, Peggy wasn't looking forward to it. Little did she know that she would soon hear a revelation so shocking that all discussion of beef would be forgotten forever. ✕

After dinner at the Lagoon Lodge, she crawled into bed, finally sinking down to the bottom of her familiar silent black lake. There she remained until her cell phone buzzed loudly.

Slowly she opened her eyes as the phone chirped away. She looked at the clock; it was a few minutes past midnight. She looked at the phone; it was Nana Kwesi. What on earth was he doing calling her at such an hour? She pushed herself up on one elbow and grabbed the phone.

"Hello," she said, groggily. "Are you all right? Is something wrong?"

There was a pause on the other end of the line. "Nana," he said, "I don't know how to tell you this so I will just say it. I just got a call from Cousin Charles, who heard it from one of the late king's nephews. The morgue has been trying to reach you for hours, but no one there has your phone number."

Peggy rubbed her eyes. Nana Kwesi wasn't making sense. "Why would the morgue be trying to reach me?" she asked. Surely they weren't going to ask for more money?

"Nana, the morgue says they gave you the wrong body. Uncle Joseph is still there, and you have buried a stranger in the royal tomb."

The morgue director, Frederick Aduako, had been doing his weekly inventory that day and was shocked to find that the king of Otuam, whom he thought had been handed over to Peggy's elders a few days before, was still floating serenely in his tank of formaldehyde. It wasn't every day relatives came by to pick up a king, and he remembered Peggy vividly because she was a female king and an American, and she had argued charmingly and successfully to have the morgue fees reduced. She had also mentioned several times that the magnificent funeral would be held on Saturday, October 9, and here it was Monday, October 11, and her uncle was still in the tank.

Mr. Aduako searched all his paperwork but found he didn't have a phone number for Peggy. He did have one for the late king's nephew, whom he called immediately with the shocking news. The late king's nephew didn't have Peggy's number either, so he called Cousin Charles, who called Nana Kwesi, who called Peggy.

Peggy was stunned. "I just can't believe it," she said, as tears started to stream down her cheeks. "After all the money I saved, after everything . . . Maybe the late king's children are spreading this rumor to embarrass me because I wouldn't let them attend. Maybe it's all a lie."

There was silence on the phone. Peggy saw before her the square head with the small eyes, when Uncle Joseph had had a long face with big eyes.

"Let's go to Otuam tomorrow and get to the bottom of it," Nana Kwesi said.

Papa Warrior was surprised to see Ekow banging on his door after midnight, telling him he had to come quick because Peggy was very upset. When he arrived at her room, he found her crying, and it took him a few moments to understand what she was saying. Finally he understood.

"Idiots!" he cried. "After all that . . . You mean they brought back the wrong body?"

Peggy sobbed.

Papa Warrior shook his head. "They're lucky we are Fantes. If this happened to an Ashanti king, those elders would disappear and no one would ever speak of them again." Peggy stood up shakily and ran into the bathroom. It seemed as if her insides had turned to mush.

In the wee hours of the morning, she and Papa Warrior had a long talk. Had everything been for nothing then? she asked him. The dancing, drumming, feasting, the five hundred guests, the rituals and prayers, had it been not a dignified funeral but a grisly farce? Should she plan another funeral, in a year perhaps when she had saved up more money, and really bury the late king the second time around?

They both agreed that that would be ridiculous, not to mention costly.

She couldn't leave the stranger in the family tomb, which was, most likely, the reason why there had been a supernatural brawl in the palace the night before. Her ancestors were shocked that there was a stranger in their midst and were punching the intruder, who had been smiling broadly at finally getting buried. Perhaps he had been punching them back, insisting that he stay.

She curled up in a ball on the bed and sobbed like a child. Papa Warrior sat beside her and laid a cool hand on her heaving back. Looking back on her life, there had been only one thing more hurtful than this—her inability to carry a child to term and William's resulting abandonment. Yes, that had hurt worse, devastating her self-image as woman, wife, and would-be mother. But then she had crafted another image, that of a king efficiently bringing progress to her people. Now that image, too, it seemed, had been sullied. She would appear a buffoon, the object of ridicule and derision. A dignified funeral indeed. For the wrong man.

Once her emotions had poured themselves out and there was nothing more to pour, she began to feel calmer. After all, it had not been her fault. She had done everything a king could do for her predecessor. Surely her uncle, and her people, would recognize that. They wouldn't blame her. Regardless of misidentified royal bodies, she had brought Otuam water and was in the process of bringing many other much needed improvements. Yes, she would get through the body switching, somehow, and continue to move her town forward. She recalled the bright smiling faces in that first town meeting, how reluctantly the people had left the throne room when Tsiami told them it was time to go home. Her people appreciated her and would forgive this mistake that had occurred on her watch.

Peggy sat up, dabbed at her eyes with a tissue, and said, "Whatever happens, my people love me."

"They do!" Papa Warrior replied firmly. "Your idiot elders can never take that away from you." He put his arms around her and squeezed. "I've never seen you so upset," he said gently.

No, she said silently. *I've never shown you that I could get upset. With you, I was always strong, in control, telling you how to run your life as if I were your mother. I wonder now how you could stand me calling from fifteen time zones away, asking about your whereabouts and how much you had been drinking, and lecturing you sternly when you told me. But tonight I am the child, you the parent, and it feels so good to have you here with me, comforting me, letting me know I am not alone and you will always be here for me.*

Being a man, and a practical man at that, Papa Warrior didn't like to linger too long in the frightening terrain of raw female emotions. He withdrew his embrace and said, "However it happened, since it seems that you have buried the wrong king, we should go to the morgue tomorrow and arrange to switch the bodies immediately, to bring our uncle home and return this other person."

Peggy nodded. But first she would go to Otuam to get to the bottom of the matter, to confront her elders and find out how they had made such an unforgivable mistake.

The next morning Peggy swept coolly into her throne room and sat regally on her stool. The room was packed as word had already gotten out that they had buried the wrong body, which was the most interesting thing to happen in Otuam since the Magic Mirror people had burned down the town three centuries earlier. Even the courtyard was packed. People leaning in through the windows of the throne room were expected to call back what was being said.

She instructed Baba Kobena and Isaiah the Treasurer to sit on her right side so she could question them, and they dragged themselves to their seats as if they had balls and chains attached to their ankles.

"I understand there was a phone call from the morgue last night that we have buried the wrong body," she began. She looked sharply at Baba Kobena and Isaiah the Treasurer. "You two identified the body. So whose body did you bring back? Whom did we bury in the royal tomb?"

Isaiah the Treasurer stood respectfully and flashed a smile. "It was the body of the late king," he said. "At least, I thought it was. After so many years in the morgue, it was hard to tell. If you find a carcass in the bush that has been there awhile, it is not always easy to see if it was a tiger or a panther."

"Baba Kobena?" she asked.

But Baba Kobena couldn't look at her. "I didn't know for sure if it was him," he said miserably. "I couldn't read the wrist band because I can't read, so I told Isaiah to read it. He said he couldn't read it because the writing was too faded, but he assured me it was our late king."

"There was no wrist band!" Isaiah cried. "What are you talking about?"

Mama Amma Ansabah stood up and declared, "There was a wristband! I saw it in the spot behind the palace where they threw the water they used to wash the body."

Peggy narrowed her eyes. "I want someone to go behind the palace and search for the wristband and bring it to me immediately." Two young men, one of them the late king's nephew, Kofi Assuman, popped out of their chairs and raced out of the palace.

A few minutes later they returned, Kofi Assuman holding out a plastic tag for Peggy. "Isaiah the Treasurer, why did you tell me there was no wristband?" she asked, snatching it and waving it in the air.

"Nana, I swear I didn't see it," he said. "It must have been on his left hand, and I was looking at his right."

The room erupted into sarcastic guffaws.

Peggy squinted at the wristband. The writing was faded, all right, and not obvious at first glance, but in the right light the letters could still be made out. The first name was easier to read than the second. Her heart sank when she saw the name *Kofi*.

"This wristband says we have buried one Kofi in the royal tomb," she said loudly, but her voice was trembling.

"The idiots!" Papa Warrior cried. After that there was stunned silence. Ekow, leaning in through the open window, shook his head back and forth in disbelief. In the right corner of the dais, Queen Mother Ameyaw pulled her gold-embroidered shawl over her head and wept.

"How can it be that no one recognized that this body wasn't your king?" Peggy cried. "You worked with him every day for twenty-five years. I hadn't seen him for eleven years before he died, but you should have recognized him."

Baba Kobena shifted in his chair and said, "We assumed he looked different because he was dead. It is well known that dead people don't look the way they did when they were alive."

"I only saw him a couple of times after I returned to Otuam," Mama Amma Ansabah countered, "but I knew the late king didn't have a hair on his bald head when he died. Since when do dead men grow white hair? When I saw the body on Saturday I told you that it was odd, Baba, but you just waved me away, saying maybe the chemicals in the tank made the hair sprout."

Several people burst into laughter as Baba Kobena cried, "I never said such a stupid thing!"

"You did, too!"

Tsiami stood up and said, "Let me tell you, down at the fishing beach all the fishermen are very upset that Nana spent so much money on the funeral but couldn't even bury the right body." Tsiami threw himself down into his chair and became a statue again.

On the dais behind Tsiami, Mama Amma Ansabah stood up waving a towel in agitation. "Was it *Nana* who went to the mortuary and brought the wrong king home? *No.* So it is not *her* disgrace." She turned to Peggy and said, "*Eye dze,* Nana. You did well." She turned back to address the audience. "If those idiot elders Isaiah and Baba were told to bring back a sheep, and they brought back a dog, it is *their* dishonor for being so stupid they didn't know the difference." She plunked her full weight back down into the groaning red plastic chair as the townsfolk burst into laughter.

As the accusations and denials flew, Nana Kwesi, who was standing near the open window with crossed arms, began to laugh. "The wrong body!" he said, as if to himself. "How could they bury the *wrong* body?" His tall frame shuddered with laughter. "I knew they were imbeciles, but *this*!"

Peggy saw nothing humorous about the situation. She felt a wave of despair threaten to wash over her, the same one from the previous night. How could this have happened? After all the money, all the years of planning and saving . . . She wanted to wail at the top of her lungs, *Why? Why?* But instead she uttered a prayer. *Jesus, help me now. Mother, guide me. Help me to deal with this, to do what is right in the face of such shame and horror. Help me to handle this like a king.* She clasped her right hand around her mother's little gold bracelet, and shut her eyes, and was still.

Suddenly a great calmness settled over her, as if she had been blanketed with grace. All anger and shame left her, and she knew what she had to do. She said, "We will return to this conversation later and get to the bottom of what happened. But right now we are going to the morgue to pick up my uncle and bring him home. Are there any relatives of the late king who are willing to identify him at the morgue? I would hate to make another mistake."

Two of his nephews stood up. "Come with me," she said. She stood up from the throne as Nana Kwesi opened a path for her through the excited crowds to the van.

25

Frederick Aduako had been horrified to find that there had been a mix-up with the bodies and desperately wanted to avoid any press exposure. Therefore, he greeted Peggy almost falling over himself with apologies.

"Terrible, just terrible," he murmured as he ushered her, Papa Warrior, Nana Kwesi, and the late king's nephews into his office and shut the door. "Of course, it does happen from time to time with the older bodies because the chemicals in the tank erase the names on the tags. That's why I insisted several times that your elders really study the body to make sure it was the right one because that tag was hard to read."

Peggy felt a rising sense of dread. "Please tell me everything that happened when they came to pick up my uncle."

Mr. Aduako nodded. "I had instructed the woman in charge of the dead kings to have the male workers pull your uncle's body from the tank and put it on a stretcher, where it was washed and draped in a cloth. I was waiting with your elders when they rolled the body in. I said, 'Make sure this is the man you are looking for because sometimes the tag is illegible.'"

"What did they say?" Peggy asked.

"That was the strange thing. From way across the room, they said, 'That's him! That's the one we want!' But they couldn't have even seen him from that distance. 'There is no rush,' I said. 'Look for distinguishing marks, scars, moles, broken fingers. Sometimes it's not all that easy to recognize the person if they have been here a long time. The chemicals change their appearance.' I rolled the stretcher up to them, and once again they said it was their late king. But there was something about the situation that made me uneasy, Nana. I said that we should remove his cloth to look for identifying marks. The smaller man with the high pants said that wouldn't be necessary, but I removed the cloth anyway. The two of them came up to look at the body, and I turned it over to show them the back, and they said, 'That's him.'"

Peggy knew that in his last year her uncle had had a growth on his back, near his right side, a cyst of some sort, and since childhood he had had a large scar on his chest that anyone could see when he wore his traditional cloth. "Did the body they took have a cyst or tumor on the back, or any scar on the chest?" she asked.

Mr. Aduako shook his head. "No, there really weren't any special marks on the back or the front of the body they identified."

How could they have missed it? At first Peggy had thought her elders had identified the wrong body out of sheer bumbling stupidity, an African version of Laurel and Hardy at the morgue, perhaps. But now she was beginning to wonder . . . had they done it intentionally?

Why, though? What would have been the purpose of it? Beneath his silver-tongued flattery, she knew that Isaiah the Treasurer had been furious that she had stopped his corruption and probably still wanted to punish her, but Baba Kobena? And how would they have known that the wrong body would be brought out? Had it been an accident due to faded wrist tags, and Isaiah the Treasurer had merely taken advantage of it? Had he managed to convince an uncertain Baba Kobena that this was the right body?

Peggy fished in her purse and removed the wristband that had been cut from the wrong body. She handed it to Mr. Aduako.

"The ID tag was faded, but I could read it well enough," she said. "The king we buried in my uncle's coffin was named Kofi, not Joseph."

"Yes," the mortician replied, "we discovered he had left us after we found your uncle still in his tank. This Kofi was a king of a village about fifty miles north of here, who has been in our morgue for twenty years. His family put him here and never paid the fees and has probably forgotten about him by now. They certainly wouldn't be able to afford the fees for twenty years."

Peggy thought of the smiling face, so happy to finally be buried long after he had given up hope. "What will happen to him?" she asked.

"We will put him back in the tank and after five more years we will be legally allowed to turn his body over to the hospital for the medical students to dissect. Even bodies this old are of interest to them."

Peggy cringed. How sad, she thought, to dig this poor man up from his rich tomb and throw him back in the tank, unwanted and forgotten. Hadn't he been a father, an uncle, a friend to anyone?

"Perhaps your elders' inebriated condition had to do with the mix-up," Mr. Aduako continued. "I do believe they had had something to drink. One of them kept dropping his black hat and could hardly pick it up. The gentleman in the high trousers walked in with one sandal on and one bare foot."

Yes, she remembered they sounded drunk on the phone the night they picked up the body. As a Muslim, Baba Kobena wasn't supposed to drink at all, and as a strict Methodist, Isaiah the Treasurer was usually abstemious. Why would they have gotten drunk unless they needed extra courage to do something horribly wicked? Had this been a plot somehow? Did they know all along they were going to pick up the wrong body?

She turned her thoughts to the matter at hand. "Mr. Aduako, how do we resolve this situation? I must bring my uncle home as soon as possible and return this other gentleman."

"We will wash and prepare your uncle's body and send it out in the ambulance within the hour," he assured her. "Then we will take the other body out of the coffin, and put your king into the coffin, and take the wrong one back with us. It will, of course, cost you nothing. Again, I apologize for this unfortunate situation, which is so terribly embarrassing for us all."

Peggy was greatly relieved. Sometimes in Ghana it took weeks of paperwork and a certain greasing of palms to accomplish anything official. But Frederick Aduako was an efficient administrator, aghast at the error and eager to make things right.

"As you know, I cannot see the body until it has been ritually purified," Peggy said. "I want my brother and these two nephews of the late king to go now to where they are preparing the body and make sure *this* king is the right one. I don't think I can go through this again."

"Yes, I will take them there," Mr. Aduako said. "And Nana, it would be helpful if there weren't many people around when we switch the bodies. We don't really want this to get out and create a scandal."

Peggy nodded. "I will call my elders and tell them to vacate the palace premises," she said. "There will be no one there."

Unfortunately, that was not to be. Peggy's van, followed by the ambulance, could hardly drive through the crowds standing around the palace. Word had cascaded through the entire town that they had buried the wrong king, and everyone was curious. The stretcher-bearers carrying the covered corpse had to shove their way through the throng to reach the secret chamber in the palace where the wrong king had been buried.

They removed the robe and jewelry from the wrong king and placed them on the right one. Then they switched the bodies. But the normal rituals that usually attended burying a king would not be carried out. Peggy didn't want to take the time to call in the Asafo to drum and line up the council of chiefs to perform their rituals. She wanted to right the wrong immediately, not wait several days for things to be done according to tradition. She merely asked Tsiami to pour schnapps for Uncle Joseph's spirit while she waited outside.

When it was done, Peggy went into the tomb and saw her uncle in the coffin. Yes, that certainly looked much more like him, the long face, the deep eye sockets. Papa Warrior had assured her at the morgue that he recognized this body as their uncle, but it was good to see it for herself.

"I'm very sorry, Uncle Joseph," she said quietly. "I'm devastated about this mix-up. I don't know how it happened, but I promise you I will get to the bottom of it. I hope that your spirit saw the splendid funeral I gave you, even if your body wasn't here. All those people were here to honor *you*; all their prayers and libations were for *you*, not for the poor man who took your place. You are home now, Uncle Joseph. So rest in peace."

There seemed to be an answer in the stillness, a thud, a throb, a pulse of emotion that said, *Thank you, my daughter.*

When Peggy, Papa Warrior, and Nana Kwesi pushed their way through the crowd toward the van, Ekow was waiting next to it but refused to step inside and take his seat. Peggy could tell from one glance that he was drunk and belligerent. He was arguing loudly with people near the vehicle, and when Papa Warrior told him to get in the car, he flat out refused. Afraid that they would be crushed by the surging crowd, Papa Warrior pushed Ekow into the van and slammed the door shut—on Ekow's finger.

Bumping over the Otuam road, Peggy's dark mood was not improved by Ekow's whimpers as he watched his nail turning black. Someone had offered him a beer, he said, and he had been so upset about the bodies that he thought a single beer might calm him down and not do any harm. Peggy wondered who had offered Ekow that beer, and if it had been done on purpose to cause trouble. Nothing would surprise her anymore.

Had the children of the late king had something to do with her burial of the wrong body? There were the sons in Houston, who had ambushed her with the morgue fees at the last minute, hoping that she wouldn't be able to hold the funeral. There were the daughters in Accra, trying to convince first Peggy and then her elders to bury the body secretly so their father wouldn't have a royal funeral. Surely it couldn't be a coincidence that their wish had come true? Yet how on earth could they have known that the morgue worker would bring out the wrong body because the tags were so faded? Had they possibly *bribed* a morgue worker? And how could Peggy ever find out?

Although the late king had finally been buried, there were still many unresolved questions. On her drive back to Winneba, Peggy called her elders and told them to organize a town meeting for the next day.

The following morning, when her van arrived in the palace courtyard, it could hardly park for all the people crowding the area. Nana Kwesi and Papa Warrior had to clear a path for her as people called her name and tried to touch her, touch her cloth, ask for her blessing, and give her their blessing.

Peggy made her way through a packed throne room and took her seat on the stool. The flies were out in full force, and she swatted at them with her handkerchief until a woman came to fan her with a towel. Isaiah the Treasurer sat in the first row of the audience, and Baba Kobena sat at her side, wedged disconsolately into the corner, wearing a black long-sleeved robe and his old black fedora with holes and worn patches, an outfit suitable for sackcloth and ashes.

She looked at the expectant faces in the crowded room. "What happened with the bodies was a very big disgrace," she began. "My elders disgraced not only me and all of Otuam; they disgraced themselves. Baba and Isaiah showed up at the morgue rip-roaring drunk. Baba's hat kept falling off, and Isaiah was wearing one sandal."

"That's a lie!" Isaiah piped up. "I had on two sandals!" Baba Kobena didn't say anything about his hat but glowered at Isaiah.

Isaiah continued, "We are very sorry for the mistake, but we didn't plan it. Really, it was the morgue's fault for rolling out the wrong body. No one should make any false allegations against me because it is not true that I did this thing on purpose."

Peggy was relentless. "Isaiah, Mr. Aduako removed the cloth from the body, even though you told him not to bother. Didn't you notice the cyst missing from the late king's back? He complained about it to anyone who would listen that last year, so you must have known. And what about the scar on his chest? You saw that every day when he was walking around in a cloth."

"That's true!" said a nephew of the late king. "Anybody could see the scar on my uncle's chest! If the body you took had a smooth chest, why did you take it?"

Isaiah the Treasurer shook his head. "I followed Baba Kobena's instructions," he said. "Everyone knows that Nana always listens to him, so when he said it was the right body, I wasn't so sure, but I just went along with him."

"That's not true," Baba Kobena thundered darkly from his perch on the corner of the dais. "You were the one who insisted it was the late king even though I wasn't sure. This whole thing is your fault."

Uncle Eshun rose unsteadily from his seat and said, "Please, Nana, forgive everyone for this mistake and move on." Shimmering tears fell from his Bambi eyes.

"First of all, it was not just a mistake," Peggy replied quickly. "It was a disgrace. A mistake is when you overcook your fish, not when you put the wrong body in the royal tomb."

Mama Amma Ansabah stood up and cried, "I don't think it was a mistake at all. The fact remains that when they brought the body back from the morgue that first night, they locked the door and wouldn't let me in! Clearly that is evidence of guilt. Why else would they have locked the door if they hadn't been hiding something?"

Peggy thought about that. It certainly was suspicious. It was also odd that people who had seen him up until his stroke didn't realize it wasn't his body sitting on the throne. "Did anyone know that it wasn't the right body?" she asked.

Numerous hands went up as several people cried, "I did! I did!"

A man stood up crying *Ah-go!* As the room silenced, he said, "My mother and I helped wash and prepare the body on Friday. My mother was one of the late king's sisters. She took one look at the body and almost fainted and said, 'It's not him. They have the wrong one.' We went outside and quietly discussed what we should do. Neither of us is an elder, Nana, so we felt we didn't have the status to make a fuss. That's why we decided to wash and dress the body of the man we didn't know." He sat back down.

Peggy pulled a handkerchief from her cloth and wiped the rivulets of perspiration from her face. Her gaze fell on Tsiami, who had been sitting motionless in the *tsiami* chair in front of her and rather looked like an embalmed corpse himself.

"Tsiami!" she snapped, and he started up with a jerk.

"Nana!" he replied.

"Did you know that the body wasn't the right one?"

Tsiami stood, carefully adjusting the folds of his cloth, and puckered his lips thoughtfully. "Remember I, too, called you when Baba and Isaiah wouldn't let me pour libations after they had brought back the king. You told me not to worry about it so I had to pour them outside the locked door. But now I know they didn't want me in there because I would have seen it wasn't the right body and I would have told you. When I did see him on the throne, along with everyone else, I knew we had the wrong one. Even an idiot could have seen that."

Peggy was afraid her heart might stop and forget to start up again. "Tsiami, why didn't you say anything?" she demanded.

Tsiami shrugged and said, "I had no say in the matter because Nana only listens to Baba so I kept my mouth shut. The past year it has always been Baba this and Baba that, and Nana can only trust Baba, and Nana calls Baba when she wants to talk about Otuam instead of calling Tsiami. I knew if I said anything, Nana would just get mad at me because she is always getting mad at me and yelling at me and sometimes threatens to do things to my balls. Squeeze them until my eyes pop out, wither them, and things like that. So I kept quiet.

"And I figured, if the king is happy, and her five hundred guests are happy, what did I care if they buried the wrong body? It wasn't *my* business. If I had said anything, it would have ruined the funeral with all the dignitaries there."

Peggy passed a hand over her face. Yes, she had made some threatening remarks about balls in the past in an effort to find out what motivated her elders to behave. But that wasn't a reason to hide the fact that she was *burying the wrong king*. How could Tsiami have possibly attended the funeral for three days performing the rituals while knowing the wrong dead man was sitting on the throne?

Slowly, Baba Kobena rose from his chair in the corner of the dais like a towering thundercloud. "I have been disgraced!" he cried at the top of his lungs. "Humiliated! You think I did this intentionally, but I did not! How can you accuse me of that?"

Mama Amma waved her towel at him as if he were a fly. "You are either very wicked or very stupid, Baba," she said. "Either way, it's not good. Sit down." Baba shook his head and sat back down.

A man in a turquoise robe stood up. "The town must unite," he said. "We must learn the lesson of the broom. When the fibers are tightly tied together, the broom sweeps well. But if you pull one out, you loosen the tie at the top and other fibers fall out, and the broom does not sweep well." Did this man expect Peggy to forgive them completely? She had been contemplating substantial jail time and a fine.

As if in answer to this question, Queen Mother Ameyaw stood up from her stool on Peggy's left side and, pulling her red and gold brocade shawl gracefully about her with a clattering of golden bracelets, addressed the assembly.

"Last night I had a dream," she said, "in which I came into this throne room and it was full of stools, ancient stools, and full of dead kings and dead elders I had never met. Nana was sitting there on her stool, and an old man leaning on a walking stick came in and sprinkled perfumed powder on her head, which as you probably know was what people did to honor victorious generals in the past. Then this old man with the stick praised her for doing so many things well, and all the dead kings and elders praised her with great praise.

"Then I saw the late king who had been in the fridge, and he too praised Nana for trying to give him a great funeral and for giving water to her people, and fixing his palace, and bringing a high school to the town. So the message of the dream is that Nana has done well, and the late king is happy with her efforts, and happy to be buried here even if it was a few days later than we planned. The message of the dream is that we should forgive those who did the wrong thing and move on." The queen mother sat down as the townspeople clapped.

Peggy knew that the ancestors had a hard time reaching her in dreams. It was as if, when she went to sleep, she hung up a sign that read: *Peggy sleeping. Ancestors, please do not disturb.* She had had only one dream that came true, though she had had it repeatedly, in her thirties, about walking behind the king's palace in Kumasi. It seemed that the ancestors, realizing an attempt to give Peggy the dream would probably be futile, had given it instead to Queen Mother Ameyaw, who evidently received dream messages more easily.

Peggy found it fascinating that the dream contained no mention of punishment or revenge, which indicated she shouldn't imprison and fine Baba and Isaiah. She suspected that the ancestors would punish the miscreants in their own way and in their own time.

More importantly, the message was a clear sign that the ancestors, even the late king, were pleased with Peggy's efforts, despite the disgrace. What else could it mean but honor and praise for Peggy? It was their way of telling her to calm down, relax, and look ahead. They knew of all her efforts, of all her expense, and were proud of her, were blessing her. It was a message straight from heaven, saying, *You have done well, Daughter.* Suddenly humbled, she bowed her head.

Then she raised it and said, "The queen mother's dream means something important, or she would not have had it. We must consider well her dream."

26

Though Uncle Joseph's body was finally at rest in the royal tomb, Peggy's trouble didn't end there. A reporter from one of Accra's main radio stations called the president of the council of chiefs in Essuehyia and said he had received an anonymous tip that the wrong king had just been buried in Otuam, and he wanted a confirmation before he broadcast the story. The president had not heard anything about it and told the reporter he would investigate the matter and get back to him.

When he called Peggy, he was doubly horrified by her explanation. First, that she had indeed buried the wrong king, and second, that she hadn't conducted the proper royal rituals when she buried the right king, but had simply let the morgue workers pull one body out of the coffin and lay the other one in.

"This is a very serious matter," the president said. "We will have to hold a tribunal to investigate your actions. Come to our hall in Essuehyia tomorrow morning at ten."

Peggy's heart sank. Though she had, every step of the way, done the very best she could, she was now facing an angry tribunal of kings. She found comfort in Queen Mother Ameyaw's dream; the dead kings, at least, were pleased with her, and as important as the council of chiefs was, even they recognized that ancestral kings had priority.

The following morning, Peggy, Nana Kwesi, Papa Warrior, and Tsiami were ushered into a small office on the side of a courtyard, where they greeted several members of the council and sat down in chairs that had been set out in a circle.

"We are very upset to hear that you buried the wrong body," the president said. "This council, which works hard to keep alive the dignity of kingship, has been disgraced by the scandal. And Nana, though you were unaware of the mistake in burying the wrong king, at least you should have contacted us the moment you knew about the mix-up."

"I was devastated," she explained. "Horrified. All I could think about was to switch the bodies as soon as possible. I never considered that I was expected to contact the council of chiefs."

"You know we performed special rituals at the coffin when we buried the wrong one," the president said sternly. "Why didn't you think we should have done the same rituals for the right one?"

Peggy sighed. "I thought that all the rituals we did, the entire funeral, were spiritually for my uncle," she replied, "even if it wasn't him lying there. I didn't think we had to do them again."

At first, the council wanted ten million cedis, some seven hundred dollars, to be her fine. Peggy countered with one hundred dollars. They argued about the fine for an hour or so, without coming to any resolution. Then the president said, "I want to know how you think this mix-up occurred."

Peggy explained that she hadn't seen the king since 1997 and, forbidden by tradition to pick up the body herself, had sent two elders to do so.

"But how did your elders not recognize that this wasn't their king?" interjected a white-haired council member, perplexed. "Hadn't they worked with him every day for, what, twenty-five years?"

Peggy nodded. "They thought that his appearance must have changed from being in the morgue. There was a wrist tag for identification, but one of my elders can't read, and the other one had trouble reading it because it was faded from all the formaldehyde."

Suddenly Tsiami, who had been staring into space, said loudly, "Oh, that wasn't it at all."

All eyes in the crowded room focused on him.

"What do you mean?" the president asked. Peggy wondered what Tsiami would reveal, as he had proven capable of keeping the most shocking secret until the last moment when it all tumbled out and left you scratching your head why he hadn't told you sooner. Now what was he going to say to all these kings?

"The children of the late king wanted to come to his funeral without paying any of the morgue fees or even for the coffin," Tsiami began, studying his hand and picking at a callus. His lower lip jutted out in seeming concentration at this task. "They never cared much for their father anyway, and they never wanted him to have a dignified royal burial. But since Nana was going to give him one, they wanted the honor of being there and setting up a table to collect the *nsawa* donations. When they learned this wouldn't be allowed, they hatched a plan to dishonor both their father and Nana at the same time."

He stopped again, picking off a little piece of hard skin and flicking it onto the floor.

"And then?" the president prodded, as everyone leaned forward.

"And then they knew that they had a relative who worked with all the dead bodies at the morgue. They knew this woman could pick out the wrong body, the body of an old man nobody cared about and would never pick up, and roll it out on a slab to the elders. But they had to be sure of the elders. That's why they approached Isaiah the Treasurer and Baba Kobena. Isaiah has always been corrupt, and though Baba hasn't, that was probably why he really needed the money. The children of the late king knew that Nana trusted Baba, so they offered him a price he couldn't turn down. Anyway, everyone has a price, as they say, and the children of the late king found what Baba Kobena's price was."

Each face of those listening bore the expression of utter astonishment—a trinity of circles consisting of two wide-open eyes and one wide-open mouth.

Unprodded this time, Tsiami continued as he started examining his other palm for calluses. "The mortuary man had no idea of any of this, and as the wrong body was rolled out by his assistant, the relative who had been bribed by the children, he advised Baba and Isaiah to look very closely at the body to make sure it was the right one, especially because the name on the wristband was so faded. They identified the wrong one on purpose, but they had to get drunk first because they knew they were doing something that the ancestors might punish them for.

"And because they had been bribed, that was why Baba Kobena and Isaiah the Treasurer wouldn't allow me or any other elders to see the body that night. Some of the king's relatives washed and prepared the body, but most of them thought he was greatly changed by being in the morgue so long, and the few who realized it wasn't him were too afraid to say anything.

"None of the others on the council—Mama Amma, Eshun, Uncle Moses, or myself—saw the late king until the funeral had started and he was sitting on the throne, and all the dignitaries had arrived, and it was really too late to switch the bodies or make a fuss. Eshun can't see that well anymore, and Uncle Moses has become brain addled, and Mama Amma didn't know the late king. But I knew it was the wrong body the second I saw it, though I figured, what difference did it make to me if they buried the wrong one? Nana would be happy with holding such a magnificent funeral; whoever the dead guy was would be happy to finally be buried; and the late king, well, he probably wouldn't be too happy still floating in the tank of formaldehyde, but what did I care? I never much liked him. Uncle Rockson was a good king, and Nana is good, but the late king really wasn't so good."

There was another long pause, but Tsiami had really finished this time.

On purpose. Peggy was horrified, all her worst suspicions confirmed. It had been done on purpose. Even Baba Kobena, her beloved, honest elder, had been involved. A word kept pulsating through her mind. *Wicked. Wicked. Wicked.*

"Tsiami," Peggy pleaded, "how do you know this? Is it just gossip, or is there any proof?"

He shrugged and brought his hand closer to his eyes for further scrutiny of the calluses. "Everybody knows," he said, squinting. "You know how people talk in Otuam. The children of the late king are very proud at having disgraced Nana, and they have been boasting about it to everyone. They think it's very funny. They think they've won."

Those in the room lowered their heads in shame at the story, except for Peggy. Her head was high, and her eyes flashing. *But they haven't won,* Peggy thought. *Because there is a God who doesn't approve of dishonoring corpses, especially that of the person who gave you life. They haven't won because there is a God who hates deceit and bribery and causing pain to innocent people, a God who will punish the wicked. Honor thy father and thy mother, God said, and he wasn't joking.*

"They didn't get to finish their plan, though," Tsiami added. "Giving you the wrong body was just part one." Several heads snapped up.

"What plan?" Peggy asked in fresh horror. There was another part to the evil plan?

"The morgue fees for the late king had been paid, you see, and he was still in the tank. Therefore, his children planned to go and get him on a day when Mr. Aduako wasn't there and their conspirator in the morgue could roll out the body and they could cart it off to an undignified burial in a secret place. They hoped that by the time you realized you had buried the wrong body in the royal tomb, you would never be able to bury the right body because it would have disappeared. And everything you did for the funeral would have been a complete waste. But Mr. Aduako found out too soon for them to do this. So at least you were able to bury the right body the second time around."

Everyone in the room was stunned. Finally, the president cleared his throat. "I think, under the circumstances, Nana, we can reduce the fine. We will fine you two million cedis for the fault, and you must pay another two million cedis to the radio station to keep quiet."

Peggy nodded. She took two million cedis, which was about $140, out of her purse and promised to wire the rest after she got home, as she was running low on cash. Then she asked, "But who told the radio station?"

"Oh, that was the children of the late king as well," Tsiami replied. "They wanted your disgrace to be broadcast all over Ghana. They bragged about that, too." He dropped both hands into his lap and stared at the wall.

"Well, that explains it," Peggy said. As she walked slowly to the van, Nana Kwesi stood close to her on her right side, Papa Warrior on her left.

A few days later when Peggy came into the throne room and sat on the stool, she looked at the crowded room and saw that Baba Kobena and Isaiah weren't there and mentioned it to Mama Amma Ansabah. Mama Amma chuckled. "They are hiding for very shame," she said. "Whenever townspeople see either of them, they laugh and point and ridicule them as the men who brought the wrong king back from the morgue. Yesterday some children threw goat dung at them."

Baba Kobena would probably never show up at a meeting again, considering his humiliation, or if he did so, no one would listen to him. Having no shame whatsoever, Isaiah the Treasurer might pop up, smiling and waving as if nothing had happened (he had a bit of Kwame Lumpopo in him), but she would instruct Nana Kwesi to tell him to stay home in future.

But there were two other misbehaving elders, and Peggy wondered what she should do to them. Uncle Moses had been very wicked, indeed, killing the late king, stealing so many fees, and threatening to burn down the palace. She would have liked to kick him off her council, though he could no longer do any harm there as no one would listen seriously to an old man wearing a woman's dress. It was evident to all that the ancestors were punishing him, and Tsiami had said they were poised to do more. The stools had told him that Uncle Joseph would come back to get Uncle Moses a month after his burial. Peggy wouldn't have long to wait to see if this prediction came true.

And then there was Tsiami himself—building supply thief, land sales thief, and fishing fees thief—who might very well outlive them all at this rate. She could picture him on his hundredth birthday, leaping through his pineapple fields, swinging a machete with his muscular arms to harvest his sweet fruit, and pausing to bounce an infant and a toddler on his knees, children he had had with his new wife. Whatever he did, the stools obviously liked him and would forgive him anything. There would be no divine retribution there, as there had been with Uncle Moses. No, she had better let Tsiami alone.

After Tsiami opened the meeting and poured libations, Peggy said, "I want to tell you that our program of sponsoring children's school fees has barely begun. We will add many more children to the program, and Shiloh Baptist will put their photos on the church Facebook page to encourage their members to sponsor them. So if the Americans haven't chosen your child yet, don't worry. Help is on the way. By God's good grace, it will come."

Those assembled nodded in approbation. "I am leaving Ghana soon," Peggy said. She never told them the exact dates of her coming and going in case someone might try to put a curse on her airplane, but she needed to let them know the time was coming. "Is there anything else to be discussed?"

A woman stood up and said, "Nana, I can tell by your face that you are very sad about the funeral. Please, let it go. It has already happened. What can we do now?"

Peggy nodded. The sadness still clung to her a bit, but it was fading. She couldn't concentrate on the failures of the past when there were so many challenges in the future.

A man rose from his seat and cried, "By the grace of God we have a good king. Nana has made it possible for water to be brought here and for the Americans to sponsor our children's education. Whoever goes to bed and whoever wakes up, their last and first thoughts should be to pray to God for Nana, to ask him to give her the strength to do everything she can for this community."

"God bless you!" several cried out in English.

"Eye dze!" You have done well.

"We are so proud of you!"

Yes, they were proud of her, these simple farmers and fishermen and grandmothers. She had worked hard for them, and despite all the obstacles and wickedness she had encountered along the way, they loved her. She floated in the happiness of that knowledge, as if it were her mother's loving embrace.

27

While many issues had been resolved, Peggy had made no decision about Ekow. If he hadn't gotten drunk at the palace the night they switched the bodies, she would already have given him the money to buy his kiosk, but after that she didn't know if she could trust him. Would he start drinking again as soon as she gave it to him? Papa Warrior thought so, telling her that clearly Ekow hadn't reformed. Just look at how he behaved the night they had buried the right king: drunk out of his mind.

Peggy considered the issue. Ekow had surely stopped for the most part, given the fact that he looked and acted like a new man. That night at the palace was a highly unusual event, after all, as the tossing about of royal corpses would have unnerved even the most dedicated reformed alcoholic. Peggy had heard that getting rid of an addiction often involved ups and downs, several steps forward and then a step or two backward. It was all part of the process, and Ekow had been drunk only one night out of the past twenty-six, of that she was sure. Though Papa Warrior tried to talk her out of it, Peggy decided to give Ekow a chance. Everyone, especially when they tried hard, deserved another chance, and Ekow was family.

After the three of them ordered their breakfast on the veranda, she said, "Ekow, here's the two hundred dollars you wanted to start your business." She held out two one-hundred-dollar bills, and Ekow lunged for them. But Peggy wouldn't let them go, so there was a tug of war until Ekow finally dropped his hand. "And if you waste this money, I'll never give you another dime," she said sternly. That probably wasn't true, she realized, even as she said it. But she didn't want him to know.

To her surprise, Papa Warrior pulled his wallet out of his pocket and removed a hundred-dollar bill. "And here's money to buy merchandise for the shop. If you spend it at a bar, when I come back to Ghana in a few months I will kick your ass from here to Takoradi and back."

"Yes! Yes!" Ekow cried, plucking the bills from Peggy and Papa Warrior. "I promise I won't waste it this time! And I swear!"

With loud cries of "O! O! O!" Ekow flew up the stairs, pausing to do a little dance on the landing, and flew back down, laughing, waving the three hundred-dollar bills in the air, and jumping up and down in utter elation. It did Peggy's heart a lot of good to see him so happy, to see how a few dollars—her first microfinance loan, come to think of it—could transform someone's life. She said a fervent prayer to the ancestors to continue to guide and help Ekow, whom she loved for her dead sister's sake, and for his pain, and striving, and joy.

Peggy and Papa Warrior were all packed, their large bags in the lobby, and waiting on the veranda for Nana Kwesi to pick them up and drive them to the airport. Her brother would be spending six weeks with Peggy in Silver Spring before returning to Australia, which made her very happy. She was already planning on cooking his favorite African dishes to fatten him up a bit.

Papa Warrior had bought a prime lot on the main road through Winneba, where he planned to build a gas station, car repair shop, and motel, though he had had difficulty purchasing land. The minute he agreed to an asking price and he showed the seller his Australian passport as identification for the transaction, the seller doubled or tripled the price, as Westerners were generally thought to be multimillionaires. Papa Warrior invariably stormed off in disgust at such chicanery. He finally found a property where the seller stuck to the original asking price even after learning that the buyer was from Australia. In a few months he would return to Ghana to start construction and help Nana Kwesi look after things in Otuam.

Peggy was delighted that Papa Warrior would move to Ghana at least part of the year to help her. He couldn't move permanently because he had four children in Australia, and besides, dealing with Otuam full-time might drive an impatient man like Papa crazy. But it was a gesture of love and support that she would always be grateful for.

Nana Kwesi would probably also be grateful for Papa Warrior's help as it would lessen his own burden. She had been sad to see him so thin and haggard, trying to keep up with her constant requests, driving here and there and doing this and that. Yes, she had issued many commands, and probably he was getting tired of them, especially with all the stress of the funeral and body switching. Now that the funeral was over and there was no great rush to put the finishing touches on the palace, she hoped things would be as they had been, that his angelic smile and the bounce in his step would return.

While Peggy and Papa Warrior sipped Star beer, enjoying the sea breeze, Peggy found it hard to believe that tonight she would leave Ghana for Silver Spring, back to her little condo and her increasing heap of American bills. In two days, she would drive her ancient sputtering car through the Rock Creek Parkway to the embassy, hoping it wouldn't stall. She would be answering the phone for the Information and Public Affairs Department, making copies, and typing letters.

Thinking back on her visit, she had to admit it hadn't gone at all as she had planned. For one thing, she hadn't seen William, or even tried to. Oh, she would always love him for what they had shared. And while it was sad to lose even the hope of a dream, it was also very good. She had a new purpose in life now.

Ekow was the greatest success story of this trip, or at least so it seemed. Only time would tell there. No sooner had he received the money than he called the man in Accra selling the kiosk and arranged to buy it later that day. He spent the next two days fixing it up and painting it blue and white, with a sign that read IN GOD WE TRUST KIOSK because Ekow knew he couldn't always trust himself, but he could trust God. On the third day he purchased his wares and opened shop. From now on, if he didn't blow it, Ekow would have regular work, a small but reliable income. He would be a man, proud of himself again. The future had never seemed as bright for Ekow as at that moment.

But along with this victory came Peggy's overwhelming feeling of failure with the royal funeral. There was just no getting around it. The children of the late king and her corrupt elders had wrought their revenge on her, a very humiliating, public revenge. For the rest of her life, would she be known as the king who buried the wrong body? Would people point and laugh at her forever? Or would the story die down over time, as stories often do?

Yes, of course it would. Her people were already grateful for the palace and the boreholes and the funeral equipment they could borrow free of charge. They would be even more grateful once she had brought them the high school, and the ambulances, the public latrine, and the bakery. While they might laugh at the story of burying the wrong king (even Peggy had to admit this tale had its comic aspects, particularly if your name wasn't Peggy), the people of Otuam wouldn't hold it against her.

There was so much more to do, she knew, and until the day she died she would be fighting to help them. Surely they would appreciate that. The love that was just beginning to grow in their hearts for her, their king, would flourish, thrive. It was overwhelming to think that thousands of people, farmers and fishermen, housewives and small business owners, would love *her,* who had felt unloved for so many years. And then there was the love and support of Papa Warrior, and Nana Kwesi, and all those people at Shiloh Baptist Church.

She suddenly recalled the ancestor who had appeared beside her bed one night during her first trip to Otuam. He had told her, "You may not be aware of it yet, but there are so many people taking care of *you* spiritually, mentally, and physically." She had thought he meant the ancestors, not the living. Yet she couldn't have been more wrong. There were many, many living people involved. She was bound to them and they to her by thick strands of generosity, kindness, and support, which made her feel even more generous, kind, and supportive to others—to the thirteen communities surrounding Otuam, to the rest of Ghana, to all of Africa. Her wildest dream was establishing a kind of grassroots movement to empower poor communities across the continent. If change had come to Otuam, why shouldn't it come elsewhere? She would need a great deal more help to do any of this, she knew, but so far whenever she needed it, help seemed to be forthcoming.

Surely there were wonderful opportunities ahead. The defining moment of this third trip shouldn't be the horror of the wrong corpse on the throne, but the triumph of the boreholes. To bring clean water from the ground was a microcosm of African transformation, a symbolic event for everything good that could happen.

The borehole ceremony had continued after the unwelcome interruption by the late king's daughters. And toward the end of the speeches, a typhoon of sorts had suddenly planted itself directly over Otuam. Looking out the large window, the crowd in the throne room had seen such cascading sheets of water that it seemed as if the palace had been built under Niagara Falls. Those who had been draped over the window ledges to watch the proceedings pushed their way inside and stood huddled and dripping along the walls. Several leaks sprouted from the throne room roof, and her townspeople quickly set out buckets.

Pastor Colleton stood up to talk again because he was very good at talking and there was, quite frankly, nothing else to do until the deluge subsided. "God is showing us the bounty of fresh water," he said in a ringing voice. "This is a sign that our well will *never* go dry."

It occurred to Peggy that the pastor was referring to the Bible story of Jesus who, standing next to a well, said, *Whosoever drinketh of this water shall thirst again. But whosoever drinketh of the water that I shall give him shall never thirst; but the water that I shall give him shall be in him a well of water springing up into everlasting life.*

It was such a beautiful thought, that her well would never go dry, and to Peggy it spoke not only of the water in the borehole, but of the font of all blessings, worldly and spiritual. It would remain fresh and clean and life-giving forever.

Eventually the downpour tapered off, then stopped altogether as the sun came out and cast its warm gaze on a world that was refreshed. The trees in the palace courtyard seemed to stand taller, their countless green arms reaching toward the golden light. The coating of golden-red dust had washed off the chickens and goats, which raced to drink deeply from the sudden puddles.

Some walking, others driving, the group inside the throne room made its way to Main Street, where they would have the ribbon cutting ceremony to officially open the boreholes. At the church borehole, Tsiami poured libations, and Pastor Colleton prayed before cutting the ribbon.

The man guarding the pump turned on the tap, filled a cup with water, and handed it to Peggy to drink.

Thank you, God, Peggy said silently as she tasted the town's water. It was cold, sweet, and clean.

Peggy's memories were interrupted by a horn beeping in front of the hotel. A moment later she saw Nana Kwesi standing in the entrance of the veranda, waving. He strode toward her with a bounce in his step and smiled.

Epilogue

Uncle Moses died on November 13, 2010, fulfilling the prophecy that the late king would come to get him a month after his burial, which occurred on October 12.

Ekow has remained sober, working sixteen hours a day at his little kiosk and making enough to support himself. He has earned the respect of all who know and love him and says this is the happiest time of his life.

Peggy is currently saving the town income from fishing fees and land sales to build a public latrine and create a library with Internet access for Otuam's kids.

In October 2011, Pastor Colleton and members of Shiloh Baptist Church will travel again to Otuam. They will hand a letter of intent to build a high school to the local government representative and interview architects and builders. During the trip, Shiloh members will meet with all children hoping for scholarships and their parents, take photos of the kids, and officially register them in the program. These photos will be placed on the church Facebook page so that anyone, even non-Shiloh members, can sponsor an Otuam child.

Peggy and Pastor Colleton will visit hospitals in Accra to determine the equipment and training Otuam's nurses require to maximize the benefit from the gently used ambulances they will purchase.

In August 2011, a third borehole was donated by the Imperial Supreme Council Ancient and Accepted Scottish Rite Masons. Several other groups have approached Peggy about helping Otuam. All charitable efforts will be coordinated by Shiloh.

In May 2011, she joined Shiloh Baptist Church.

Peggy still works at the embassy and still drives her 1992 Honda Accord.

Authors' Note

This is the very real story of Peggielene Bartels, king of Otuam, Ghana, and the first two years of her reign. The names of some people have been changed to protect their privacy, and one minor character is a composite of two real people. All the events and conversations occurred, though for purposes of conciseness some scenes have been abbreviated, others combined from several related events into fewer scenes, and a few details altered. Some characters who were present have been left off the page if they did not participate significantly in the events portrayed. Notably, Eleanor Herman traveled with Peggy to Ghana in September 2009 and September 2010 and was personally present at the events in those sections of the book. But because this is Peggy's story, one not greatly enhanced by a writer sitting next to an interpreter in the corner of the room, taking notes, Eleanor does not appear in the book.

Otherwise, *King Peggy* is the account of the transformation of an impoverished African village by its American lady king, a tale of challenges and triumphs that is often stranger than fiction and made more poignant by virtue of being real.

Acknowledgments

When I first became king of Otuam, I had no idea that people would find my story interesting. It was my co-author, Eleanor Herman, whom I happened to meet at a Ghanaian embassy reception, who convinced me that my journey was indeed fascinating and many people would like to read about it. Thanks to Eleanor for seeing what I could not see and making this book possible. Thanks also for her good humor, encouragement, and friendship along the way.

I am grateful to Elizabeth Koranteng, the embassy colleague who insisted I take the kingship of Otuam despite my initial reservations. I would certainly be remiss if I neglected to thank my regent, Nana Kwesi Acheampong, for so beautifully renovating my palace and dealing with Otuam's many headaches during my long absences, and his nephew, Francis Bondzie-Quaye, for his logistical support during my visits. Neither can I forget Casely Kweku Mensah, known as Nana Tufu, for sponsoring my gazetting, and my beloved brother, Papa A. Warrior, for being there when I needed him most.

My nephew, Richard Ekow Blavo, known as Ekow, holds a special place in my heart. I am so darned proud of him. In a place without rehab clinics or Alcoholics Anonymous, he has become clean and sober through sheer determination and the power of prayer.

I am overwhelmed by the kindness and generosity of Shiloh Baptist Church of Landover, Maryland, and its wise and charismatic pastor, Be

Louis Colleton. Surely God has answered my prayers to help my people by sending Pastor Colleton my way. I know I can count on his leadership as we move forward with additional improvements to Otuam—the school, children's scholarships, library, latrine, and ambulance. I would also like to thank Reverend Clarence Brock, head of Shiloh's Foreign Missions Ministry, who visited Otuam twice, for his devotion to improving the lives of my people. May God bless them and the church for their tireless efforts to help those less fortunate. Many religious organizations talk the talk, but Shiloh Baptist walks the walk.

I dedicated this book to my mother, Madam Mary E. Vormoah, who passed away at the age of eighty-four in Sekondi, Ghana. She taught me the values I live by, and I am strong, honest, and loving because of her. She also taught me not to be afraid of anyone except Almighty God, and to have a basket full of iron balls to swing around as needed. I miss her dearly. May she rest in peace.

Lastly, I am grateful to my people, the citizens of Otuam, for their loyalty, support, and love. May I continue to prove worthy of it.

—PB

In February 2009 I attended a reception at the embassy of Ghana in Washington, D.C., where I didn't know a soul. Suddenly feeling an awkwardness unusual for a life-of-the-party author, I decided to play a game I had invented years earlier: scrutinize everyone, decide which individual looked the most interesting, march up with hand extended, and introduce myself.

My gaze rested on a robust woman of indeterminate age, wearing African attire and standing alone on the side, calmly surveying the party as if she owned the place. Struck by her dignity, I chose her as my victim and introduced myself. "Peggy Bartels," she replied. "I'm a secretary here."

Somehow it disturbed me that she wasn't eating or drinking while the party was rapidly descending into a bacchanalia. "Can I get you some food or a glass of wine?" I inquired.

She shook her head. "I'm a king, you see, and we are not supposed to eat or drink in public."

"King?" I asked, thinking perhaps I had misunderstood. "King of what?"

"King of a community in Ghana called Otuam," she replied. "A few months ago, my uncle died, and I became the king."

As an author fascinated by the intersection of women, royalty, and power, I knew I had found the subject for my next book.

Naturally, writing this book required me to spend substantial time in Ghana with the king. My first thank-you goes to my husband, Michael Dyment, who, as Africans familiar with the story say with wonder, "allowed" his wife to go to Otuam. It sounds strange to a middle-aged, liberated American woman for her husband to *allow* her to do something, but he ended up supporting this project, feeding my cats, cleaning their litter, walking the dog, and doing all the household chores I normally do, without complaint and despite his hectic business schedule. I was absolutely delighted that he joined me for a few days on my second monthlong trip to Otuam. Thanks also to our kids, Sam, Phil, and Rachel Dyment, for their fascination with this constantly unfolding "very cool" story.

My initial interest in Africa was inspired by Alexander McCall Smith's No. 1 Ladies' Detective Agency series. Utterly charmed by the stories, I fantasized of going on African adventures with his charming protagonist, Mma Ramotswe, even though that clearly was impossible since she didn't exist. Little did I know that my dream would, in a way, come true.

I also extend my sincere gratitude to my amazing agent, Dorian Karchmar of William Morris Endeavor, and my editor, Kris Puopolo at Doubleday, for their enthusiasm and excellent editorial advice. I couldn't have done it without them.

When I first cheerfully got on a plane headed for Ghana I had no idea that the experience would be life-changing. There are many Americans—I myself was one of them—who live in big houses with every luxury money can buy and who are, nonetheless, stressed, depressed, and take for granted so much of what we have. Until my trip to Otuam, I was never grateful for the faucet that brought me clean water, hot or cold, at a touch. For flush toilets. For the ambulance that arrives at our doors within minutes of a 911 call. For food and clothing, heating and air-conditioning. Yet most of the people of Otuam, despite their poverty and their lack of water, health care, and educational opportunities, are grateful for every blessing and find joy in their faith, families, and friends in a way that those of us trapped in suburban depression can't imagine. I have learned much from them, and they have my heartfelt thanks for teaching me life's most valuable lesson.

Last but not least, I am grateful to King Peggy, who has become a dear friend. I want to thank her for taking the strange, annoying white woman to Otuam despite her initial shock at the request. I admire her stubborn determination to make a better life for her people and her spunk, wisdom, and humor, all of which made writing this story a very great pleasure.

Having witnessed firsthand the myriad difficulties of being king—and particularly the king of Otuam—I am more than satisfied in my position as royal scribe and have no aspirations to a throne. Honestly, I couldn't begin to do what King Peggy does. This realization causes me to look at her with wonder, respect, and not a little awe.

—EH

ALSO AVAILABLE FROM
VINTAGE BOOKS AND ANCHOR BOOKS

THE EDUCATION OF A BRITISH-PROTECTED CHILD
by Chinua Achebe

From the celebrated author of *Things Fall Apart* comes a collection of autobiographical essays—his first new book in more than twenty years. Chinua Achebe's characteristically eloquent and nuanced voice is everywhere present in these seventeen beautifully written pieces. From a vivid portrait of growing up in colonial Nigeria to considerations on the African-American Diaspora, from a glimpse into his extraordinary family life to his thoughts on the potent symbolism of President Obama's election—this charmingly personal, intellectually disciplined, and steadfastly wise collection is an indispensable addition to the remarkable Achebe oeuvre.

Essays/Autobiography

FACING MOUNT KENYA
by Jomo Kenyatta

Jomo Kenyatta, the grandson of a Kikuyu medicine man, was among the foremost leaders of African nationalism and one of the great men of the modern world. In the 1930s he studied at the London School of Economics and took his degree in anthropology under Bronislav Malinowski, one result of which is this now famous account of his own Kikuyu tribe. *Facing Mount Kenya* is a central document of the highest distinction in anthropological literature, an invaluable key to the structure of African society and the nature of the African mind. *Facing Mount Kenya* is not only a formal study of life and death, work and play, sex and the family in one of the greatest tribes of contemporary Africa, but a work of considerable literary merit. The very sights and sounds of Kikuyu tribal life presented here are at once comprehensive and intimate, and as precise as they are compassionate.

History

MANDELA
The Authorized Biography
by Anthony Sampson

Nelson Mandela, who emerged from twenty-six years of political imprisonment to lead South Africa out of apartheid and into democracy, is perhaps the most admired and beloved man on earth—a leader whose life has been led with exemplary courage and inspired conviction. Now Anthony Sampson, who has known Mandela since 1951 and has been a close observer of South Africa's political life for the last fifty years, has produced the first authorized biography, the most informed and comprehensive portrait to date of a man whose dazzling image has been difficult to penetrate. With unprecedented access to Mandela's private papers (including his prison memoir, long thought to have been lost), meticulous research, and hundreds of interviews—from Mandela himself to prison wardens on Robben Island, from Walter Sisulu and Oliver Tambo to Winnie Mandela and F. W. de Klerk, and many others intimately connected to Mandela's story—Sampson has created an authoritative, objective, and, above all, wonderfully readable biography.

Biography

VINTAGE BOOKS AND ANCHOR BOOKS
Available wherever books are sold.
www.randomhouse.com

Helen Canna
808
Caroline apts
Denton Md.

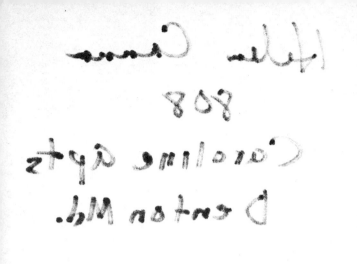